Sociology

Developing Skills Through
Structured Questions

We would like to dedicate this book to our families, our friends and most of all to our students.

> Sociology . . . necessarily has a subversive character . . . because sociology deals with problems which are the major controversies and conflicts in society itself, the study of sociology . . . cannot remain a purely academic subject, if 'academic' means a disinterested and remote scholarly pursuit.

A. Giddens, *Sociology: A Brief but Critical Introduction*, Basingstoke: Macmillan, 1986.

Sociology

Developing Skills Through Structured Questions

Mark Kirby, Francine Koubel, Nick Madry

Collins Educational

Published by
Collins Educational Ltd.
77–85 Fulham Palace Road
Hammersmith
London
W6 8JB

First published in 1993
Reprinted 1994

British Library Cataloguing in Publication Data is available on request from
the British Library.

ISBN 0 00 322336 1

Typeset by CG Graphics, Aylesbury, Bucks
Cover designed by Ridgeway Associates, Project Editor: Emma Kemsley
Printed in Great Britain by Scotprint Ltd, Musselburgh

Contents

Foreword

This book has been written to help students develop the necessary skills to gain an A level in sociology with the AEB, through which the great majority of sociology students sit their exams.

The AEB syllabus (first examined in June 1991) adopts a skills-based approach to sociology and this is reflected in the structure of our book – hence its subtitle 'Developing Skills Through Structured Questions'.

The book will enable students to develop the skills they need to negotiate Paper 1 of the exam successfully. Paper 1 is entirely made up of structured questions based on items of stimulus material drawn from a variety of sources. Increasingly, the A and AS level sociology exams of all the boards are adopting this style of question.

Special features of the book

- a comprehensive introduction, using examples from past exam papers
- up-to-date stimulus material on each subject area
- a developmental approach which enables students to practise those all-important skills
- marginal notes to help develop skills and provide some hints on further reading
- fully-referenced extracts, allowing students to investigate any topic in greater depth
- a full Author and Subject Index
- a reference list.

We hope that you, the student, find the book useful and enjoy your sociology as much as we do.

Acknowledgements

The authors would like to thank all those people whose help has made this book possible. First, there are the countless other sociologists whose work we have used for material in the book. We have acknowledged these instances throughout, and we would like to thank them for permission to reproduce their work. Throughout this book there are extracts from the *Guardian* newspaper which have been reproduced by kind permission. Readers are advised that, in many instances, these extracts appear in abridged form only and so may not fully reflect the views of the writer. For the full original texts, readers are referred to the *Guardian*. Photographs by kind permission of Photofusion.

We would also like to thank our colleagues for their help, support and encouragement in this venture and in particular the following: John Clossick, Kris Cobbe, John Cosby, Richard Dunn, Steve Farrell, Rob Fletcher, Paul Healy, Tina Healy, Tony Jewson, Maria Lenn, Eddie Sanderson, Helen Smith, Lisa Taylor, Helen Tucker, Andy Willis, and the Computer Unit at Amersham and Wycombe College. We would also like to thank the Library staff at Amersham and Wycombe College who have always provided us and our students with a fantastic service.

Tony Lawson has given invaluable advice on the material and Pat McNeill in the role of commissioning editor has provided constant encouragement and patience throughout this project. Jenny Batt and Emma Kemsley at Collins Educational have played a great part in the production of the finished book and its style is a testimony to their skills.

Finally and most importantly, we thank our A level students at Amersham and Wycombe College who provided constant, critical and helpful comments on earlier drafts of this material and pointed out some of our stupidities.

Needless to say the stupidities which remain are the sole responsibility of the authors of this work.

Introduction

Developing skills through structured questions

THE AEB EXAM

The majority of you will be sitting the AEB's sociology exams and so in this section we will concentrate on the structure of the AEB's syllabuses. However, the advice given here is relevant to those of you studying the syllabuses offered by any of the other exam boards.

Paper 1 of the AEB A level exam includes five structured questions, one on each of the areas of **Theory and Methods**, **Family**, **Education**, **Work and Leisure**, and **Stratification**. Although there is only one question on each area, it will usually cover more than one topic within that area. For the AS level, the paper contains three questions, one on **Theory and Methods**, and two on **Stratification**.

The best way to familiarize yourself with the style of the exam papers is to obtain copies of past papers from your examining board. You will find that most of the boards also provide copies of their mark schemes which show how marks are allocated and provide some clues as to what points the examiners are looking for. Another useful document is the Chief Examiner's Annual Report which indicates what the Examiner considers to be good and not so good points in exam answers.

THE CONTENTS OF THIS BOOK

Unlike the AEB's exam, this book provides ten questions on each of the five areas, each covering a main topic within that area. The reason for this is that exams are taken at the **end** of a course while this book is intended to be a help to you right from the **start**. By providing you with examples of structured questions which cover one topic at a time, we ensure that you do not have to wait until you have studied the whole of an area in sociology, e. g. the family, before you can attempt one of these questions. As an added bonus, the stimulus material provides you with extra knowledge and ideas in that topic area.

In every other respect, the questions in this book have been written using the criteria and guidelines laid down by the AEB syllabus. These criteria are explained in articles in *Social Studies Review* in January 1990 and January 1991 by Tony Lawson, the current Chief Examiner for AEB. You should try to obtain copies of these and other articles he has written on the subject. For example, in *Sociology Review*, November 1992, he provided a detailed set of notes for a question on Sociology and Science, which appeared in Paper 1 of the AEB exam in June 1992.

A skills-based approach to sociology

The current AEB syllabus is relatively new and is intended to provide students accustomed to GCSE-style exams with a relatively smooth transition to A level. The AEB's current Chief Examiner has written 'The new syllabus is designed to draw upon and further develop the types of skill which many students have acquired in doing GCSEs, while keeping the strengths of the traditional assessment pattern of the A level'. (Lawson, *Social Studies Review*, January 1990)

Again, this section will be of particular relevance to those of you taking the AEB's exam, but the practices it outlines will improve exam performance for any of the other boards.

It is important to understand that three types of skill are tested in the AEB's structured question paper (and, in effect, by all A level sociology syllabuses), these are:

1   knowledge and understanding
2   interpretation and application
3   evaluation

Let us examine in more detail what these terms mean.

Knowledge and understanding
To demonstrate the skill of knowledge and understanding, you must show that you are familiar with and understand sociological concepts and approaches, and that you are aware of and understand sociological theories, methods, studies and evidence. It is likely that this skill will be combined with other skills in the question set. Remember that a question may require you to introduce material (knowledge) which is not included in the stimulus material, but which you have become familiar with in the course of your study.

Interpretation and application
Interpretation and application tests your ability to interpret sociological and other material and to apply your sociological knowledge and understanding in a particular context. This type of skill is particularly appropriate to the structured questions paper because you are given a number of items of information, presented in a variety of forms. For example, you may be presented with a table of official statistics taken from, say, *Social Trends*. The question may ask you to interpret trends within the data, in other words, to explain what this particular item tells you about society and/or changes within it.

The skill of application requires you to demonstrate that you can select material and apply it **relevantly** to the question asked. It is important to note that marks for application can be gained for applying relevant material both from the items you are presented with *and* from elsewhere. When you do include material from elsewhere in an answer, you should give not only the details of the study (which will gain you knowledge and understanding marks), but also show how this information is relevant to the question being asked. This approach will gain marks for application. You can also gain application marks by using relevant examples or referring to personal experience, as long as it is related to substantive sociological points. There could also be marks for application of material from the items contained in the question, even where you are not specifically directed to incorporate this material. You must, however, avoid the old trap of 'writing down everything you know': this would, as always, be a disaster.

Evaluation
The skill of evaluation concerns your ability to consider the validity of points made by the items and also your ability to relate this to your wider sociological knowledge. You need to examine the strengths and weaknesses of particular approaches and evidence and come to a conclusion. For example, you might be asked to discuss the advantages and disadvantages of a particular research method, or to question the conclusions reached by the author(s) of an item, or to consider the overall validity of a particular sociological theory or perspective. The wording of the question should alert you to the fact that one person's evaluation of the relevance of, say, Marxist theory to contemporary Britain, might not be the same as another person's evaluation. There are no right or wrong answers. For this reason, we have not provided a model answer to any of the questions in this book – we cannot evaluate for you.

The skill of evaluation often causes problems and you will find that there are many disagreements among sociologists. As long as you are able to show awareness and understanding of the main arguments on each side, you will have the basis for a good evaluation. Only you can decide what your own conclusion is, but the more evidence you have to back it up the better.

THE MARKS AVAILABLE

Success in structured stimulus-response questions requires you to demonstrate **all** the skills outlined above. Marks are allocated to each skill. The approximate weighting for marks available in Paper 1 of the AEB exam is as follows:

Skill	*Marks* (%)
Knowledge and understanding	20
Interpretation and application	40
Evaluation	40
Total	**100**

The allocation of marks is not precisely fixed, but candidates are expected to demonstrate the skills in roughly these proportions. From this you can calculate that an answer which demonstrates only your knowledge and understanding will give you a maximum of 20 per cent. This is why we said earlier that a simple write down everything you know approach would be a disaster – you would fail your exam. However, the questions we have provided will give you plenty of practice in developing the multi-skilled approach required.

How the Exam is Organized

The AEB exam paper is split into two sections. Section A contains the question on Theory and Methods and is compulsory. Section B contains four questions taken from the other areas, i.e. Family, Education,

Work and Leisure, and Stratification. You are required to answer two questions from these four. Parts of these questions may relate to issues of sociological Theory and Methods.

In total then, you must answer three questions; the compulsory question from Section A and two of the four questions in Section B.

In the AS Level exam, the format and skills requirements are the same but there are only three questions on the exam paper. You have to answer the compulsory question in Section A (Theory and Methods) and one of the two in Section B (on Stratification).

CROSS-REFERENCING

It is important to look for opportunities to cross-reference between the topics. These links exist in the real world and part of the skill of application is being able to show them in your answers. This is something which all the chief examiners are trying to encourage and it was a central point made in the interviews conducted with them by Mike Moores and Tony Breslin in their article 'In search of good sociology' which we would strongly recommend you to read (*Sociology Review*, September 1991).

We have tried to show where we think there are links between different topics both within each chapter and across the book as a whole (such links are shown in the marginal notes and notes to questions).

The questions on the exam paper have a clear structure and it is important to be familiar with this. Although, as we said before, this book does not provide specimen exam questions, the questions in the book do correspond to the format of those questions and will therefore help you to become familiar with them (again, we have the AEB paper specifically in mind here).

The Stimulus Items

In each of the fifty questions in this book, there are between two and five items clearly identified by a letter for each – Item A, Item B, Item C, and so on. In this respect the questions in the book are identical to those on the exam paper, though we believe we have provided longer items of stimulus material than are likely to be included in the exam. The aim is to provide you with plenty of material to develop your skills.

In the book, as in the exam, the material is taken from a variety of sources: official statistics; sociological studies or books written by sociologists; textbooks; newspaper reports, etc.

The material may also be presented in a number of formats: text; tables; graphs and so forth.

CLUES AND CUES

Each question contains several distinct parts, all of which must be answered. Each part is clearly identified by a letter – **a**, **b**, **c**, etc.

The exam paper contains important clues about the type of skill required and the approximate length of answer demanded and, therefore, the amount of time to be spent on it. We have followed this format, so that the questions in this book contain all the clues that the exam paper will. Using this book will enable you to become fully conversant with the vital skills of decoding and understanding these clues.

THE WORDING OF QUESTIONS

The wording of questions contains important clues to the construction of your answer. As the AEB's Chief Examiner Tony Lawson has stated: 'The structured question approach requires that each part of the question be targeted on a particular skills or any combination of skills, and therefore the wording of questions will give you important clues as to which skill(s) is being asked for.' (*Social Studies Review*, January 1991). For example, the phrase 'Referring to Item B' directs you to a particular Item and so your answer must contain explicit reference to that Item; a general answer that is not particularly related to Item B would gain very few marks. A question phrased in this way targets the skill of *interpretation and application*.

The phrase 'Using material from the Items above and elsewhere' also targets the skill of *interpretation and application*, but additionally requires that you refer not only to material in the Items but also to other relevant sociological material not contained therein. If you refer exclusively to material in the Items, you will not obtain full marks. The question therefore also targets *knowledge and understanding* ('and from elsewhere').

ACTION VERBS

The examiners are very clear about what type of skill(s) they want you to demonstrate, so you must become familiar with the clues which tell you exactly what the question is looking for. One of the key clues is the use of 'action verbs' – words which direct you to a particular action. Each of these verbs is related to a particular skill and its inclusion in a question tells you what skill the examiners are testing and therefore indicates how you should respond. Below are some examples of action verbs associated with each skill:

Knowledge and understanding
State, Name, List, Outline the view, Explain the view, What do you understand by, etc.

Interpretation and application
Summarize, Examine, Identify, Illustrate with reference to Item C, Describe, Using material from Item A, According to Item C, What trend, What sociological perspective is illustrated in Item D? Referring to Item C, Using only the material in the Items, Identify the patterns shown in Item B, etc.

Evaluation
Assess, Evaluate, How valid, What criticisms, To what extent, How convincing, How useful is, Consider the arguments for and against the view, How far do you agree, etc.

This is not a comprehensive list. It is also important to remember that the action verbs must be considered in the context of the whole question asked.

EFFICIENT USE OF TIME

In this book and in the exam each part of a question will show in brackets the number of marks available for that part. It is very important that you take account of this information, since it gives a rough guide to how long an answer is needed, and therefore to the amount of time you should spend on it. In the exam you are required to answer three questions in three hours. This means that you should spend approximately one hour answering each question. Each question has a total of 25 marks available and the marks available for each *part* of the question should act as a rough guide to the length of time spent answering it. If there is only one mark available then you cannot gain more than one mark by writing pages and pages of good sociology. If you do over-write on a one-mark question you will use up time which would be better spent attempting a 10-mark question where this wealth of sociological understanding would, if applied in a relevant way, gain credit and therefore more of the available marks. We have provided marks in this book so that you can practise the skill of time allocation as you prepare for the exam.

PAST EXAMINATION QUESTIONS

It is important to remember that each question can test more than one skill and that the clues above may therefore be combined in actual questions. You must consider the whole question and identify all the clues. This is best illustrated by looking at some past examination questions. For this purpose, we do not need the items on which the questions are based and so they are not included here.

What explanations have sociologists offered for the differences between male and female patterns of non-manual employment, as shown in Item B?   (6 marks)

(AEB, June 1991)

This question targets the skills of *knowledge and understanding* and *interpretation and application*. You need to interpret the material provided in Item B (not shown here) and identify what the patterns of employment are and you then need to apply your own relevant sociological knowledge of the explanations sociologists have given for these patterns. As there are six marks available this will need to be done in some detail.

What trend in divorce is indicated by Item C?   (1 mark)

(AEB, June 1991)

This question targets only one skill, namely that of *interpretation*. The answer is to be found in the material in the item referred to (not reproduced here). The answer in fact is a rising trend in divorce. This question offers only one mark. You should not spend long on this type of question. In fact all you need to write is that the divorce rate is increasing. Most one-mark questions in the exam will be interpretation questions.

What criticisms, other than those raised in Item A, could be made of the Hall-Jones and Registrar-General's classifications of occupations?   (6 marks)

(AEB, June 1991)

This question targets *knowledge* ('other than those raised in Item A') but also includes marks for *interpretation* since you need to be clear which criticisms are included in Item A. There is also an element of *evaluation* in the phrase 'what criticisms', although you are not asked to evaluate the criticisms.

How have government policies concerning the family responded to changes identified in the passages?   (7 marks)

(AEB, June 1991)

This question targets *interpretation and application* ('changes identified in the passages') and *knowledge and understanding* ('how have government polices concerning the families responded to'). If the question were 'How successfully have . . .' there would be *evaluation* marks available, but it isn't.

Using information from Items A and B and other sources, assess the argument that power relationships in the family have fundamentally changed.   (12 marks)

(AEB, November 1991)

This question targets all three skills. The clues are as follows: 'Using information from Items A and B' tells you there are marks for *interpretation and application* and you must therefore incorporate and specifically refer to the points made in those items to demonstrate this skill; the phrase 'and other sources' tells you that you are expected to bring in sociological knowledge not incorporated in the items and this therefore tests the skill of *knowledge and understanding*. It also tests *application* since you will be given marks for applying relevant material and not just describing it. Finally, the word 'assess' tells you that your answer must include the skill of *evaluation*. You must consider the points which support the argument and those which do not and come to your own conclusion. This must be consistent with the points you raise.

Using information from the Items and from elsewhere, assess whether it is possible for sociology to be a science.   (9 marks)

(AEB, June 1992)

Again a three-skill question. *Interpretation and application* ('Using information from the Items'), *knowledge and understanding* ('and from elsewhere'), *evaluation* ('assess').

Which sociological perspective is illustrated by Item A?   (1 mark)

(AEB, June 1992)

Interpretation, and a very short answer.

Item C states that 'in most societies, the two people who produce a child are expected to take responsibility for its upbringing' (lines 10–11). How far is this view supported by sociological evidence? (5 marks)

(AEB, June 1992)

You need to *interpret* Item C (not reproduced here) to contextualize the quote and you then need to *evaluate* whether it is supported by sociological evidence. You can therefore also gain *application* marks for using relevant sociological evidence, rather than just simply producing a long list, and for applying it relevantly to your overall answer.

With reference to information in Item B and elsewhere, assess sociological explanations of the role of private education in Britain. (6 marks)

(AEB, November 1992)

Firstly, you need to refer to Item B (not reproduced here) to ensure that you incorporate material from that extract in your answer. This will gain *interpretation* marks and also *application* marks for using the material relevantly. Secondly, there are marks for *knowledge* ('and elsewhere') and *application* marks available for applying whatever knowledge you have in a relevant way. Thirdly, you must provide *evaluation*. Notice you are required to evaluate sociological explanations of the *role* of private education, not simply private education.

Item C suggests that alienation will decrease with the introduction of automation. To what extent do sociological studies support such a view?   (8 marks)

(AEB, November 1992)

There are *interpretation* marks available for incorporating material from Item C and *application* and *knowledge* marks for introducing knowledge of sociological studies on the subject of alienation in a relevant way which helps you to answer the question. 'To what extent' is a phrase which shows that the examiner is asking for your *evaluation*.

Identify three criticisms that interactionist sociologists might make of the type of approach adopted in Item A.   (3 marks)

(AEB, November 1992)

Here you need firstly to identify the approach adopted in Item A (not reproduced here) which requires the skill of *interpretation* and you then need to apply relevant *knowledge*, in this case knowledge of the methodological beliefs of interactionist sociologists, to come up with the three criticisms. Notice the question is quite specific. Three criticisms are required so make sure you give three. If you don't you will lose marks. Look at the mark allocation for this question. You are not asked to evaluate the criticisms, so don't.

With reference to the Items and elsewhere, assess the advantages and disadvantages of the longitudinal strategy adopted by the survey begun in 1946 (Item C).   (8 marks)

(AEB, June 1993)

This question targets all three skills. You first need to interpret the material in Item C (not reproduced here) and then also 'use material from the Items' (*interpretation* and *application*) 'and elsewhere' (*knowledge* and *application*) and you then need to *evaluate* longitudinal surveys as a research method ('assess the advantages and disadvantages of').

Assess the extent to which school factors, such as those identified in the Items, explain differential educational achievement between social classes.   (10 marks)

(AEB, June 1993)

This questions tests *evaluation* ('Assess the extent to which'). It also tests *interpretation* ('such as those identified in the Items') and *application* since the information selected needs to be made relevant to the issue of social classes and educational achievement.

Although you are required to use information from the Items, you are not required to bring in knowledge from outside, but the wording ('such as those identified in the Items') does not preculde it as long as it is relevant to the issue.

Using this book

This book is intended to be used from the start of your course and we have therefore provided comments in the margins and below the questions which we hope will be helpful. In each chapter these comments are more numerous in the earlier questions. As you gain more experience we will allow you to become more self-sufficient and we'll provide you just with some typical structured questions on which to practise your increasing skills.

The function of marginal notes is two-fold. Firstly, the notes will help you to identify the skills required by each question. This will familiarize you with the many ways in which examiners signal each particular skill or combination of skills. The notes will encourage you to get into the habit of identifying the skills for yourself, so this information will gradually tail off. Secondly, the marginal notes provide suggestions as to where you might find sociological knowledge that is relevant to the question. It is important to remember that you must not provide answers to the questions based solely on the material provided because *interpretation and application* accounts for only 40 per cent of the marks. You would be missing out on some of these marks if you used only the material in the items since some of the *application* marks are for the way you apply the knowledge you already have. You can get *application* marks both for the way you use the material provided and for the way you use material from elsewhere (your *knowledge*).

We have searched long and hard for material which we believe is relevant, up to date and covers some of the key sociological arguments of the 1990s, so we hope you might wish to read some of the articles and books from which we have extracted material. We have therefore provided full references below each extract to enable you to follow ideas up if you wish.

Answering structured questions

Like anything else that is new, your first attempts take much longer than when you are fully prepared, so you should not worry if at first you take longer than an hour to complete one of the questions in this book. The sociology will be new to you and the skills required are also new. However, over time and with plenty of practice, you will be able to approach the exam confident that you can complete three questions in three hours. These guidelines are therefore based on your having one hour to answer each question. Remember, however long you take, it is vital that you use the mark allocations as a guide to divide your time up in answering the question.

When the exam starts:

1   Read the data and the questions in Section A. Allow yourself 5 minutes.
2   Read all the data and the questions in all four questions in Section B. Allow yourself 15 minutes. In Section B you have to answer two of the four questions. In order to make the best choice, and therefore maximize your chances of obtaining a good mark, you should spend this much time reading all the data and all the questions before making your choice. Do not rush this stage. It is an important point. When you are ready, make your choice.
    Note: *in this book you are not required to make a choice and we have therefore felt able to incorporate more material than would normally appear on an exam paper. This also helps us to provide a comprehensive picture of sociology in the 1990s. You will therefore need to spend longer reading the material in the book than you would in the exam.*
3   When you have selected your two questions from Section B, carefully reread the items and the questions, in relation to all *three* of your questions. The urge to start writing an answer, particularly in the stressful atmosphere of an exam, may feel overwhelming. Resist it. Spend up to ten more minutes on each of your three questions, rereading the items and the questions to make sure you understand what they are showing or saying, identifying which skills are required in each part of the question and making notes for your answer. Refer to these notes constantly to make sure you are demonstrating the correct skills.
4   About 45 minutes have now passed, so you have 135 minutes left in which to write your 3 answers – that's 45 minutes each. Since there are 25 marks available for each question this means you can calculate the approximate time you should spend on writing an answer to each part of a question by multiplying the marks available by 1.5. For example, a typical question might allocate marks to its parts as follows: **a** – 5, **b** – 1, **c** – 2, **d** – 9, **e** – 8. In this case you should roughly allocate your time as follows: Answering **a** 7.5 minutes, **b** 1.5 minutes, **c** 3 minutes, **d** 13.5 minutes, **e** 12 minutes. This leaves about eight minutes to read over your answers to check that they make sense and actually say what you want them to say.

So, for each question the total approximate time allocation is as follows: reading, thinking, noting and planning – 12 minutes; answering – 40 minutes; checking answer – 8 minutes; total time available – 60 minutes.

You should not worry about sticking rigidly to this (except perhaps in the case of reading time) but use it as an approximate guide. Clearly it should take more time and effort to answer a question offering ten marks than one offering two. Make sure, however, that you get those two marks.

In order to make sure that the examiner knows which question or part of a question you are attempting, clearly mark the number and letter for that part in the margin. Tony Lawson (*Social Studies Review*, May 1991) says you need to make it 'easy for the examiner to give marks', and he should know since he is a Chief Examiner. It is always wise to follow their advice. They award the grades.

Conclusion

We have tried to cover what we think are most of the important points to be aware of when approaching the exam. Developing the habit of tackling questions in this way will ensure that you can approach the exam with confidence knowing precisely what you need to do, and how to do it and how to avoid the possible pitfalls. The rest, as they say, is up to you.

Exercises

The way to learn how to tackle structured questions is to gain plenty of practice in answering them. You cannot learn to swim without getting in the water. The more you practise, the more you will improve. Here are suggestions for a couple of exercises which you can do on your own or together with other students to help you with this essential practice.

1   We have provided the marks available for each part of a question. Why not try to develop a mark-scheme showing how these marks would be allocated? If you find a part of a question that gives 9 marks try to decide what kind of answer would gain 9 and what kind would gain 5. This exercise will make you consider what the question is really looking for. It would be helpful to obtain a copy of an actual mark-scheme from the AEB to see what they look like and what they include.

2   Why not develop your own database? We hope the material in this book is up to date but you will need to keep your knowledge continuously up to date to ensure success at this level. There are lots of sources of information for your database. You could start by using a standard A level sociology textbook or you could look up copies of *Sociology Review* or its predecessor, *Social Studies Review*. Another good publication containing lots of tables and graphs is the yearly *Sociology Update*. Good sources for official data are *Social Trends*, *Regional Trends*, the *General Household Survey*, the *Labour Force Survey* and the *New Earnings Survey* (all published by HMSO). You

might also look out for material emerging from the 1991 Census There is also a lot of informative material contained in the quality newspapers. In short, there is data all around you and being aware of it can only enhance your sociological skills.

Identifying skills in questions – some examples

EXAMPLE 1

ITEM A

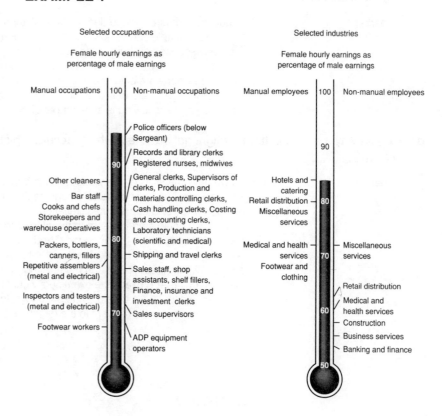

'Source: New Earnings Survey' quoted in *Social Studies Review*, March 1990.

a According to Item A, in which industry was there the greatest percentage difference between male and female hourly earnings?

(1 Mark)

This question targets the skill of *interpretation and application*. The answer is to be found in Item A and you need to interpret the table correctly to find it. The question is only worth one mark; most of the questions worth one mark will be *interpretation* questions. If however we wanted to target *knowledge and understanding* as well, we might ask:

b   What explanations have sociologists offered for the patterns shown in Item A?

(5 marks)   There is still some *interpretation* here as you first have to work out what patterns (note the plural) are shown in Item A. However other marks will be for *knowledge and understanding* as you introduce relevant sociological knowledge relating to gender inequalities in pay, and *application* marks for showing how it is relevant. If we now wanted to bring in the third skill of *evaluation* we could reword the question as follows:

c   What explanations have sociologists offered for the patterns shown in Item A? Which do you find the most convincing, and why?

(8 marks)   This question requires you to demonstrate all three skills in order to obtain full marks. This example shows how a question for 8 marks using all three skills can be devised starting from a one mark question testing only one skill. It is important to note however that this progression would not happen in an exam as all the questions are checked to ensure there is no overlap between them.
   One point to be aware of is that the source of material is potentially the basis for questions. The following is an example of this:

d   Explain why the data in Item A might not provide a wholly accurate picture of gender inequalities in pay.

(5 marks)   Here we have the skills of *interpretation and application* and *knowledge and understanding*. The key here is to recognize that the data comes from the *New Earnings Survey* and that this has limitations. If you are not sure what they are, find out – you could start by reading the extract from Susan Faludi's book *Backlash* in the question on Work and Gender in this book (p. 157). Never ignore the source of any piece of material – it may tell you a lot and the examiner might expect you to comment. Although it is likely that, in line with the whole style of the AEB exam, the examiners would be very explicit if they wanted you to comment on the source of an Item you would in any case be rewarded for any such comment if it is relevant to the question. So always make a note of this information.

EXAMPLE 2

ITEM B   The majority of people in Britain are not in employment of any kind. Many are children who must stay in school until at least the age of sixteen. They presumably fall outside the scope of class analysis altogether. Even excluding the under-sixteens, however, 54 per cent of women and 22 per cent of men were classified in the 1981 Census as 'economically inactive'. Twenty-one per cent of the total are other economically inactive people, 99 per cent of whom are women who in everyday language would be referred to as housewives. None of these people (who together make up 39 per cent of the adult population) can easily, or perhaps sensibly, be accommodated within conventional class analysis.

Source: adapted from P. Saunders, *Social Class and Stratification,* London: Routledge, 1990.

In recent years, the idea has developed that some of these people who do not regularly participate in the formal economy might validly be said to represent an 'underclass' in British society.

e What percentage of men were classified as 'economically inactive' in the 1981 Census?

(1 mark)   This is another example of the one-mark question which targets the skill of *interpretation.* If we wanted a question that sought to test your *application* skill also, we might have set the following question:

f The author of Item B refers to people being classified as 'economically inactive'. Suggest two groups of people, other than those mentioned in Item B, who might fit into this category.

(2 marks)   This is *application,* because you need to apply your knowledge to a particular requirement. If however we decide to add the skill of *knowledge* and *understanding* (as well as retaining *interpretation*), we might devise the question below:

g Using material from the Items above and elsewhere, explain the meaning of the term 'underclass'.

(3 marks)   The answer to this question is not contained in detail in the material selected, although it does contain the start of an explanation 'do not regularly participate in the formal economy' so there will be a mark for *interpretation.* However the rest of your explanation must come from your sociological *knowledge* and *understanding* ('and elsewhere'). The third mark is for *applying* the *knowledge* in a relevant way. If you want to consider what this might be, look at the extracts contained in the question on the Underclass in this book (p. 190). If a fuller definition of the underclass was contained in the data this might become a wholly *interpretation and application* question which shows that the skill tested is a function of both the question and the material selected. In this case the words 'and elsewhere' would not appear.

Let us look at a three-skill question on this piece of material:

h Using material from the Items above and elsewhere, assess the usefulness of the concept of the underclass in explaining the position of women in contemporary Britain.

(9 marks)   This question targets all three skills as follows: *knowledge and understanding* ('and elsewhere'); *interpretation and application* ('Using material from the Items above'); *evaluation* ('Assess the usefulness'). It is also important to note here that the concept of the underclass is related to a specific social group, namely women, though we could easily substitute ethnic minorities and the question would still be valid. The point of noting this is that it is a conscious attempt on the part of the examiners to discourage 'Write down all you know type' answers since you are required to apply relevant knowledge to a very specific question. An alternative question which tests all three skills and looks at a different aspect of the material is as follows:

i   The author of Item B argues that 39 per cent of the adult population cannot 'easily be accommodated within conventional class analysis'. To what extent does this weaken the usefulness of the concept of class?

(8 marks)   You need *interpretation and application* to fully understand the significance of the argument and you will then use a lot of *knowledge and understanding*, but make sure you come to a conclusion since you are required to evaluate. Note that although this question does not require you to use material from the items, there is nothing in the wording of the question to stop you from doing so, and you would gain credit for any material applied in a relevant way.

EXAMPLE 3

ITEM C   **Percentage unemployment by ethnic group**

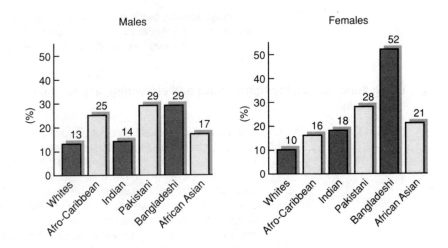

Source: 1982 PSI Survey quoted in *Social Studies Review*, March 1986.

j   Referring to Item C above, identify one ethnic group where the percentage of males unemployed is higher than the percentage of females unemployed and one where it is lower.

(2 marks)   In this case we have a question which targets *interpretation* but instead of being for one mark, it is for two. However, the two answers you are asked to give are contained in the table so both marks are for *interpretation*. If we wanted a one-mark question it might be as follows:

k   According to Item C, which social group had the highest level of unemployment?

(1 mark)   If we wanted to add in some *knowledge and understanding* we might have:

l   What explanations might sociologists offer for the different levels of unemployment of the social groups shown in Item C?

(6 marks)   And then if we wanted to add the skill of *evaluation* we could change the question to:

m Using material from the Items above and elsewhere, assess sociological explanations for the different levels of unemployment between social groups.

(10 marks)

EXAMPLE 4

ITEM D

Source: adapted from S. Lukes, 'The future of British socialism?' in B. Pimlott (ed.) *Fabian Essays in Socialist Thought*, London: Heinemann, 1984

The distinction between manual and non-manual labour is less and less relevant. Labour or work itself, and the sphere of production seems to be becoming less central to the identity and consciousness of workers, while consumption, especially with respect to housing and transport, has become more central to their interests.

n The author of Item D argues that 'the distinction between manual and non-manual labour is less and less relevant'. Using material from the Items above and elsewhere, assess the extent to which this is supported by sociological evidence.

(7 marks)

This question illustrates an important example of the style of question asked on the AEB paper. Here a quote is taken from a piece of material and you are asked to evaluate it. You will notice from the wording of the question that all three skills are being tested here.

Another example of this style taken from the same piece of material is:

o To what extent have sociologists agreed with the assertion in Item D that consumption is becoming more central to the 'identity and consciousness of workers'?

(9 marks)

Again all three skills will be tested here since you need first to consider the context of the quote (*interpretation and application*) and you must then show *knowledge* of this debate, *apply* this *knowledge* in a relevant way and *evaluate* it. However we can ask questions on this piece of data targeting just one skill, for example:

p What does the author of Item D argue is becoming more central to the identity and consciousness of workers?

(1 mark)

This is a question which targets *interpretation* for 1 mark. If we wanted a question which combined *knowledge and understanding* with *interpretation and application* we could try:

q Explain the difference between manual and non-manual labour (Item D) and suggest an example of each.

(4 marks)

The knowledge here comes in the first part since there is no definition of the terms manual and non-manual in the material presented, so here you would be drawing on your sociological knowledge. However, the second part, asking you to provide an example, requires you to consider the knowledge you have – types of occupations/jobs – and then apply these correctly, one manual and one non-manual.

We have tried to show how the wording of questions varies depending on the skill which is being targeted. We have also illustrated a number of different styles of question.

We hope that this section has illustrated some of the key clues which are present in the wording of the questions because it is vital for success that you are able to recognize and act upon these clues.

Some dos and don'ts

Dos

DO refer to the syllabus to make sure you have information on all possible areas on which questions may be set.

DO practise your skills throughout your course and revise thoroughly and regularly.

DO obtain copies of past papers and mark-schemes from the exam board.

DO ask your teacher/lecturer to clarify any confusing aspects of these documents.

DO refer to the Question and Answer section in *Sociology Review* regularly.

DO attempt to hear the Chief Examiner speaking at a conference and use the opportunity to ask him/her lots of questions.

DO revise.

DO read all the parts of a question to make sure you can attempt all parts. It is no good selecting a question on the basis that you can answer the part that gives you one mark and then finding you haven't got a clue about the part worth 9 marks.

DO spend some time planning your answer. You only really need to be writing for about 130 minutes in a 180 minute exam. Use the rest of the time to plan, think and check.

DO plan your whole answer so you do not use material in one part which is more appropriate to another part.

DO read the question carefully to ensure you are clear about what the examiner is looking for.

DO look out for action-verbs: these are clues to the type of skill required.

DO look out for clues in the question as to whether you are expected to stick only to material provided in the items or whether you should incorporate other relevant knowledge.

DO answer the question set in all respects. If you are asked to suggest three reasons give three not two or six.

Don'ts

DON'T rush to put pen to paper. Your work will inevitably be poor quality and will gain few, if any, marks.

DON'T underestimate the importance of planning in answering questions.

DON'T forget to read and re-read all the material contained in the question.

DON'T attempt to answer the questions by using pre-written model answers. The questions are very specific, so must the answers be.

DON'T assume each question tests only one skill. It is quite possible for one question to require demonstration of two or even three skills.

DON'T forget the mark allocation in terms of skills. Any answer containing only knowledge will gain a maximum of 20 per cent – a solid fail.

DON'T assume you can answer a question only on the basis of the material provided. There are five marks available for *knowledge and understanding* and more marks available for the relevant *application* of that knowledge.

DON'T read more into a piece of material than is actually there. You must respond to what the material provided actually says.

DON'T ignore the material in planning your answer. There are often important points included in the material. It has been selected for a reason. The material is there, use it, but use it relevantly.

DON'T copy out the question. This is a waste of time and will gain you no marks.

DON'T write answers to the question 'Write down everything you know about … ' This question has never appeared and never will.

DON'T use 'common-sense' notions as part of an answer. This is not socioloogy and will gain no marks in a sociology exam.

DO make sure you correctly signal to the examiner which question and which part of the question your answer relates to. A surprisingly large number of people forget to do this.

DO use the material from the items when asked to. The importance of this cannot be stressed enough. This lies at the heart of a skills approach and therefore at the heart of success in the exam.

DO use the material provided in the items where appropriate in attempting your answer. According to the Chief Examiners' reports this is an area of weakness among candidates.

DO use other material relevantly.

DO provide explicit evaluations when required to do so, by providing both sides of an argument and coming to a conclusion.

DO give your answers a clear structure.

DO divide your time appropriately.

DO read over your answer to make sure it answers the question set.

DO remember examiners can only mark what you have written, not what you thought you had written. So read your answers to make sure they say what you want them to say.

DO provide note-form answers if you are really rushed for time but try not to be by good planning.

DO read the rubric on the exam paper. The rubric is the set of instructions telling you how many questions you need to answer and how. Obviously you should then follow these instructions. A surprising number of candidates break basic rules.

DO remember there is more than one way to obtain full marks on a question so beware of model answers.

DO read all the material through once to try to get a feel for what it is about.

DO read the material a second time more carefully so that you are clear about what is contained in it and what the examiner is looking for.

DON'T copy out huge chunks from the material provided. All this proves is that you can read and write.

DON'T try to write essay-style answers to short structured questions. You will run out of time and will possibly fail the exam.

DON'T write long answers to questions with few marks allocated.

DON'T write short answers to questions with many marks allocated.

DON'T worry too much about poor handwriting but do try to write in a clear, logical well-structured way.

DON'T forget to read over your answers after you have written them.

DON'T forget to check that you have correctly identified which question and part of a question your answer refers to.

DON'T panic!

1

Theory and methods

1.1 Consensus theory

ITEM A

Durkheim is a key writer on consensus theory. Like other functionalists he believes that value consensus (a general agreement on norms and values) is essential to hold society together. All of the following major A level textbooks cover Durkheim's contribution to functionalist sociology: *Sociology: Themes and Perspectives* (3rd Ed.), by M. Haralambos and M. Holborn; *Introductory Sociology* (2nd Ed.), by T. Bilton *et al.*; *Sociology* by A. Giddens; *A New Introduction to Sociology* (3rd Ed.), by M. O'Donnell. These textbooks are referred to frequently in these notes. For further details, see the Select Bibliography on pp. 209–10.

Source: T. Bilton *et al.*, *Introductory Sociology*, 2nd Ed., London: Macmillan, 1987

Unlike some politicians who cling to mythical notions of a past golden age, no sociologist believes that society is, or could be, really like this. However, many, beginning with Emile Durkheim, believe that society approximates to this model. Durkheim and his followers have been concerned with consensus theory's one basic and overriding preoccupation – how society can continue as an integrated whole and not collapse into a mass of warring individuals. Their answer to this 'problem of social order' is in terms of socialisation into a consensus of norms and values. For them the key to societal continuity is conformity due to learnt rules of conduct. Individual people may come and go, but society carries on continuously – because it can shape the incoming individuals to fit the existing state of affairs.

From this point of view, societal characteristics cannot be explained as the product of actors' choices, since the choices are themselves the product of socialisation. If this is so, how do societies come to be organised in the way they are? For most consensus theorists, the answer lies in a theory of social structure made famous by Durkheim in the nineteenth and early twentieth centuries and developed to such an extent by Talcott Parsons and his followers in the USA between the 1930s and 1950s that during these years it came to be seen as the sociological theory. This theory is called functionalism.

ITEM B

Brown is focusing on one of the main problems with consensus theory, if almost everyone agrees with the *status quo* (existing order) how does change occur? You need to look in more detail at the concepts of 'dysfunction' – something which works against the maintenance of social order (see Giddens (1989) p. 697 and Haralambos and Holborn (1991), pp. 777–8) and 'dynamic equilibrium' (movement out of and back into social stability) to understand the way consensus theorists explain social change. Talcott Parsons' views of equilibrium and change are discussed on pp. 774–5 of Haralambos and Holborn (1991).

Source: adapted from C. H. Brown, *Understanding Society*, London: John Murray, 1981

Functionalism does not seem to be very good at explaining social change. The whole thrust of its argument is in understanding society as it is now. It gives a static picture; rather like a still photograph compared to an animated film. It is true that Durkheim gives us an evolutionary perspective on social change through the concepts of mechanical and organic solidarity, but these describe the course of social change rather than explain why societies changed in the way they did.

Merton introduced the concept of 'dysfunction'. Just as functions are 'observed consequences which make for the adaptation or adjustment of a given system' so dysfunctions are 'those observed consequences which lessen the adaptation or adjustment of the system'. Parsons, too, has introduced the concept of 'dynamic equilibrium'. By this concept he means that when the equilibrium of society is upset, whether by some factor within the system or outside it, processes may be set in operation which restore equilibrium but at a different level from before.

ITEM C

A useful definition of consensus, taken from a long list which appears at the back of Giddens' (1989) book. If you get stuck with a sociological term or concept, see if there is an entry in his glossary or make use of a dictionary of sociology such as the one published by HarperCollins.

*Source:*A. Giddens, *Sociology*, Cambridge: Polity, 1989

Consensus: agreement over basic social values by the members of a group, community or society. Some thinkers in sociology strongly emphasize the importance of consensus as a basis for social stability. These writers believe that all societies which endure over any substantial period of time involve a 'common value system' of consensual beliefs held by the majority of the population.

5

ITEM D

This item suggests that all sociological approaches recognize order in social life, but differ in their views on the nature and extent of that order. Consensus theorists focus on what is necessary for society as a whole to exist and survive over time, they talk of the 'functional prerequisites' of society. Try to find out what these are by referring to Haralambos and Holborn (1991), pp. 768–9.

Consensus theory has been criticized for being deterministic – i.e. assuming that what happens in society is somehow limited by the existing structures and patterns, thus denying the potential for change through social action – and for producing what has been called an 'over-socialized' conception of humans. See O'Donnell (1992) pp. 499–501 and Haralambos and Holborn (1991) p. 780.

Source: adapted from E. E. Cuff, W. W. Sharrock and D. W. Francis, *Perspectives in Sociology*, 3rd Ed., London: Routledge, 1992

Most sociology, in one respect or another, can be seen as a contribution to our understanding of the ordered, patterned and predictable nature of the social world. However the notions of 'order' and 'predictability' to which sociologists generally refer are not those which would imply that social relationships and events are fixed or inevitably predetermined. Rather the conception of order referred to derives from the observation that by and large both our expectations of our own behaviour and our expectations of the activities of others are generally fulfilled in our experience. That is not to say we know exactly what others may do in any given situation, but we generally have a good idea of the range of probable actions.

A focus on the ways in which the 'ordered' nature of social life is organized is something all sociological perspectives have in common. Where the perspectives tend to differ is in their conceptualization of the nature of the achievement and management of social order.

Those sociologists who have developed an approach in sociology which we are calling the consensus perspective have explicitly focused on the 'problem of order' at a societal level. Their theoretical and empirical analyses have generally been based upon the assumption that societies can be seen as persistent, cohesive, stable, generally integrated wholes, differentiated by their cultural and social–structural arrangements.

5

10

15

20

QUESTIONS

a Explain what is meant by the 'problem of social order' (Item A, lines 8–9).

(2 marks)

These two marks are for your *interpretation* of the material in Item A. Two points are made immediately before the reference to 'the problem of social order'. Explain them carefully. Don't be tempted to write more than is necessary to get the marks on offer in a short answer like this.

b   Using material from Item D and elsewhere, explain how consensus theorists might account for social stability.

(4 marks)

This question is asking you to demonstrate both the skill of *interpretation* of material in the item and the *application* of your *knowledge*. So make sure that you refer to Item D (there are some clues in the note to the Item) and that you also bring in material from outside. Look at the writers mentioned here, such as Durkheim and Parsons. See Haralambos and Holborn (1991), pp. 770–81.

c   Explain briefly the meaning of 'the concept of dysfunction' (Item B, line 9).

(2 marks)

This is an *interpretation* question so the answer is in the Item. However, you may find it easier if you have read up on Merton's theories before you attempt an answer. Use your own words.

d   Using material from the passages above and elsewhere, assess the validity of the notion that a 'common value system' exists in contemporary British society (Item C, line 5).

(10 marks)

This question demands a long answer and requires you to use all three skills. This is indicated by the wording of the question: 'material from the passages above' requires *interpretation and application* skills; 'elsewhere' expects you to show *knowledge and application* skills; and 'assess' expects you to *evaluate*. Always back up your criticisms with sociological material or other evidence. The question refers to contemporary British society so you will be rewarded for the application of relevant topical examples in your answer. Abercrombie and Warde (1988) might provide some ideas here, notably their discussion of the 'dominant ideology thesis', pp. 365–7. Reference to the findings of the latest *British Social Attitudes Survey* would also be illuminating.

e   The author of Item B argues that 'Functionalism does not seem to be very good at explaining social change' (line 1). With reference to the material in the passages, and any other material you are familiar with, examine the arguments for and against this view.

(7 marks)

Like question **d**, this question is also worded to indicate that you need to use all skills. As requested, refer both to the Items (*interpretation and application*), and also to a variety of relevant sociological studies (*knowledge and application*) – in this case it specifies 'material you are familiar with'. Examining 'the arguments for and against' (*evaluation*) involves looking at both sides of the argument *and* reaching a conclusion. Beware of simply producing lists of points with no direct comparisons or analysis.

Longer answers like this and the one above should always be planned. The references listed throughout this question are a helpful guide to relevant sources of information.

1.2 Conflict theory

ITEM A

This outline of Marxist theory comes from O'Donnell (1992). O'Donnell uses this format to explain the functionalist and social action approaches. Make sure you understand the Marxist terminology used in this passage. For example, the means of production are those things needed to produce goods, such as land, factories and raw materials. The relations of production are the ways people get together in order to produce anything, such as employers and employees or landowners and farm labourers. Both are needed for production to occur.

Source: adapted from M. O'Donnell, *A New Introduction to Sociology*, 3rd Ed., Walton-on-Thames: Nelson, 1992

Marxism

1 How is society constructed?
According to Marx, society is constructed from classes. In all societies, except the most simple, there are two major classes. It is people's relationship to the means of production that determines which class they belong to. The most powerful class is that which owns the means of production (land, factories, etc.) and the least powerful is that which has to sell its labour to make a living.

2 How does society 'operate' or function?
In Marx's view, society operates mainly through class conflict. In particular he argues that in capitalist society the bourgeoisie and the proletariat are fundamentally opposed.

3 What causes social change?
Social change occurs as a result of class conflict. The victory of a new class introduces a new historical period. Thus the rise of the bourgeoisie introduced the capitalist epoch.

4 Is society normally in orderly balance or in conflict?
Society is in a state of fundamental conflict between the classes. Marx recognized, however that periods of social order and equilibrium can occur, in which class conflict is temporarily submerged. He argued that such periods benefit the rich and powerful more than others.

ITEM B

Max Weber is often described as 'having a debate with the ghost of Marx', although he shared many of Marx's basic ideas. Weber agreed with Marx that conflict is inevitable and that it is based on class differences, but he added that conflict also arises from other differences which have to do with status and power. The end result is therefore a very different version of conflict theory from Marxist theory. See Giddens (1989), pp. 211–13, O'Donnell (1992), pp. 10–11, and Haralambos and Holborn (1991), pp. 42–5, for further information.

Source: adapted from C. Townley and M. Middleton, 'Sociological Perspectives' in P. McNeill & C. Townley (eds), *Fundamentals of Sociology*, London: Hutchinson, 1986

Whereas functionalism emphasizes consensus, shared norms and shared values, and uses concepts like order, harmony, cohesion, integration and equilibrium, conflict theory takes a different view. This perspective emphasizes differences between interest groups, and uses concepts like control, conflict, power, constraint, domination, coercion, dissensus and change. The central theme or thesis of conflict theory is that conflict is an inevitable fact of life

Max Weber's contribution to conflict theory, like Marx before him, represents only one part of his enormous contribution to sociological theory. He is sometimes referred to as 'the bourgeois Marx' because so much of his work was concerned with testing, reassessing or developing Marx's ideas. Like all the major theorists of class structure, Weber began with Marx's formulation of the question and accepted that class is economic in origin. For Weber, however, stratification was much more than an economically-determined class position; it also involved a consideration of, status, power and political parties.

ITEM C

The ideas of Dahrendorf expressed in this Item are more Weberian than Marxist. While Marxists claimed that capital would be concentrated in fewer hands, Dahrendorf suggests that the owners have less control over industry. He also suggests that Marx was unable to predict the increasing differences between groups of workers, the growth of the middle classes and the expansion of social mobility which all led to a more heterogeneous and fragmented class structure. Remember that Dahrendorf was writing in the 1950s and 1960s – a time of economic growth. Dahrendorf's ideas are discussed by O'Donnell (1992), pp. 130, 135 and 473. See also Haralambos and Holborn (1991), pp. 352–3 and 793–5.

Source: adapted from E. E. Cuff & G. C. F. Payne (eds), *Perspectives in Sociology*, Hemel Hempstead: George Allen & Unwin, 1981

Dahrendorf suggests that the following changes of the social structure have been sufficient to produce post-capitalist society:

The decomposition of capital
With the growth in the scale of business companies due to technological advances and to the development of the joint stock limited liability company, the link between the ownership and control of industry has been weakened.

The decomposition of labour
The workers have become more differentiated. Far from becoming homogenized in terms of class consciousness, the workers are becoming increasingly aware of the differences between themselves.

The development of a new middle class
The new middle class is a category rather than a class in terms of Marx's use of this concept and it is made up of white-collar workers such as teachers, accountants, surveyors, nurses, clerks, etc.

The growth of social mobility
There is much more inter-generational mobility between occupations.

The growth of equality
Social and economic inequalities have been reduced.

Dahrendorf concludes that society can be characterized correctly in terms of conflict between competing interest groups. In the light of these arguments Dahrendorf points out what he considers to be the weaknesses of Marx's theories. For him, the basic weakness of Marx's approach is in the way Marx ties power – economic, social, political – to the ownership of the means of production.

Dahrendorf argues that most people in society are unlikely to be engaged in one mighty political-economic-social-industrial conflict which is generated from one structural source, property relationships. Instead, changes in social structure create the social structural basis for a plurality of interest groups and hence a plurality of bases for conflict.

QUESTIONS

a   State the names given by Marx to the two fundamental classes in capitalist society (Item A).

(2 marks)   This is a simple *interpretation* question taken from Item A, although you might know the answer anyway.

b   What social characteristics other than class did Weber identify as a basis for stratification and so for conflict between groups (Item B)?

(2 marks)   A similar question based on information from Item B. The answer is clearly to be found in the Item.

c Referring to Item C, explain in your own words Dahrendorf's criticisms of Marx's theory.

(4 marks)

Again, the (rather complex) answer lies in the text but you are required to put the criticisms in your own words, do not think you can simply copy them out. The skills here are mainly *interpretation* again, but you must give a fuller answer to get all four marks. Identify four separate points.

d Using material from the Items and elsewhere, assess the view that 'conflict is an inevitable fact of life' (Item B, line 7).

(9 marks)

This question clearly signals that all skills are needed. You are asked to use 'material from the Items' (*interpretation and application*), 'elsewhere' *(knowledge and application)* and then you must 'assess' it (*evaluation*). Your *knowledge* should include an awareness of such fundamental Marxist concepts as 'contradictions', 'exploitation' and 'oppression' and their role in producing social change.

Criticisms of this view come from a number of sources, especially consensus theorists. Say what you think at the end, and why, in the form of a brief conclusion.

See Haralambos and Holborn (1991), pp. 11–14 and O'Donnell (1992), pp. 502–3.

e Using material from the Items above and elsewhere, assess the view expressed in Item C that 'changes in social structure create the social structural basis for a plurality of interest groups and hence a plurality of bases for conflict' (lines 35–7).

(8 marks)

This is another question which requires a planned and structured answer using all skills. The hardest part here is to interpret the question. What it means is that the author thinks that class differences are not the sole source of conflict, but that conflict is still expressed between other social groups. Many neo-Marxists would agree and they point to struggles by environmentalists, women and ethnic minority groups. This is certainly an area of debate between Marxists and Weberians. The debate is linked to the question of the nature and distribution of power, a key theme in the 'Power and Politics' topic on AEB Paper 2. It is also relevant to discussions of social stratification (see the Stratification section of this book, particularly Is Social Class Still Central?, p. 176).

Follow up the references listed next to Item C.

1.3 Social action theory

ITEM A

This item refers to several approaches which exist under the 'umbrella' term social action theory. Make sure you are familiar with these and the differences between them. The table on p. 767 of Haralambos and Holborn (1991) may be of help here.

Social arrangements are to some extent arbitrary ways of orga- nizing human life – there is an apparently endless range of varia- tions in social rules, ideas and conventions.

Social action theory emphasizes these aspects of human life. 'Social action theory' is a general term within which several soci- ological approaches can be identified. They range from Weber's micro-sociological work (though Weber was by no means just an action theorist), to symbolic interactionism, on to the most recent radical and action perspectives – phenomenology and eth- nomethodology.

Action theorists pay close attention to the ways in which 'defi- nitions of reality' are used and sustained by actors. They show how these definitions may be disputed by individuals or groups, and how actors negotiate shared rules and ideas. What this implies is neatly summed up by the famous saying of W.I.Thomas (1966): 'If men define situations as real, they are real in their consequences.'

Source: adapted from T.Bilton *et al.*, *Introductory Sociology*, 2nd Ed., London: Macmillan, 1987

ITEM B

This relates to Weber's concept of *Verstehen*. *Verstehen*, the German word for 'understanding', refers to the procedure in which a sociologist has to develop an empathy or meaningful understanding with those s/he is studying in order to gain access to the meanings of others. Cuff and Payne (1981) stress the importance of qualitative methods such as participant observation if such an understanding is to be achieved. See Haralambos and Holborn (1991), pp. 707–8 on this.

The idea that the sociologist should 'understand', should 'take the actor's point of view', is not universally popular and there are many who regard it with considerable suspicion. They view it as a mythical notion whose application must be antithetical or opposed to the possibilities of rigour in sociology. By attempting to apprehend someone else's point of view, by trying to under- stand someone else's state of mind, we may seem to be trying to 'put ourselves in his place' and to be engaging in a kind of emo- tional speculation about him. As emotional speculations cannot be checked or verified, we may be seen to be operating in an unscientific manner.

One implication of the policy of taking the standpoint of the actor is that research should be both intensive and typically accomplished through the acquisition of a detailed and rich acquaintance with the life, circumstances and ways of those being studied. Consequently, qualitative methods are likely to provide the most congenial ways of applying such a policy.

Source: adapted from E. C. Cuff and G. C. F. Payne (eds), *Perspectives in Sociology*, Hemel Hempstead: George Allen & Unwin, 1981

ITEM C

In this passage Freund is explaining in more detail the importance of subjective understanding in the social action theory of Max Weber. Remember

Weber introduced the interpretive method. He was not the inventor of the interpretive method. Weber's merit is to have elaborated this method conceptually with more rigour, applying it to sociology.

Given that social activity can have different meanings, distinc- tions must be made among them – all the more so since an

that positivists would interpret this as biased and unreliable, arguing that the study of 'observable facts' is more important than the study of motives. Refer to p. 721 and pp. 795–6 of Haralambos and Holborn (1991) for a discussion of this.

individual is never isolated in that he acts in a vacuum because he is always influenced by others' behaviour. What then is social activity? 'By activity,' says Weber, 'we mean human behaviour (it matters little if it is an exterior or an interior act, the omission of an act, or the toleration of an act) which is given a subjective meaning by its agent or agents. By social activity we mean activity directed by its agents in reference to the behaviour of others for the consequent orientation of its development.' 10

Given that the subject matter of natural science is without meaning (which is not to say absurd), its methodology cannot simply be transferred to the social sciences where the problem of meaning plays a capital role. Natural inert phenomena can be accounted for satisfactorily by causal explanations, that is by other, antecedent phenomena. An extra effort is required, however to grasp social phenomena, because, to account for them, it is also necessary to understand their motives; that is the reasons which have led men to act and the goals which they are pursuing. 15 20

Source: adapted from J. Freund, 'German sociology in the time of Max Weber' in T. Bottomore and R. Nisbet (eds), *A History of Sociological Analysis*, London: Heinemann, 1979

ITEM D

Haralambos and Holborn (1991) outline some of the main issues in the positivism/phenomenology debate in the last two chapters of the book from which this extract is taken. Hindess takes a quasi-positivist stance here.

To phenomenologists, it is impossible to measure objectively any aspect of human behaviour. Humans make sense of the world by categorizing it. Through language they distinguish between different types of objects, events actions and people. Statistics are simply the product of the opinions of those who produce them. Thus crime statistics are produced by the police and the courts and they represent no more than the opinions of the individuals involved. The end product of phenomenological research is an understanding of the the meanings employed by members of society in their everyday life. 5 10

Although there are differences between those who support social action theory and phenomenological views, they agree that the positivist approach has produced a distorted picture of social life.

Phenomenological views have themselves been subject to criticism. Barry Hindess points out that the criticisms of suicide statistics advanced by phenomenologists can be turned against the sociological theories of phenomenologists themselves. If suicide statistics can be criticized as being no more than the interpretations of coroners, then studies such as that done by Atkinson can be criticized as being no more than the interpretation of a particular sociologist. Hindess therefore dismisses the work of such sociologists as being 'theoretically worthless' and he says of their work 'A manuscript produced by a monkey at a typewriter would be no less valuable'. If phenomenological views were taken to their logical conclusion no sociology would be possible, and the attempt to understand and explain would have to be abandoned. 15 20 25

Source: adapted from M. Haralambos and M. Holborn, *Sociology: Themes and Perspectives,* 3rd Ed., London: Collins Educational, 1991

QUESTIONS

a   Explain the meaning of the term 'symbolic interactionism' (Item A, line 8).

(2 marks)

These two marks are for *knowledge* because Item A itself does not explicitly define symbolic interactionism. There are however general hints in the Item. An example from someone like W. I. Thomas or G. H. Mead might make your definition clearer. It is defined very briefly in the glossary of Giddens (1989).

b   Illustrating your answer with information from Items B and C, explain why social action theorists prefer qualitative methods of social research.

(3 marks)

There are three marks here for *interpretation and application.* Make sure you make three clear points in your answer to get all the marks. Use the data included in the specified Items as much as you can.

c   Explain and assess the view that 'if men define situations as real, they are real in their consequences' (Item A, lines 16–17).

(7 marks)

This question requires you to use all three skills. You can get marks for *interpretation and application* by explaining the term and using material from the Items to support or criticize that view. You will get marks for knowledge if you bring in other material to back up arguments on both sides of the debate. Howard Becker, for instance, has written a lot about this. *Evaluation* marks come from your criticism of the view expressed.

Look at Merton's argument about manifest and latent functions as an example of a positivist criticism (see Giddens (1989), p. 697 and also O'Donnell (1992), on interactionism). A discussion of interactionist theories of labelling is also pertinent to this question. See Haralambos and Holborn (1991), pp. 610–19 in relation to deviance – a Paper 2 topic – and pp. 272–82 on education. There are also references to labelling in the section of this book on teacher–pupil interaction (p. 123). It is also worth following up the source from which the Item is taken – Bilton *et al.* (1987), p. 22.

d   Using material from the Items above and elsewhere, assess the view that the sociologist should 'take the actor's point of view' (Item B, line 2) when engaged in sociological research.

(7 marks)

This question requires you to *evaluate* the qualitative research methods that are associated with the social action approach. You need to produce a well-structured discussion of the advantages and disadvantages of the participant-observational method and arrive at a conclusion. These arguments are summarized in Haralambos and Holborn (1991), p. 721 and pp. 743–6.

Remember two unconnected lists will not do. Reference to specific sociological studies to illustrate your answer will gain you marks for *knowledge* and *application.* You are also instructed to refer to the Items. (The information and references contained in the question on Participant Observation on page 41 are also relevant to this particular question.)

e   Assess the view contained in Item D that 'if phenomenological views were taken to their logical conclusion no sociology would be possible' (lines 25–6).

(6 marks)

This question is about the criticisms of phenomenological approaches; that they are so 'relativist' that they deny the existence of reality at all. The issue of relativism is discussed in general terms by writers such as Barry Hindess, Alvin Gouldner and in more specific terms by Gerald Bernbaum in his criticism of the 'new' sociology of education. A key writer in this area is Michael F. D. Young whose book, *Knowledge and Control* (1971), is discussed in Haralambos and Holborn (1991), pp. 295–6.

Use all skills in this answer to discuss problems associated with social action theories.

The issue of relativism also underlies the arguments surrounding postmodernism as can be seen from the question on Modern Social Theory on page 48. The question on The National Curriculum on page 116 also includes a debate arising from the work of Michael F. D. Young.

1.4 Questionnaires

ITEM A

There are many terms here which you need to be familiar with. If you do not know what terms like 'quantitative' (using numbers), 'sample' (a selection from the population being studied) and 'representative' (whether the group of people we are studying is typical of others) mean, then you will be unable to answer the questions. On representativeness, see the article by J. Platt in *Sociology Review*, February 1993.

Source: adapted from M. Williams: 'Finding out about society', in *Society Today*, London: Macmillan, 1986

Quantitative research methods

Surveys These are of two types: censuses, where every member of the population under study is questioned; and sample surveys, where a proportion of the population is questioned, and the results generalized from the sample to the whole population. Sociologists almost never use census techniques because of their 5 cost, unless a very small population is being studied. In this sense population is the term we use to describe the group we want to study – with the national census for example, the census population is the same as the population of the UK. But a population might only be a small social group. 10

A sample is a small section of a population: sociologists usually try to set up random samples in order to have a representative group to study. If a sample has been drawn up properly, and everybody in the study population has an equal (or random) chance of being included in the sample, then the sociologist can 15 be reasonably sure that the data collected from the sample will be representative of the wider population.

Surveys and censuses normally use questionnaires to collect data; these are simply lists of questions that the researcher wants answered. Questionnaire design is a very important and skilled 20 part of survey research: the questions must relate directly to the variables in the study and be unambiguous.

ITEM B

Patrick McNeill highlights some of the problems which arise when trying to draw up and administer a questionnaire. The study mentioned illustrates clearly the problematic nature of research findings based on questionnaires.

The wording of questions, especially closed questions and those asked in a postal questionnaire, must be clear, precise, and unambiguous. The language used should be as simple as possible. Questions must not presume that respondents have any more knowledge than in fact they have, and must not lead 5 respondents towards a particular answer. This is much more difficult than it sounds, and requires a great deal of skill and practice.

As an example of the pitfalls involved in drafting questions, we can consider the fuss there was in 1983 when Hill announced 10 that he had found that as many as 40 per cent of six-year-old children had seen video-nasties (i.e. video films of horror, violence, and sadistic sex). In his questionnaire, he named some of the more famous such videos and asked the children to say whether they had seen them. His findings produced a lively press confer- 15 ence, and questions in the House of Commons, and certainly contributed to the passage of a bill through Parliament to limit the availability of such films. Cumberbatch and Bates repeated the research, asking another sample of children, eleven-year-olds this time, whether they had seen certain such videos. They 20 achieved a figure of 68 per cent of the children claiming to have seen these films. The point was, however, that Cumberbatch and

Bates had named a number of video-nasties that did not in fact exist, and yet the children claimed that they had seen them. What Hill had found was that children would claim to have seen video-nasties, rather than that they had actually seen them. This is a very good example of the validity problem. 25

Source: P. McNeill, *Research Methods*, London: Routledge, 1985

ITEM C

This item points out that people may interpret questions differently at different times. This is an example of the reliability problem of questionnaire-based surveys, particularly when dealing with people's attitudes.

British Social Attitudes aims to monitor public attitudes to a wide variety of social, economic, political and moral issues during the 1980s and 1990s. Our task is to keep the 'camera' still so that we end up recording rather than creating movement. But we are never able to control the fact that the background keeps shifting. 5 Governments, for instance, insist from time to time on introducing new policies for the nation with little consideration for how they affect social science measurements!

So, however desirable it may be in theory that all questions about all topics should be the same between readings, it is not 10 always possible in practice. And even when the question is the same, we cannot ensure that its meaning is constant. No question or set of questions can be asked in a vacuum; how respondents answer will depend to some extent on what they think a question is actually getting at, not only on what it says. Identical questions 15 may well convey different messages at different times.

Source: adapted from R. Jowell *et al* (eds), *British Social Attitudes*, the 5th Report, Aldershot: Gower, 1988

ITEM D

This is an example of the kind of questionnaire that is sometimes produced by non-social scientists.

IT'S YOUR VERDICT

1 I believe that capital punishment should be brought back for the following categories of murder: Children ☐ Police ☐ Terrorism ☐ All murders ☐

2 Life sentences for serious crimes like murder and rape should carry a minimum term of: 20 years ☐ 25 years ☐

3 The prosecution should have the right of appeal against sentences they consider to be too lenient ☐ *Tick boxes of those statements you agree with, then post the coupon to: VIOLENT BRITAIN, Daily Star, 33 St. Bride St., London EC4A 4AY.*

Source: the *Daily Star*, 11 February, 1985

ITEM E

This item illustrates the many problems, as well as some of the advantages, of collecting information with questionnaires. You could also use this material in your answers to the question on page 44 on Official Statistics.

Pat McNeill: The British Crime Survey was set up in 1982 to investigate crime through a sample survey which asks people their experience of crime. What is the design of the survey?
Pat Mayhew (Principal Research Officer at the Home Office Research and Planning Unit): Many forms of crime are rare, so 5 we have to have a big sample, about 11,000 households. In 1982 the only feasible sampling frame was the Electoral Register. Today, PAF (the Post Office Address File) is a better frame and in 1988 we thought about whether to switch to it. But we found that this might mean a loss of comparability. Anything that jeopar- 10 dizes comparability over the years has consequences which cannot be precisely quantified.
P.McN.: How satisfied are you with the sample?

P.M.: In terms of age and sex distribution it is really quite good. But the sample doesn't cover people in institutions, who may be 15 disproportionately victimized. There is an ethnic minority 'booster sample' in the 1988 Survey, but there are no population statistics to check its representativeness. The response rate is nearly 80 per cent which is very good.

P.McN.: How do you draft the questions? 20

P.M.: In drafting the questions and in designing the structure of the questionnaire we learned a lot from the earlier surveys. For example, we used 'screener' questions. If you ask people if they have been the victim of a particular crime and, when they say 'yes', you immediately ask for more details, they quickly learn 25 that to say 'yes' means they will have more questions to answer. So you ask about all the possible crimes in a list. If they say 'yes' to any of the crimes, only at the end do you question further.

P.McN.: Are you aware of any particular weak areas in the data?

P.M.: Yes, the measurement of domestic abuse and sexual assault, 30 because of the problem of respondents being too reticent to answer frankly. Our first attempt didn't work well, but we changed the wording of the question. The rate of reported sexual assault actually doubled, though from a very small base. The interview also covers some self-reported offences, because we 35 wanted to investigate the overlap between victims and offenders, the largest group in both cases being young males.

People were sceptical about whether respondents would cooperate, but this itself was not a problem, though respondents may none the less have concealed offences. When we analysed the 40 1982 data, we found very low admission rates. so we changed the procedure in 1984, and asked first 'How many people do you think did this?' When they had said, for instance, that most people had fiddled their income tax returns, it was much easier for them to admit it. 45

The point of the survey is to show crime as it really is, and the truth is that a great number of crimes are relatively trivial property ones, despite what people imagine and the media suggest. We have shown that the upwards trend of crime is slower than police statistics show. 50

Source: adapted from P. McNeill, *Society Today 2*, London: Macmillan, 1991

QUESTIONS

a   State briefly what sociologists mean by 'sample surveys' (Item A, lines 2–3) .

(1 mark)   A simple mark for *interpretation*, use your own words.

b   Explain why the study by Cumberbatch and Bates referred to in Item B is 'a good example of the validity problem' (lines 26–7).

(2 marks)   *Interpretation* skills again here. The Cumberbatch and Bates study throws doubt on the validity of the study by Hill. Explain why this is so by clearly stating what is meant by validity in sociological research findings. McNeill's book (1991) from which this item is taken has a clear explanation of 'validity' on p. 20, as does O'Donnell (1992), p. 25 and Haralambos and Holborn (1991), p. 721.

c How valid is the assertion in Item C that 'No question or set of questions can be asked in a vacuum' (line 12)?

(7 marks)   Look at both sides of the positivist/anti-positivist debate regarding the extent to which it is possible to carry out sociological research which classifies the world in an objective, value–neutral way. Illustrate your answer with material from Item C and bring in other relevant studies, such as Dohrenwend in Haralambos and Holborn (1991), p. 739. In particular, point out the difference that political and economic conditions in particular can make. Consider the notion of 'experimental effect'. (This question also relates to the issues of 'interview effect' and 'interviewer effect' which is mentioned in the next section on Interviews, page 28.)

d To what extent would data produced by the questionnaire contained in Item D be valid and representative?

(6 marks)   This questionnaire can be criticized on grounds of both validity and representativeness. The questions themselves all have a common problem affecting their validity and there is a twofold problem of unrepresentativeness due to the way in which the questionnaire is administered. Would you have responded to such a questionnaire?
If not why not?

e Using material from Item E and elsewhere, evaluate the advantages and disadvantages of questionnaires in social surveys.

(9 marks)   This requires a discussion which relates to positivist and phenomenological views on the reliability and validity of the data produced by questionnaires. Illustrate your answer with reference to a number of social surveys (you can find plenty in textbooks or in the sources of the items). This question requires all skills and a clear structure to identify the advantages and disadvantages before supporting them with studies. See Haralambos and Holborn (1991) pp. 731–4, O'Donnell (1992), pp. 31–2. Steve Taylor's article on 'Measuring child abuse' (*Sociology Review*, February 1992) offers a detailed critique of the use of questionnaires in this field. An extract from this article is contained on pages 194–5 of this book.

1.5 Interviews

ITEM A

McNeill's book (1985) is a useful introduction to all research methods and it provides some good examples. Here McNeill outlines some of the problems which occur because what people say and what they do are sometimes different. This raises the whole problem of validity. There is also a good section on interviews in Bilton *et al.* (1987), pp. 529–41.

Source: adapted from P. McNeill, *Research Methods*, London: Routledge, 1985

The interview is an artificial situation. There is no guarantee that what people say in interviews is a true account of what they actually do, whether they are intentionally lying or whether they genuinely believe what they are saying. People are quite capable of saying one thing and doing another, and of being unaware of this. 'Interview effect' is as important as 'interviewer effect'. Oakley (1979) has a very interesting discussion of the effect that the interview has on the person doing the interview, as well as on the interviewee.

The interview schedule means that the researcher is setting limits to what the respondent can say.

It is unlikely that anyone will give full or truthful answers in an interview to questions that concern sensitive, embarrassing, or possibly criminal aspects of their lives.

Fundamentally, the survey method finds out what people will say when they are being interviewed or filling in a questionnaire. This may not be the same thing as what they actually do or think.

ITEM B

This provides a useful summary of the range of interview types and the various degrees of control which the researcher can have in interview situations.

Source: Bilton *et al.*, *Introductory Sociology*, 2nd Ed. London: Macmillan, 1987

In interviews the degree of structure of questions can vary:
1 The most structured interview is the sort where the order and wording of the questions are predetermined and each respondent is asked exactly the same questions in exactly the same way with the questions following the same order every time.
2 The focused interview, as its name suggests, is the sort where the questions are focused on particular topics but where the interviewer can choose the words he/she uses to ask them as well as the order in which they are asked. (Usually then this sort of interview schedule – as the list of questions an interviewer is to ask is called – simply lists general areas of interest the interviewer is to get the respondent to talk about.)
3 The completely unstructured or discovery interview involves the interviewer simply engaging the respondent in conversation, and then following up particular points of interest as they develop.

ITEM C

This item highlights the fact that the interview situation is always part of an interaction and, like any other, it involves issues of perception and meaning. It is not only the question but also the questionner that can affect an answer. Class, ethnic and gender differences between the

The meaning of the interview for middle-class correspondents is posed like this: although the interviewer is a stranger, an outsider, he is a well-spoken educated person. He is seeking information on behalf of some organization, hence his questioning not only has sanction but sets the stage for both a certain freedom of speech and an obligation to give fairly full information.

In contrast the lower-class person infrequently meets a middle-class person in a situation anything like the interview. Here he must talk at great length to a stranger about personal experi-

interviewer and interviewee may all affect the answers given and therefore the validity of the exercise.

Source: adapted from M. Bulmer, *Sociological Research Methods,* London: Macmillan, 1984

ences. He can as a rule assume that words, phrases and gestures   10
are assigned approximately similar meanings by his listeners. But this is not so in the interview, indeed, in any situation where class converses with class in non-traditional modes.

These same scholars are aware that as middle-class observers they may be unable to recognize lower-class classifications.   15
Secondary analyses of previously published 'scales' do suggest that sometimes the categories imposed by the investigators are indeed unlike those in the minds of the subjects.

ITEM D

Think of some of the problems involved in researching 'sensitive' topics such as child abuse. This item from *New Society* suggests that a variety of research methods may be needed to supplement an interview. This is sometimes called **triangulation**.

Source: P. McNeill, *Society Today 2,* London: Macmillan, 1991

Pat McNeill: What is the subject of your research?
Steve Taylor (lecturer at the London School of Economics): I'm researching child abuse, and in particular how various experts, such as social workers and doctors, come to 'recognize' that a child has been abused or is 'at risk'.   5
P.McN.: What research methods are you using?
S.T.: First, we did formal interviews with the various professional groups involved. We asked them how they defined child abuse, and how they recognized something as a case of child abuse. But sociologists should not just reproduce what people   10
say, and you cannot conduct research purely on interviews. So, having identified some of the things professionals saw as problematic about child abuse, we did some participant observation. This meant going out with social workers on visits, going to case conferences and to court with social workers in order to see their   15
ideas put into action.

ITEM E

Haralambos and Holborn (1991) has a particularly good section on interviews on pp. 734–40. Here the authors explore the different types of interview. You might like to look at and keep notes of some sociological examples of different types of interviewing as well as the ones mentioned here. Think about the problems of reliability and validity in relation to different types of interview.

Interviews take a number of forms depending on how structured they are. A completely 'structured interview' is simply a questionnaire administered by an interviewer who is not allowed to deviate in any way from the questions provided. The interviewer simply reads out the questions to the respondent. At the other   5
extreme a totally 'unstructured interview' takes the form of a conversation where the interviewer has no predetermined questions. Most interviews fall somewhere between these two extremes.

Interviews of a more structured variety may allow the inter-   10
viewer to probe the respondents' answers so that they can, if necessary, be clarified. The interviewer may also be allowed to prompt the interviewee, that is, give them extra guidance to help them answer the question. For example, Goldthorpe and Lockwood's team of researchers was able to prompt interviewees   15
who could not decide how to answer a question by suggesting that they might have read job adverts in local newspapers.

In unstructured interviews the conversation develops naturally, unless the respondent fails to cover an area in which the researcher is interested. Eventually the interviewer will direct the   20
conversation back to the areas he or she wishes to cover. Hannah Gavron, for example, in her study, *The Captive Wife,* interviewed 76 housewives. She had a schedule of areas she wished to cover

Source: M. Haralambos and M.
Holborn, *Sociology: Themes and
Perspectives*, 3rd Ed., London:
Collins Educational, 1991

in each interview, but she did not direct the wives to these areas
unless it became essential. In this way she hoped to avoid direct-   25
ing the interview too much, and so to avoid influencing the
responses. At the same time, however, she achieved some stan-
dardization of the data collected, and direct comparisons
between the women became possible.

QUESTIONS

a Explain the difference between 'interview effect' and 'interviewer effect' (Item A, line 6).

(2 marks)   Two marks for *interpretation* of the information in the item. There is more
                         information given on 'interview effect' than on 'interviewer effect', but read
                         carefully and the distinction between the two should become clear.

b With reference to Item B, identify the type of interview which falls somewhere between a
structured and an unstructured interview.

(1 mark)   A simple *interpretation* mark.

c Illustrating your answer with material from Item E and elsewhere, assess the relative
merits of both structured and unstructured interviews.

(9 marks)   This question requires you to use all three skills. You can get marks for
                         interpretation by explaining the views expressed in Item E, but make sure you
                         look at both types of interview. *Application* marks are available for using the
                         material in a relevant way. *Knowledge* and *application* marks can be gained
                         by bringing in relevant examples from other sources than those in the item.
                         Evaluation skills can be demonstrated by comparing the advantages and
                         disadvantages of each method, and saying in the end which is more useful.
                         An answer like this benefits considerably from planning.

d Referring to Item C, describe how the social class of an interviewer might affect the validity
of an interview.

(4 marks)   This question asks for *interpretation* skills using the information from Item C
                         only. Be careful to stick to the question asked and do not bring in issues
                         which are irrelevant to this particular question, such as gender or ethnicity.
                         You might consider the type of social class background from which
                         sociological researchers usually come and any problems that flow from this.

e Assess the view expressed in Item D that sociologists 'should not just reproduce what
people say, and you cannot conduct research purely on interviews' (lines 10–11)

(9 marks)   This should be a lengthy discussion leading to a brief conclusion in order to satisfy
                         all three skill requirements, particularly that of *evaluation*.
                             Interpret Taylor's remarks carefully. Note that he shows the importance of not
                         relying just on what people say. The question also requires you to look at the value
                         of interview data and what sort of research methods may be used to supplement it.
                         Does Taylor's remark mean research conducted using only interviews is invalid?
                             A key concept is triangulation (i.e. use of a number of different methods to
                         crosscheck the accuracy of data produced) in order to get data which is both
                         reliable and valid. Alan Bryman's book *Quantity and Quality in Social Research*
                         (1988) includes a helpful discussion of triangulation, which is summarized in
                         Haralambos and Holborn (1991) on page 754.

1.6 Participant observation

ITEM A

Pryce argues convincingly for the use of participant observation. Particularly important are the arguments about seeing things the way the people involved see them and the insight this gives. Can you think of any arguments against his views? A more lengthy extract from this book is contained in Trowler (1987) pp. 88–90.

Source: K. Pryce, *Endless Pressure,* Harmondsworth: Penguin, 1979

The main method adopted for the research on which this study is based was participant observation. Participant observation, because it deposits one inside the culture of the group studied and forces on one the role of involved actor and participant, affords the academic researcher a unique opportunity of getting the right leads and following through situations whereby he can replace superficial impressions with more accurate insights. By 5 combining his 'outsider' perception with an insider's view of life under consideration, the researcher can thus get behind the statistical shapes and patterns and explore at first hand the wide variety of adaptive responses he encounters, studying them from the value position of the people themselves, in their own terms 10 and on their own ground. All the time he does this through prolonged, intensive direct exposure to actual life-conditions over a relatively long period of time. Not only can the findings of this intensive approach supplement and add significance to data gathered by more quantitative techniques, they can generate 15 fruitful hypotheses which quantitative research can later refine and test.

ITEM B

This fictional example from a novel refers to one very practical problem of certain forms of participant observation! It also hints at the ethical problems a researcher might encounter when studying 'deviant' groups. This has been explored by 'J. Patrick' in his study of a Glasgow gang (*A Glasgow Gang Observed*, 1973). Moral, legal and ethical questions, particularly in relation to covert participant observation, are discussed in all the main textbooks.

Source: adapted from the novel *The Men's Room* by Ann Oakley, London: Flamingo, HarperCollins, 1991.

The next event of that spring was a scandal in the department. Ivan Swinhoe was caught shoplifting. He liberated six bottles of washing-up liquid from the shelves of Tesco's in Sydenham High Street.

Why had Swinhoe done it? By the time the news reached the department he'd constructed a plausible story. Everyone knew he'd been doing research on shoplifting for years. He occasion- 5 ally wrote a languid paper about it, but mostly it just dragged on. So now he said he'd needed to expand his methodological approach to the study by engaging in participant observation. Thus like Jenner who injected himself with cow pox, Swinhoe had caused himself to be afflicted with the crime of shoplifting. 10 This account made him a great hero; someone pinned on the noticeboard in the hall the headline from the *Sydenham Star*: 'Local Man's Research into Shoplifting Lands him in the Dock'.

Naturally, the ethical implications remained to be thought out: what needed to happen was that the names of social scientists 15 studying society by such means should be cleared of all criminal associations. Their behaviour was professional, not personal. However it was hard to see how the British Sociological Association would easily defeat the police and the law courts on that. 20

ITEM C

Non-participant observation is quite often neglected in the debate about research methods. The key question here is whether just by observing someone you are part of the interaction or not, and whether you can observe without people changing their behaviour. David Hargreaves had a useful discussion of this problem in the classic *Social Relations in a Secondary School.*

Source: New Society, 24 June, 1988

Pat McNeill: You have published a great deal of work on your research in schools, often using the technique of non-participant observation. What does this involve?

Peter Woods: It is important not to exaggerate the difference between participant observation and non-participant observation. As a participant, you undertake a role within a group or institution. In non-participant observation you observe a situation from a detached position which doesn't intrude nor take over any of the roles of the people interacting in that situation. A term often used is a 'fly on the wall'. The problem with this model is that observers are not flies and, with schools in particular, the observer inevitably influences the interaction to some degree.

5

10

ITEM D

O'Donnell (1992) has provided a neat summary of the relative strengths and weaknesses of participant observation which revolve around the fact that the undoubted benefits of this method can be at the expense of objectivity. The Frankenberg example suggests, however, that the problem can be overcome to some extent.

Source: M. O'Donnell, *A New Introduction to Sociology*, 3rd Ed., Walton-on-Thames: Nelson, 1992

The main advantage and disadvantage of participant observation are opposite sides of the same coin: the method can bring all the insight and understanding that comes with subjective involvement but also all the possible loss of objectivity. Ronald Frankenberg, himself the author of a participant observational study of life in a Welsh village, has usefully suggested three stages of research for the participant observer which offer some safeguard against excessive subjectivity. Each of these stages involves a different degree of involvement with the subject matter. Firstly, the research project must be set up – a relatively objective process. Secondly, the sociologist becomes subjectively (personally) involved with those s/he wishes to study. Thirdly, s/he withdraws to consider and assess his/her experience and findings.

Authors of participant observational studies are not uncommonly accused of sentimentalising and over-romanticising the deviants, criminals and youth groups which are typically the subjects of their research. Certainly, there is a strong suggestion of identification with 'the outsider' in a number of classic participant observational studies but on the credit side such studies often have an authenticity which could scarcely be achieved by survey work.

5

10

15

20

QUESTIONS

a Explain in your own words why Pryce adopted participant observation as his main method, (Item A).

(2 marks)   Make two clear points to get both *interpretation* marks for this question. Use your own words, as requested, to show your understanding.

b Using material from Item B and elsewhere, explain the problems sociologists might face in collecting sociological data using participant observation.

(4 marks)   This question tests skills of *interpretation*, *knowledge* and *application*. You must specifically refer to the problems mentioned in Item B, and bring in

examples of actual studies from elsewhere. The following extracts from participant-observational studies would be a good starting point: Corzine and Kirby in Trowler (1987) pp. 24–6, Ball also in Trowler (1987), pp. 206–10, Whyte in Haralambos (1986), pp. 39–43 and Hargreaves in the same book pp. 43–6. Another example which raises moral issues is Laud Humphreys' study of homosexuality in public toilets in the United States, *The Tea Room Trade* (1970).

c Illustrating your answer with material from the Items above discuss the merits of qualitative research methods.

(4 marks)   This question calls for a fairly short discussion in which you must use the information provided in the items alone to look at the advantages of participant observation (*interpretation and application*). As you are asked to 'discuss the merits' you can also get marks for *evaluation* when you look at criticisms.

d Assess the view that 'non-participant observation' (Item C, line 2) is possible.

(6 marks)   This relates to the problem of whether it is possible to carry out observational research without affecting those being studied. The term 'Hawthorne Effect' has been used to describe the way in which knowledge of being the subject of study affects behaviour. (See Haralambos and Holborn (1991) p. 705). The cartoon on p. 45 of Haralambos (1986) may give you some ideas. See also O'Donnell (1992), p. 32. On the positive side think of situations in which observation might be unobtrusive. Look at both sides of the argument and refer your conclusion directly back to the question to get all *evaluation* marks available.

e The author of Item D suggests that 'Authors of participant observational studies are not uncommonly accused of sentimentalising and over-romanticising . . . the subjects of their research', (lines 15–18). Assess the extent to which this means that participant observation leads to totally subjective conclusions

(9 marks)   This question relates to the positivism/phenomenology debate concerning the extent to which sociology should produce findings which are objective and quantifiable. Because participant observation is one of the main methods of the phenomenological approach it has come under criticism from positivists for its unreliability because there is no way of replicating such research. The fact that the researcher has to interpret what they observe introduces the risk of subjectivity. There are however arguments that suggest that participant observation can be rigorous and 'scientific'. These arguments are covered in Haralambos and Holborn (1991) pp. 745–6. Note that this question is an evaluative one so reach a conclusion. Remember also that information in the items is there to be used.

1.7 Official statistics

Newspapers are a good source of up-to-date information and you can collect a lot of data from them. It is useful to record this information somewhere, maybe on index cards, and use the information to answer questions and revise for exams. This article is especially useful, as it talks in some detail about the problem connected with collecting official statistics and the effect that this has on their validity.

Why the Census doesn't make sense. One of the temporary staff employed on the 1991 Census explains the flaws in the system . . .

The object of the exercise, as you may recall from literature pushed through doors with the Census forms last April, is to enable government departments, national and local, to plan resources for public services . . .

Beyond the statistics lies an interesting set of pointers to the state of society, which we came across in our door-to-door work and which often made form collection difficult. They are perhaps as important to take note of as the figures themselves . . . In general terms this is what we found.

The forms themselves appeared to have been designed for the convenience of those feeding the statistics into the computer rather than the consumers. Householders had to be fairly well educated and literate to fill them in without making mistakes. Enumerators spent hours helping people bemused by the questions and guidelines, and supplying forms in different languages as necessary. That was part of our job, but it didn't leave time to check back over every omission and error in other forms . . .

Some people made themselves hard to find . . . Some may have been dodging poll tax bailiffs, out in strength in our area during the census period. Other properties may have been illegal sublets or harbouring people who for one reason or another shouldn't have been there.

There were also those who while prepared to accept that the census was confidential doubted that statistics would be used in any effective manner . . .

Elderly people and others were simply afraid to answer the door. There were also flats with intercoms which crackled with a child's voice . . .

There were people who worked long hours even at weekends and were never there. Even in multi-occupied property often the person in Bedsit One had never seen his neighbour in Bedsit Two.

Source: abridged from a report in the *Guardian*, 25 July, 1991

5

10

15

20

25

30

Another article critical of official statistics, showing in a more detailed way how some social groups are either left out of statistics or under-recorded in them. The article also shows that there is even more of a problem if there are no statistics available. It

There are three ways in which women and their lifestyles are invisible in government statistics; areas in which data is simply not collected at all; areas in which some data is collected but is available only at local authority or health authority level and not broken down nationally by sex, race, age or other categories; and areas such as employment in which, although some national data is collected and published, it under-represents women because it is based upon assumptions that can exclude them.

For example, people earning under the National Insurance

5

also illustrates the idea that official statistics are 'social constructs'.

threshold of £52 a week – the majority of them part-time women workers – never appear on the New Earnings survey, the key government statistics on earnings. The survey counts only those who are actually paying National Insurance, so it can never give an accurate picture of low pay or true average wages, particularly for women . . . 10

15

The government's trend to decentralize those statistics that are already available applies to information on health care, as Jo Richardson MP, the shadow Minister for Women, found out last month. When she put parliamentary questions asking for national figures on the provision of sterilizations, treatments for infertility and provision of pregnancy tests, Virginia Bottomley stated in written replies that such information is 'not held centrally' or 'routinely collected'. 20

Source: abridged from a report in the *Guardian*, 24 July, 1991

ITEM C

This is an article from the same newspaper, treating various crime statistics as relatively unproblematic. This shows that even serious newspapers do not always question the source of the statistical data they use. Look at Slattery (1986) to see some of the problems involved with the collection of criminal statistics. Also the article from which Item D is taken.

The crime rate continues remorselessly on its upward trend with 4.9 million offences recorded in the 12 months to last June, an 18 per cent rise, the Home Office reported yesterday.

One of the biggest increases was in car crimes, up by nearly a quarter and accounting for more than a third of the overall increase . . . Although the crime surge contrasts with an average annual 6 per cent rise for the past 10 years, government and police officials say that the latest statistics risk giving a distorted impression 5

The 5 per cent increase in violent crime, for instance, was relatively small, according to the Home Office, compared with an average 10 per cent annual increase in the three previous years. The public's increased readiness to report crimes also contributes to the increases . . . 10

Of the 4.9 million offences recorded in the year to June, 4.6 million (94 per cent) were crimes against property, while 256,000 (5 per cent) were violent crimes against the person, sexual crimes and robbery. The remaining 33,000 (1 per cent) were other types of crime. 15

Just over half of all recorded crime involved theft of or from vehicles (1.4 million or 29 per cent) or burglary (1.1 million or 23 per cent). 20

Source: abridged from a report in the *Guardian*, 14 September, 1991

ITEM D

Lewis' article, taken from *Social Trends*, highlights one of the major problems, that of unrecorded or unreported crime. For some activities this 'dark figure of crime' might make the data almost meaningless and certainly highly unreliable. Make sure you are aware of the difference between the official figure given for crimes known to the police and the statistics presented in the *British Crime Survey*.

Reports of crime figures, though useful, should always be regarded with a critical eye. The relationship between recorded crime and the level of real crime is influenced by community attitudes, levels of policing, legislative change and the statistical definitions used. The relationships between these factors are complex and changing. The one thing that can be said is that police recorded crime statistics do not provide a simple picture of trends in crime. Despite all this, statistics on recorded crimes, together with the results from the British Crime Surveys remain the only regular basis on which we can infer crime trends. If they can be analysed with all the considerations discussed here kept in mind, they can yield valuable insights into crime trends and 5

10

This issue is discussed in R. Matthews, 'Squaring up to crime' in *Sociology Review*, February 1993.

the demands placed on police and criminal justice resources. If, however, they are analysed carelessly they simply foster uninformed public debate.

15

Recorded and unrecorded crime: by type, 1987, England and Wales

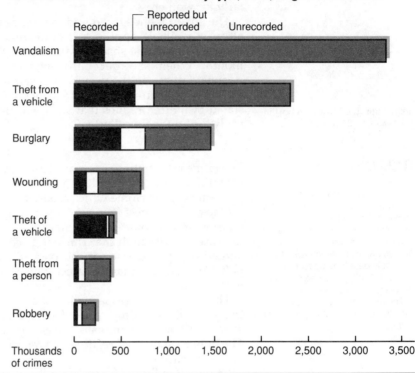

Recorded | Reported but unrecorded | Unrecorded

Source: adapted from C. Lewis, 'Crime statistics: their Use and misuse' in *Social Trends 1992*, London: HMSO, 1992

ITEM E

In this article Slattery links the control of statistical information with power, based on the ways that sociologists have theorized the concept of power, for example the work of S. Lukes. You will find reference to this in any good textbook. Slattery (1986) from which this extract is taken is the key book to get hold of for this topic.

Source: M. Slattery, *Official Statistics*, London: Tavistock, 1986

All forms of social knowledge represent power: the power to inform or mislead, the power to illuminate or manipulate. Whoever controls the definition of official statistics controls what is collected and how much; whoever controls the interpretation of official statistics controls public debate (and criticism); whoever has the power to withhold official data (or not collect it in the first place) has the power to prevent public discussion from arising.

5

QUESTIONS

a With reference to Item A, examine the problems that might arise in using the data from the 1991 Census to plan public services.

(3 marks) This is a question asking you to interpret how the reliability problems in data collection, such as the ones highlighted in this Item, might affect the validity of projections made on the basis of such data. Use the relevant material in the Item and put it in your own words. To get all three marks you must identify three separate points.

b Assess the validity of the argument that women are 'invisible in government statistics' (Item B, line 2).

(7 marks) This question is asking you to use all skills, interpreting the views in Item B, backing them up with other studies (*knowledge* and *application*) and then looking at data which contradicts that view (*evaluation*). For example, women may be under-represented in the unemployment statistics but they may be over-represented in health statistics as sometimes they make trips to the doctor for other members of the family. You could also look at the points made by S. Faludi in the question on Work and Gender on page 157. A discussion which touches upon this issue is contained in Abbott and Wallace (1990) on pp. 202–12.

c Assess the validity of the view put forward in Item C that official crime statistics 'risk giving a distorted impression' (line 8).

(7 marks) This is asking for a well-structured argument about the validity of official crime statistics. Although many sociologists agree that official statistics are distorted, positivists in particular see them as less subjective than other ways of collecting information. Make sure you are clear what is meant by the term validity. This, along with the two other crucial concepts of representativeness and reliability are discussed in some detail in McNeill (1985). Item D contains several points on the ways in which crime statistics are influenced by the processes of collection and interpretation. The diagram is also pertinent to this discussion. Victim surveys may not be without their faults however. (See the question on Questionnaires on page 34 for some information on this.)

d Identify the type of offence where recorded crime most approximates the true level of crime (Item D).

(1 mark) A simple *Interpretation* question – make sure you get it right!

e Using material from the Items and elsewhere, assess the validity of the argument put forward by the author of Item E that 'all forms of social knowledge represent power' (line 1).

(7 marks) Look in Haralambos and Holborn (1991) pp. 748–51, or Bilton *et al.* (1987), pp. 526–9, or any other textbook, to explore ideas about the relationship between social knowledge and power. The idea that the ruling class control the knowledge in society is a Marxist concept and is associated in particular with the work of Antonio Gramsci and his concept of hegemony, explained in Haralambos and Holborn (1991), p. 155, might be useful, but it can be challenged from a pluralist viewpoint. They accept that knowledge gives power, but suggest that different groups hold knowledge on different issues and therefore power is not confined to one particular group in society.

1.8 Modern social theory

ITEM A

Postmodernist thinking emphasizes 'relativism', the idea that there is no such thing as 'objective' truth; there are only competing ways of looking at things and competing ways of knowing about things. So all sociological accounts of reality have equal validity. This implies that we have gone beyond the time when we could believe that a theory which tries to explain everything can have any credibility. Postmodernism is therefore critical of the kinds of attempts to provide such an explanation which were at the heart of the founders of sociology. The founders were very much modernists, believing that it was possible to understand the world and that it was also possible to use that understanding to change the world for the better. These themes are clearly central to the work of Comte, Marx, Weber and Durkheim.

If postmodernists are right, we must therefore accept that we are in a postmodern world where such grand theoretical designs are obsolete and where multiple claims for truth compete for our support. These ideas were around in the nineteenth century in the work of Nietzsche, but the most important modern origin is Foucault. Sociological writers who tend towards support of postmodernism are Scott Lash and John Urry. Others who prefer to argue that we are in a period of late-modernity rather than postmodernity include Anthony Giddens and Jurgen Habermas.

You could consult O'Donnell (1992) pp. 511–12 or Jones (1993) pp. 102–11.

Source: adapted from 'What is postmodernism?', Research Roundup, *Social Studies Review*, September 1990

The words 'postmodern', 'postmodernism', and 'postmodernist theory' have appeared ever more frequently in social science texts.

A little thought will show that the idea of the postmodern involves the complimentary idea of the 'modern': the postmodern is something that is different from and comes after the modern. There is also the implication that the postmodern emerged as a reaction to the modern.

The idea of the modern originated as a description of the forms of thought and action that developed with the decline of medieval society in Europe. The principal features that came to be identified as modern can be seen in the three areas of economic, political and cultural processes. Economically, modernity involved the capitalistic process of a market economy. Politically, modernity involved the consolidation of the centralized nation state and the extension of bureaucratic forms of surveillance, and democratic political party systems. Culturally, modernity involved a challenge to 'tradition' in the name of 'rationality' and a stress on the virtues of scientific and technical knowledge.

These themes are familiar from the writings of the classical sociologists, who saw their task as that of describing and explaining the emergence and development of modern society. The works of Marx, Weber and Durkheim took these ideas as their central concerns.

The idea of the postmodern involves some kind of claim that some or all of these key features of modern society have disappeared. This can be seen most clearly in the realm of culture, where self-proclaimed 'modern' thinkers and artists were challenged from the late 1960s by 'anti-modernist' ideas attacking the dehumanization of modern society. This coincided with the challenge to orthodox 'positivist' sociology by new schools of thought which rejected its claims to a scientific status.

This cultural postmodernity became the basis of a whole school of social theory. Whereas the classical sociologists sought to transcend the relativity of social situations and to establish some rational standpoint from which 'reality' could be described, the postmodern writers embrace diversity and fragmentation. Their argument is that there is no 'objective reality' behind social meanings. Accounts and definitions have no objective or external reference. They are elements in a free-floating system of images which are produced and reproduced through the media of mass communication. People live in an 'artificial' world which is created and defined by the cultural processes of mass communication.

ITEM B

Feminists have been very influential in the development of more modern social theories. You need to be quite clear on the differences between different feminist perspectives which are outlined here and in Abbott and Wallace (1990) and Maynard 'Current trends in feminist theory' in *Social Studies Review*, Vol.2, No 3.

Theory is the basis of sociology. Theories determine the ways in which we make sense of the world – the questions we ask and the range of answers that are permitted. In this sense feminism is a theory; a world view. However, it is not a unified one; feminists do not agree on the ways in which we can explain women's sub-ordination or on how women can be emancipated. There are a large number of feminisms, and any attempt to classify feminist theories is fraught with problems.

We have identified four feminist perspectives: liberal/reformist, Marxist, radical, and socialist. All these perspectives address the question of what constitutes the oppression of women, and all suggest strategies for overcoming it. All argue that women are oppressed in British society, but they differ in their explanations of the oppression's cause and their suggested strategies for overcoming it. Liberal feminism is concerned to uncover the immediate forms of discrimination against women in Britain and to fight for legal and other reforms to overcome them. Marxist feminists argue that the major reason for women's oppression is the exclusion of women from public production and that women's struggle for emancipation is an integral part of the fight of the proletariat (working class) to overthrow capitalism. Radical feminists see male control of women (patriarchy) as the main problem and argue that women must fight to free themselves from this control. Socialist feminists argue that women's oppression is both an aspect of capitalism and of patriarchal relations. An end to capitalism, they argue, will not lead automatically to the emancipation of women; women also need to fight to free themselves from control by men.

Source: adapted from: P. Abbott and C. Wallace, *An Introduction to Sociology: Feminist Perspectives,* London: Routledge, 1990

5

10

15

20

25

ITEM C

This diagram shows the differences between two different strands of New Right theory although, as the passage states, in practice they often overlap in the formation of policy, particularly as applied in Britain under the Thatcher Governments. Sociologists associated with the New Right include Peter Saunders, David Marsland and Charles Murray. Their work has affected a number of debates included in this book. See for instance the questions on Bias in Sociology, The Underclass, New Vocationalism and The Family and Social Policy. The most comprehensive coverage of their ideas in a textbook is in O'Donnell (1992).

Source: adapted from A. Belsey, 'The New Right, social order and civil liberties' in R.Levitas (ed.), *The Ideology of the New Right*, Cambridge: Polity, 1986

Like a great deal of social and political theory the New Right is very exercised by the problem of social order, its creation and maintenance, and its views on this have considerable consequences for a wide range of civil liberties issues.

This is true whether the New Right is considered under its 'neo-liberal' or its 'neo-conservative' aspects. I take these terms to refer to two ideal types, each produced by means of a list of important points or principles. The contrast between the two sides is illustrated in the diagram below.

5

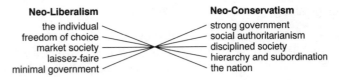

Neo-Liberalism
the individual
freedom of choice
market society
laissez-faire
minimal government

Neo-Conservatism
strong government
social authoritarianism
disciplined society
hierarchy and subordination
the nation

New Right political practice, such as Thatcherism, involves both sides. On the one hand it draws on the conservative discourse of authority and discipline and on the other on the liberal discourse of freedom and justice. The two sides seem distinct, but in political practice there is much cross-over and no clear separation can be made.

10

ITEM D

Read Giddens (1989), pp. 704–5 to understand more about structuration theory. He is trying to overcome the action/structure argument which lies at the heart of much sociological theoretical debate. Ian Craib's article 'Structure and action in modern social theory' in *Social Studies Review*, Vol. 4, No. 5, offers the best explanation and critique of Giddens' theory.

Source: M. Haralambos and M. Holborn, *Sociology: Themes and Perspectives*, 3rd Ed., London: Collins Educational, 1991

Over recent years the British sociologist Anthony Giddens has attempted to overcome the division between structure and action. Although the details of his argument are complex, the basic point is simple. Giddens claims that structure and action are two sides of the same coin. Neither structure nor action can exist independently; both are intimately related. Social actions create structures, and it is through social actions that structures are produced and reproduced, so that they survive over time. Indeed he uses a single word, 'structuration', to describe the way that structures relate to social actions, so that certain sets of social relationships survive over space and time. Giddens talks about the 'duality of structure' to suggest both that structures make social action possible and at the same time that social action creates those very structures. He says that 'structure has no existence independent of the knowledge that agents have about what they do in their day-to-day activity'. In other words, it is you, I, and every other individual that creates structures.

QUESTIONS

a Identify three key features of the 'modern society' (Item A).

(3 marks)

b Briefly explain the difference between 'radical feminism' and 'Marxist feminism' (Item B).

(2 marks)   There are only two *interpretation* marks here so be brief, as requested.

c Compare and contrast the neo-conservative and neo-liberal versions of New Right theory (Item C).

(4 Marks)   You are being asked to interpret material from the passage. Make sure you show similarities (compare) as well as differences (contrast). Notice the diagram shows the contrasting positions on various areas at the opposing ends of each arrow.

d In Item D, Anthony Giddens suggests that structure has no existence independent of social action. Using information from the Items and from elsewhere, assess the extent to which sociological arguments support this notion.

(7 marks)   The wording of the question shows that you need to demonstrate the use of all skills. Remember to explain the theory before you evaluate it. You can answer this question by looking at Giddens' theory and then bring in Craib's critique, and/or look at structuralist and interactionist viewpoints. A detailed commentary on this debate is included in Haralambos and Holborn (1991) pp. 814–19.

e How valid is the postmodernist notion that 'key features of modern society have disappeared', (Item A, line 26)?

(9 marks)

An apparently intimidating question requiring all skills. It is most easily answered by identifying what the key features of modern society are and looking at what postmodernists believe them to have been replaced by. Look around the world you live in to see which theory makes more sense to you. A number of articles in *Sociology Review* have covered this debate. See, for example, articles by Fulcher and Jewson in the November 1991 issue, and articles by Strinati and Clegg in the April 1992 issue.

1.9 Bias in sociology

ITEM A

Sociology (especially Marxist sociology) has often been seen as extremely critical of capitalism. Here the author suggests that sociology is inherently anti-capitalist, as most sociologists ignore the benefits that it has produced because they are so biased, and in particular he argues that sociology ignores entrepreneurship.

Similar remarks were made by Professor D. Marsland and his criticisms and some criticisms of him were contained in 'Bias against business?' in *Social Studies Review*, Vol. 3, No. 2.

Source: adapted from an article in the *Guardian*, 18 June, 1991

In the 1990s, sociologists are compelled to do more than simply offer a critique of capitalism, which seems to have won the day.

Capitalist corporations are usually portrayed as enjoying excessive influence over international, national and local economies, with effects for wage rates, levels of employment and standards of living. But their domination is far less complete than that which was exercised by the state bureaucracies behind the old Iron Curtain. It is hardly surprising that most people prefer to be exploited and feel free, rather than be subjected to tight forms of bureaucratic control . . . 10

Sociologists have tended to ignore entrepreneurship in their discussions of capitalism. The fact that 12 per cent of the gainfully employed population are self-employed . . . seems to be of little interest to them . . . Capitalism is exploitative and it does create great inequalities, but it has other features which sociologists have neglected because of their personal values . . . 15

Sociologists, because of their implicit values and their hidden agendas for an alternative non-capitalist social order, have been preoccupied with the exploitation to the neglect of capitalism's advantages. 20

ITEM B

A further area of discussion about bias in sociology relates to the whole question of value freedom. Gouldner argues here that the complete rejection of subjectivity by the logical positivists was actually immoral because, in the case of Project Camelot, sociologists ignored the moral implications of reporting their findings to the government. His writings on this subject are contained in a book called *Anti-Minotaur: The Myth of a Value-Free Sociology*. This is discussed in some detail in Haralambos and Holborn (1991), pp. 762–4.

The potential consequences of positivism were furthest developed within logical positivism. Their opposition to 'metaphysics' went so far that they condemned any statements which did not have direct empirical content as literally meaningless and nonsensical. Scientists must rigorously distance themselves from such distractive outbursts and concentrate on producing value-neutral knowledge. Not only must value-judgements be excluded from *scientific* statements which claim truth, but the scientist must also be ethically neutral. As positivist sociology came to imitate the natural sciences more and more slavishly, the discipline became increasingly divorced from any ethic of social responsibility. American sociology in particular became wedded to this principle of ethical non-responsibility; it reached its nadir in the notorious Project Camelot of 1964.

By the early 1960s American social science had succesfully established an image of scientific and political responsibility, and as Gouldner has argued, the commitment to value-neutrality was partly motivated by a desire to be seen as 'safe' and non-threatening to the established order. As Lundberg had proclaimed, social scientists were often technicians researching topics defined as 'problems' by others; usually they were certainly not social critics. Such self-defined roles encouraged the US Army to recruit social scientists for a huge research programme in Latin America, designed to discover the causes of social instability. In

its natural concern for social order in the lower half of the conti- 25
nent, the Pentagon wished to discover the causes of revolt and
remove them. In order to achieve this, they planned to spend up
to six million dollars and recruit a huge team of political scientists and sociologists to work in the countries concerned. Their
employer made the aims clear in a recruiting letter: 'The US 30
Army has an important mission in the positive and constructive
aspects of nation-building in less-developed countries as well as
to a responsibility to assist friendly governments in dealing with
active insurgency problems'. The aims were equally clear to the
South American governments concerned, and they rapidly 35
forced the abandonment of the project, with accusations of spy-
ing and covert intervention by the United States. All this came as
a shock to those who agreed to take part, for they believed that
they were aiding those countries by advocating policies such as
land reform which would remove the need for revolution. It is a 40
sad comment on social scientists that they could be so naive
about the intentions of the powerful.

Source: T. Bilton *et al.*,
Introductory Sociology, 2nd Ed.,
London: Macmillan, 1987

ITEM C

Roger Scruton is a well-known critic of sociology. He suggests that the constant questioning of values by sociologists may be harmful, particularly for young people. Professor Platt clearly disagrees with him and sees questioning as an important aspect of sociological research.

Dr. Christopher Pole (Department of Sociology, University of
Warwick): Dear Punters, yet again, sociology is the butt of your
humour. Why is it that this respectable academic pursuit is so
frequently derided by the media? ... Why is it that sociology
receives such a bad press, from programmes such as this and 5
from journalism?

Radio 4 Presenter: Professor Scruton, why do you think that sociology gets a bad press? Do you think it does?

Roger Scruton (Professor of Aesthetics, Birkbeck College,
University of London): Yes, I think it does and I suppose I think it 10
deserves it. ... The subject has concentrated on those areas of
enquiry which are interesting to someone with a socialist agenda;
obsessed with class, with domination, hierarchy, exploitation, all
those old ghastly nineteenth-century ideas. All this amounts to, I
think, a case to be answered by the sociological establishment. 15

R4: Why is it, do you think, that so much criticism does come,
perhaps from right-wing newspapers or from more right-wing
journalists?

Jennifer Platt (Professor of Sociology, Sussex University): It's hard
to avoid saying that it's because they don't wish certain things to 20
be inspected, or they don't wish certain things to be questioned
in the sort of way that one is bound to question them if one looks
for explanations of things about society which all of us in our
everyday lives take for granted.

RS: I think that's a very good point, actually, and that there are 25
certain things that people object to being researched in the first
place and they're not necessarily wrong. ... I suspect that a lot of
people feel this about sociology, that there are certain matters
which should not be pried into, least of all by half-baked lefties
from universities. ... It would explain very well the public atti- 30
tude. It may be right or wrong. But I would sympathize with it
myself because I think this endless quest for knowledge about

trivia of the kind that sociologists pursue might actually be something which we were not made to pursue and which is harmful to pursue.   35

There is also something which people might object to in sociology, that it does teach this constant questioning especially of values and the established principles whereby a parent might want to bring up his child and if you keep asking that question about all your values you cease to have them and in that sense a lot of   40
people feel that sociology might be corrupting.

CP: But surely by the virtue of the fact that it is questioning it isn't corrupting, it can't be corrupting?

RS: Well it's a prejudice of yours that all questions are valid. Some things maybe should not be questioned.   45

JP: It's a bit hard to know which they are, however, without asking a question perhaps.

R4: But I thought that questioning was part of being healthily sceptical about things.

RS: I was trying to ask and answer the question why people   50
might be hostile to sociology. I would say also because of this relentless questioning of human institutions and human realities it may be inappropriate for young people to study it.

Source: extracts from the Radio 4 programme, *Punters*, 8 August, 1991

ITEM D

The writer of this article suggests that the study of sociology does not make people more biased, but more tolerant of others. What do you see as his 'hidden agenda'? How has the study of sociology changed your own understanding and treatment of others?

Source: adapted from Z. Bauman, *Thinking Sociologically*, Oxford: Blackwell, 1990

By its nature sociology is singularly ill suited to the 'closing down' and 'sealing' job. Sociology is an extended commentary on the experience of daily life; an interpretation which feeds on other interpretations and is in turn fed into them. Sociological thinking does not stem, but facilitates the flow and exchange of   5
experiences. From the point of view of powers obsessed with the order they have designed, sociology is part of the 'messiness' of the world; a problem, rather than a solution.

The great service sociology is well prepared to render to human life and human cohabitation is the promotion of mutual   10
understanding and tolerance as a paramount condition of shared freedom. Sociological thinking cannot but promote the understanding that breeds tolerance and the tolerance that makes understanding possible. Sociological thinking helps the cause of freedom.   15

QUESTIONS

a Identify two of 'capitalism's advantages' (line 19) which 'sociologists have tended to ignore' (line 12) according to the author of Item A.

(2 marks)   Two interpretation marks, so make two clear points in your own words. Use only the material provided in Item A.

b What do you understand by the phrase 'value-neutrality' (Item B)?

(1 mark)   Use the Item to explain your understanding of this term to get one *interpretation* mark. An example can make a definition clearer.

c With reference to Item B and elsewhere, suggest what problems might be associated with the principal of 'ethical non-responsibility' (line 13) in social science.

(4 Marks) Explain what this term means and then put the criticisms contained in the passage in your own words to get marks for *interpretation and application*. Application of *knowledge* is also required, so bring in examples with which you are familiar.

d Assess the validity of the argument put forward by Roger Scruton in Item C that sociology is obsessed with 'old ghastly nineteenth-century ideas' (line 14).

(8 Marks) This question requires the use of all skills, so you need to explain what Professor Scruton is saying and find material to support his argument as well as criticizing it. The crux of this question is whether concepts derived from the founders of sociology who were writing in the nineteenth century are still relevant today. Examples of these ideas could be Class and Exploitation (from Marx) and Authority, Rationality and Bureaucracy (from Weber) and also the Division of Labour (from Durkheim). However there are also plenty of criticisms from neo-Marxist and neo-Weberian thought and again you could look at the material contained in the question Is Social Class still Central? (p. 176). Say what you think about this, and why.

e Illustrating your answer with material from the Items above and elsewhere, consider the arguments for and against the view contained in Item D that 'sociological thinking helps the cause of freedom' (lines 14–15).

(10 Marks) This question requires all skills, as you can see from the way it is worded. There is relevant material in the Item so make sure you use it, as well as looking at other views about values in sociology in your textbooks. Giddens (1989) contains an important section on this issue.

Bauman argues that through promoting mutual understanding and tolerance sociology helps to generate freedom. Do you think studying sociology has made you more tolerant of other people and their opinions or more argumentative, dogmatic and ideologically biased? Think also about what effect adopting a particular sociological perspective has on levels of tolerance. The concluding sections of the chapters of Haralambos and Holborn (1991), discuss the significance of values in sociology. The section on methodology and values, pp. 762–4, is particularly useful here.

1.10 Is sociology a science?

ITEM A

It is worth looking at back copies of *Sociology Review*, and its predecessor *Social Studies Review*. One article to search out is 'In the shadow of science' by Tony Lawson in *Social Studies Review*, Vol. 2, No. 2. The article by Hilary Burrage from which this extract is taken neatly summarizes the main debates about science as ideology (a set of ideas and assumptions) being like religion rather than some sort of 'objective truth'. It argues that social scientists and scientists, like everyone else interpret the world they study in terms of their own assumptions and beliefs.

Most people hold in their minds a model of the operation of science as 'objective', that is both empirical and autonomous. Science is believed to operate on the basis of 'factual' data alone, and independently of its social setting. Historical, social and psychological analyses all tell us, however, that this simply cannot 5 be. Science and technology, as 'organized knowledge', have been geared to meeting the 'problems' of government, the military and large industrial concerns. It is clear, therefore, that modern science and technology is to a critically important degree integrated with economic direction and with socio-political definitions of 'problems'. 10

For much of the time scientists work within what Thomas Kuhn and others call paradigms – sets of theory, method, data and instrumentation – which predispose them to address given 'problems' in particular ways. It is only very rarely that really 15 interesting and surprising 'discoveries' are made, quite often by people in some way on the margins of their discipline. It is from these unexpected findings that real shifts in theoretical and methodological understanding tend to arise.

The discussion so far has taken 'science' as equivalent to the 20 'natural' sciences. But what about social science? It will already have become apparent that natural science is inevitably ideological. But ideology, of course, has a part in everything which people do. To say that science is ideological in this sense, then, is simply to acknowledge social reality. There is, however, another 25 sense in which science is ideological. Science, as we have seen rests very fundamentally on a particular set of assumptions about what is appropriate and admissible in terms of evidence and procedure. The natural sciences allow only consideration of demonstrable evidence – i.e. 'hard', and usually quantifiable, 30 data. The ideology of natural science is therefore empiricist.

Like natural science, social science is based upon observation, but with one important proviso. For all social scientists, interpretation is important at each and every stage of research. Knowledge in the social sciences is not founded simply on 'hard' 35 quantifiable observations. The social sciences, broadly speaking, are about the behaviour of conscious beings, whilst the natural sciences are concerned with inanimate, or at least non-conscious, 'behaviour'.

Source: H. Burrage, 'The sociology of science and the science of society', in *Social Studies Review*, November 1988

ITEM B

Whether or not sociology is a science depends on what is meant by science. The best answer is to see science as a method rather than a body of knowledge. What distinguishes both social and natural science from non-science, from common sense and from ideology, is method. 5

Good sociology is logically derived from empirical evidence.

The desire to show that sociology was as scientific as natural science claimed to be has resulted in the accounts of how research was done being idealized.
10

The situation has changed recently. As both natural and social scientists have become more prepared to acknowledge what research is really like, so several collections of papers have appeared that give a 'warts and all' account of previously published research studies. In addition, recent original studies often now include a frank account of the trials and tribulations of the research. Such accounts do not necessarily cast doubt on the scientific status of the work done. If the ideal of natural scientific method is in fact a myth, then sociologists cannot be criticized for failing to match up to it. Instead, we have to revise our view of what science is.
15

20

Source: adapted from P. McNeill, *Research Methods*, London: Routledge, 1985

ITEM C

This table shows the links between theories and research methods very clearly. Epistemology means theories of knowledge and ontology means theories of existence, so, loosely translated, Epistemological/Ontological position means what various perspectives think about how people exist and how we can gain knowledge of their existence. A similar diagram is included in O'Donnell (1992), p. 35.

Source: A. Dale and A. Clarke, 'Theory, method and practice', in *Social Science Teacher,* Summer 1988

Idealized versions of positivist and anti-positivist approaches in social research

	POSITIVISM	ANTI-POSITIVISM
Theoretical perspective	structuralism	interactionism
Epistemological/ ontological position:	social phenomena are like natural phenomena; causal relationships can be established and universal laws discovered	social phenomena are unlike natural phenomena; social reality only exists as meaningful interaction between individuals
Methodological position:	deductive (theory testing)	inductive (theory generation)
Methods/techniques:	structured social survey	participant observation
	QUANTITATIVE	**QUALITATIVE**

QUESTIONS

a Describe what is meant by the term 'paradigms', (Item A, line 13).

(1 mark)   A simple *interpretation* mark here.

b Using material from Item B and elsewhere, assess the view that acknowledging 'what research is really like' (Item B, line 13), does not necessarily make the findings unscientific.

(9 marks)   A long answer requiring all skills. You need to explain what the author of Item B is saying and then suggest sociological arguments against it, mainly from a positivist viewpoint. Make sure you relate your conclusion directly back to the question.

c Illustrating your answer with material from Item C, describe how different views on the nature of science affect the research methods adopted by sociologists from different perspectives.

(4 marks)   This is a simple *interpretation* question but make sure you answer it fully to get all four marks available. Make sure you clearly refer to the link between theory and methods.

d Using material from the Items and elsewhere, evaluate the view that science is 'inevitably ideological' (Item A, line 22).

(11 marks)   This requires another long answer which needs to be structured carefully to demonstrate all the skills. A clear understanding of the terms used must be shown, plus an analysis of both sides of the debate. Look at different definitions of ideology (Mannheim is particularly useful) and bring in a number of sociological examples such as Popper and Kuhn to explore the question fully. Useful material is included in O'Donnell (1992) pp. 21–4 and pp. 38–40, Haralambos and Holborn (1991), pp. 755–61 and pp. 20–1, Bilton *et al.* (1987), pp. 405–14, Giddens (1989), pp. 21–2, Lee and Newby, (1983) pp. 340–5.

2

Family

ITEM A

Just because something is 'widely believed', it does not mean that it is true. Anderson's work challenges a number of assumptions about change in family structure as you can see by looking at this book by Wilson or the summary in Giddens (1989), pp. 388–91.

Source: adapted from A. Wilson, *Family*, London, Tavistock, 1985

It is widely believed among sociology students that in the period before the Industrial Revolution, the dominant form of family life was the extended family. Michael Anderson traces this back to the work of the nineteenth-century French sociologist, Fréderic Le Play. Le Play describes a model of a stem family which was common in rural areas of Europe. The family was strongly patriarchal. The eldest son assumed the family responsibilities when his father became too old or died. The household was usually limited to the patriarch and his wife, one married son and his family, and any other unmarried children of the head of household. Such a family might have up to eighteen members. This stem family is the basis for the belief in a stable self-sufficient extended family.

5

10

ITEM B

Fletcher is a functionalist and so he believes that changes in the industrial structure brought about extensive changes in the family. This is because functionalists regard all institutions as interrelated.

Source: R. Fletcher, *The Family and Marriage in Britain,* Harmondsworth: Penguin, 1973

Industrialization brought with it an increasing degree of geographical and occupational movement, and an increased degree of social mobility (i.e. movement between social classes, and changes of social status between the generations). Geographical and occupational movement was made possible by the mechanized modes of transport and communication during the nineteenth century, and the increased availability of means of transport – the motor-bus, the motorcar, the motorcycle, and the bicycle – during the twentieth century. These latter developments in transport largely promoted the growth of suburbs, since people could now live at greater distances from their work. It seems plausible to maintain, despite some criticisms of this view, that these forces must have had the effect of loosening the ties between the individual family and its wider kinship relationships, and diminishing the degree of social life which the family shared with groups of wider kindred. The family would no longer live within a particular locality and within a stable and wide network of kinship relationships to the same extent that it did before industrialization.

5

10

15

ITEM C

This material from Anderson contradicts the functionalist view that industrialization brought about a move from extended to nuclear family structures. His evidence suggests that, in Britain at least, the nuclear family was the norm in pre-industrial times and it was the hardships caused by industrialization which led many working-class families to adopt an extended family

Further historical evidence suggests that far from encouraging the formation of nuclear families, the early stages of industrialization may well have strengthened kinship ties beyond the nuclear family. Using data from the 1851 Census of Preston, Michael Anderson found that some 23 per cent of households contained kin other than the nuclear family, a large increase over Laslett's figures and those for today. The bulk of this 'co-residence' occurred among the poor. Anderson argues that co-residence occurs when the parties involved receive net gains from the arrangement.

Anderson's study of Preston indicates that in the mid-nineteenth century, the working-class family functioned as a mutual

5

10

network. And therefore if anything the move was from nuclear to extended families and not as functionalists have suggested

Source: adapted from M. Haralambos, *Sociology: Themes and Perspectives*, 2nd Ed., London: Unwin Hyman, 1985

aid organization. It provided an insurance policy against hardship and crisis. This function encouraged the extension of kinship bonds beyond the nuclear family. Such links would be retained as long as they provided net gains to those involved. Anderson concludes that the early stages of industrialization increased rather than decreased the extension of the working-class family.

15

ITEM D

Lasletts' work suggests that family size has always been quite small in most of pre-industrial Europe due to late marriage and a high death rate. You can find more details about this in any recent textbook, for example Haralambos and Holborn (1991), pp. 474–88; Abercrombie and Warde *et al.* (1988), pp. 299–301 and Bilton *et al.* (1987), pp. 259–69.

Source: adapted from T. Bilton *et al., Introductory Sociology*, 2nd Ed., London: Macmillan, 1987

One of the foremost sources of data on kinship in pre-industrial Europe is the work of the Cambridge Group for the History of Population and Social Structure, of whom Peter Laslett is a prominent representative. Laslett and his associates emphasize the use of quantitative data in the historical study of the family, and one of their primary sources of data is the quasi-censuses, or listings of inhabitants of communities, compiled in periods ranging from the sixteenth to the nineteenth centuries. After examining the data for one hundred English communities, Laslett launched a profound attack on the view that industrialization bought about a decrease in average family size.

During the period surveyed, his data suggest, average household size in the communities analysed stayed fairly constant at approximately 4.75 persons per household.

5

10

QUESTIONS

a   What is meant by the term 'extended family' (Item A, line 3)?

(1 mark)   This is an application of *knowledge* question: answer – parents and children plus other kin members.

b   Identify the main factors given by the author of Item B to explain the loosening of family ties.

(5 marks)   These marks are all for *interpretation*, but they require you to outline five clearly different points from the information provided in Item B, use only the material provided and put the different points in your own words. Numbering the points will help make your answer clearer and make sure you get all five points.

c   Explain in your own words the meaning of the term 'co-residence' (Item C, line 7).

(2 marks)   These two marks are for *interpretation* but notice here that the explanation of the term comes before the term itself in the extract, so read it carefully.

d   Using information from the Items and elsewhere, discuss the problems sociologists face in using historical data to study family structure.

(7 marks)   This question is mainly about research methods. Look at the different

problems of validity associated with using records which were drawn up many years ago. Laslett, for example, looks at parish records which may not be representative, or may be incomplete.

This question expects you to use *interpretation* skills so make sure you relate your answer back to the material in the items as well as other studies. Useful reading here includes O'Donnell (1992), pp. 36–7, Giddens (1989), pp. 675–7, or you could refer to two books both titled *Research Methods*, one by Patrick McNeill (1985) and the other by Robert Burgess (1993).

e   **Assess the evidence and arguments for and against the view that 'industrialization brought about a decrease in average family size' (Item D, lines 10–11).**

(10 marks)

This question is clearly requiring all skills. You need to plan your answer and structure it carefully. Much of the information is provided in the items, but there is more in your textbooks, and we have provided page references for most of the material that is relevant earlier in this question. You will need to look up the functionalist argument for more detail as well. Relate your conclusion back to the question in order to answer it fully. One final source of information is a book called simply *Families* by Diana Leonard and John Hood-Williams (1988).

2.2 Marriage and divorce

ITEM A

Note all the points in this article carefully to show the variables that seem to lead to higher rates of divorce.

Sociologists have clear evidence about some of the factors which contribute to the breakdown of a marriage. A marriage between two people from very different backgrounds is more at risk of divorce. The divorce rate is higher in urban than rural areas. Marriages after a very short acquaintance are also risky. But the most crucial factor could be age. One in two teenage brides, and six out of ten teenage bridegrooms can expect their marriage to end in divorce. 5

In 1982, 42,000 of the couples who were divorcing had no children. Nevertheless there were 158,000 children under the age of sixteen involved in parental divorce in 1982. 10

The rise in the divorce rate does not mean people have lost faith in marriage as an institution. In 1982 about 64 per cent of all marriages were first marriages for both partners. In 19 per cent of marriages one partner was remarrying and in 16 per cent both partners were remarrying. Unfortunately, the divorcee who marries again is almost twice as likely to get divorced again! 15

Source: adapted from A. Wilson, *Family*, London: Routledge, 1985

ITEM B

This is a complicated but useful graph from *Social Trends*. You can get a lot of up-to-date statistical material from this source and you should locate the nearest copy quickly as it will be invaluable for all your sociology. Spend time looking at this graph and identify the main trends in the grounds cited by people wanting to divorce. Look at the gender differences too.

Divorce – party granted decree: by grounds[1]

England and Wales

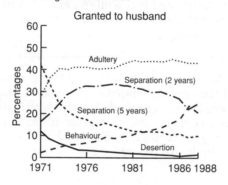

Granted to husband

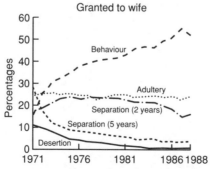

Granted to wife

Source: Social Trends 1990, London: HMSO, 1990

1 Decrees granted to one party on more than one ground are included in the 100 per cent base but have not been plotted.

ITEM C

This extract shows that a lot of useful information can be obtained from newspapers, particularly when they report official statistics as here. However, it is wise always to treat newspaper reports with caution. They, like all other sources of material need to be evaluated on their representativeness, validity and reliability. See also Chandler in *Sociology Review*, April 1993.

The marriage rate has fallen by more than half since 1971, while the number of divorces is reaching new records, and one in 12 couples is cohabiting.

In the 12 months to September 1990, the rate of people marrying for the first time in England and Wales fell below 40 per 1000 single people aged over 16. This compares with a rate of 82.3 in 1971 and 51.7 in 1981, while the rate of remarriage among divorcees has fallen even more steeply.   5

According to an analysis published by the Government's Office of Population Censuses and Surveys (OPCS), 34 per cent of divorced men and 22 per cent of divorced women are cohabiting.   10

The OPCS says the number of marriages is falling by about 4 per cent a year. The rate, which is falling more steeply and now stands at 39.6, is estimated to have dropped by 31 per cent for men and 26 per cent for women during the 1980s.   15

The remarriage rate among divorcees has plummeted from 227.3 in 1971 to 129.5 in 1981 and 68.3 in the 12 months to September 1990.

In a study of cohabitiation, the OPCS calculates that 1.2 million of a total of 13.9 million couples were living together outside marriage in 1989. Where the man was in his twenties, three in 10 couples were cohabiting; where he was in his thirties, the ratio was one in 10.   20

On divorce, the OPCS reports that there were 153,000 decrees made absolute in 1990 and that there were almost 81,000, a record in the first 6 months of this year, a rise of 2.6 per cent.   25

It is estimated that while 6 per cent of marriages in 1974 ended in divorce within 5 years, the incidence rose to 10 per cent among 1984 marriages.

Source: adapted from an article in the *Guardian*, 6 December, 1991

ITEM D

Think at this stage whether you agree that the divorce law reforms are the cause of marital breakdown. This is an argument generally associated with the New Right. Do laws cause changes or are they merely a reflection of changes taking place in society?

Source: adapted from T. Bilton *et al.*, *Introductory Sociology*, 2nd Ed., London: Macmillan, 1987

As laws and procedures regulating divorce have altered, the divorce rate has tended to increase by leaps and bounds. Many people have suggested that the higher divorce rates reflect an underlying increase in marital instability. Some commentators have gone further, and argued that more permissive divorce laws in themselves cause marital breakdown.   5

ITEM E

This table seems to show that, paradoxically, for men, those who have been divorced are more likely to get married. Look this up in *Social Trends* to see in detail what the table means.

Marriage and remarriage: by sex

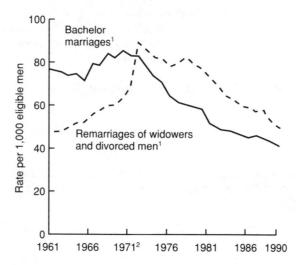

Source: Social Trends 1993,
London: HMSO, 1993

1 Irrespective of partners marital status.
2 The Divorce Reform Act 1969 came into effect in England and Wales on 1 January 1971.

QUESTIONS

a According to the author of Item A, what could be the most crucial factor in leading to the breakdown of marriages?

(1 mark)

b How do the grounds for divorces granted differ between husbands and wives (Item B)?

(4 marks)   This requires you to interpret the material in Item C and then apply the information in a relevant way. Make sure you identify four clear separate points in your own words in order to get all four marks. Be careful not to bring in any irrelevant arguments or points.

c Identify the percentage changes in the rate of marriage for men and for women in the 1980s (Item C).

(2 marks)

d Using information from the Items above and elsewhere, assess the arguments for and against the view outlined in Item D that 'more permissive divorce laws in themselves cause marital breakdown' (lines 5–6)

(8 marks)   Question **d** and question **e** are asking you to produce structured answers using all the skills. You are asked to explain the argument in the relevant item (*interpretation* and *application*) and then use relevant sociological studies that you know (*knowledge* and *application*) and material from the other items (application) in order to consider (*evaluation*) the views expressed. You will need to give your opinion about the arguments in your conclusion in order to get all the marks available for evaluation. To make sure you answer the question fully it is best to do a short plan. Also note that although the questions are about similar issues they are different questions. Question **d** focuses on whether changes in the law cause divorce or whether they merely allow divorces caused by other factors to take place (see Item A).

e Using material from Item E and elsewhere, assess the view that the 'rise in the divorce rate does not mean people have lost faith in marriage as an institution' (Item A, lines 12–13)

(10 marks)   Question **e** is centred on the debate over whether divorce indicates that people are losing faith in the idea of marriage or whether it simply indicates they are losing faith in the individual person they married. Material you might wish to consider in relation to this is question is included in Giddens (1989), pp. 393–405, O'Donnell (1992), pp. 64–6, Abercrombie and Warde (1988), pp. 290–9 and Haralambos and Holborn (1991), pp. 509–517. Wilson (1985) will also be useful here.

ITEM A

You can get a lot of useful and up-to-date statistical material from the *General Household Survey* and *Social Trends*. Use them to update and illustrate your answers, but remember the problems involved in using official statistics in an uncritical way. For a very full discussion of these problems see Slattery (1986).

Men and women aged 16–59: percentage cohabiting by age; Great Britain, 1990

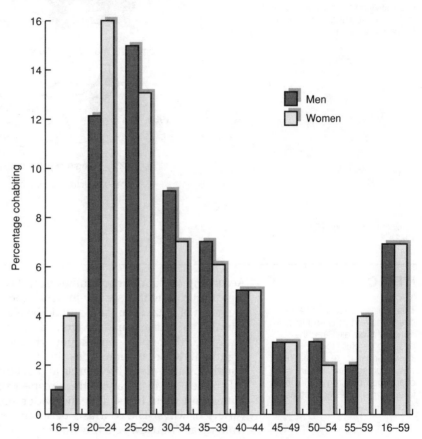

Source: General Household Survey 1990, London: HMSO, 1992

ITEM B

This is an unusual way to display material but very effective in showing the increase in single registrations, between 1969 and 1985. Make sure you notice that figures for single registrations and joint registrations are provided separately on the diagram. Also make sure you understand what these terms mean.

Outcomes of extra-marital conception, England and Wales

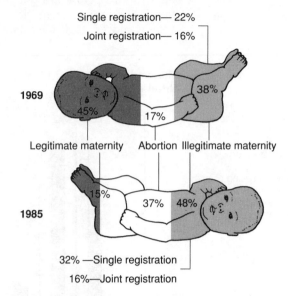

Single registration— 22%

Joint registration— 16%

1969

45%

17%

38%

Legitimate maternity   Abortion   Illegitimate maternity

15%

37%   48%

1985

32% —Single registration

16%—Joint registration

Source: New Society, 15 January, 1988

ITEM C

This outlines a variety of family structures and you need to be aware of them all. Read the passage carefully to get information in more detail. The view expressed in this item is challenged by many sociologists, for example, Chester, Fletcher and other functionalists.

According to Rapoport, 'families in Britain today are in a transition from coping in a society in which there was a single overriding norm of what family life should be like to a society in which a plurality of norms are recognized as legitimate and, indeed, desirable' (Rapoport and Rapoport, 1982). Substantiating this argument, Rapoport identifies five types of diversity: organizational, cultural, class, life-course and cohort.   5

Families today organize their respective individual domestic duties and their links with the wider social environment in a variety of ways. The contrasts between 'orthodox' families – the woman as 'housewife', the husband as 'breadwinner' – with   10
dual-career or one-parent families, illustrates this diversity. Culturally, there is greater diversity of family beliefs and values than used to be the case. The presence of ethnic minorities (such as West Indian, Asian, Greek or Italian communities), and the   15
influence of movements such as feminism, have produced considerable cultural variety in family forms. Persistent class divisions, between the poor, the skilled working class, and the various groupings within the middle and upper classes, sustain major variations in family structure. Variations in family experi-   20
ence during the life course are obvious. For instance, one individual may come from a family in which both parents had stayed together, and herself or himself become married and then divorced. Another person might be brought up in a single-parent family, be multiply married and have children by each marriage.   25

The term cohort refers to generations within families. Connections between parents and grandparents, for example, have probably become weaker than they were. On the other hand, more people now live into old age, and three 'ongoing' families might exist in close relation to one another: married grandchildren, their parents, and the grandparents.

5

Source: A. Giddens, *Sociology*, Cambridge: Polity, 1989

ITEM D

Social Trends with another useful and interesting up-to-date statistic, this time on births outside marriage. Notice the clear regional dimension here. You should also remember that while it is not legally possible for women to get married until they are 16, it is biologically possible for them to become mothers before that age.

Percentage of live births outside marriage: by age of mother and region, 1990

	Under 20	20–39	40 and over	All ages
United Kingdom	80.2	23.5	19.6	27.9
North	85.9	26.6	22.1	32.8
Yorkshire & Humberside	80.1	25.0	22.9	30.6
East Midlands	81.6	23.0	21.6	28.0
East Anglia	74.5	19.0	16.7	22.8
South East	76.8	23.0	20.2	25.9
South West	79.7	20.5	22.2	24.3
West Midlands	77.7	24.3	18.6	29.1
North West	85.3	28.8	19.5	34.4
England	80.2	24.0	20.4	28.3
Wales	81.2	23.7	21.7	29.3
Scotland	80.3	22.2	18.7	27.1
Northern Ireland	76.1	14.6	4.8	18.7

Live births outside marriage as a percentage of all births

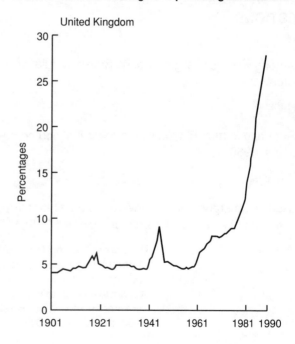

Source: Social Trends 1992, London: HMSO, 1992

ITEM E

This extract from the key book on feminist perspectives in sociology questions whether the level of diversity highlighted by some sociologists really does represent a development in diversity or not. This points to the important point that sociological knowledge relies not only on facts and figures but interpretations placed upon them, and therefore the importance of sociological theory in all aspects of the subject.

Within contemporary Britain, there is a diversity of family forms and ways of organizing roles within the family. Nevertheless, families that do not conform to the nuclear family norm are seen as a deviant, strange, and less desirable form of living arrangement. This applies not only to those who choose not to get married, but to families of Asian origin who choose to live in extended families or to retain close family connections, to West Indian families who are often assumed to be matrifocal (mother-headed), and to those families in which the mother chooses to work full time, especially when the children are young.   5 ... 10

More and more households do not conform to conventional norms. More people are cohabiting (living together without formal marriage); the proportion has risen from 2.7 per cent of couples aged 18–49 in 1979 to 5 per cent in 1985. Illegitimacy rates are rising, as more people have children without being married. Perhaps some of the stigma associated with illegitimacy has vanished. Also, the fact that these births are increasingly registered in the father's as well as the mother's name implies they are taking place within stable relationships, perhaps to couples who are cohabiting.   15 ... 20

However, these *de facto* relationships are of a form which mirrors the conventional nuclear family, including its sexual fidelity. Children may now be born outside of marriage, but traditional roles of motherhood are usually the same, and, indeed, children are now more likely to be brought up by their biological mothers than to be sent away for adoption as in the past.   25

Source: adapted from P. Abbott and C. Wallace, *An Introduction to Sociology: Feminist Perspectives,* London, Routledge, 1990

QUESTIONS

a Among which social group in the British population was cohabitation most popular in 1990 (Item A)?

(1 mark)

b Referring to Item B, identify the *least* likely outcome of extra-marital conception in 1969 and in 1985.

(2 marks)

c Assess the argument put forward in Item C that 'Persistent class divisions . . . sustain major variations in family structure' (lines 17–20).

(5 marks)   The work of the Rapoports is neatly summarized in Item C. You need to interpret this material to understand the context of the quote in the question and then use this and other material to evaluate the importance of class in relation to family structure. Useful material here might include Haralambos and Holborn (1991), pp. 484–95, Abercrombie and Warde (1988) pp. 299–306, O'Donnell (1992), pp. 48–9.

d Using material from the Items above and elsewhere, evaluate sociological explanations for the patterns of extra-marital births shown in Item D.

(7 marks)

Refer to Item D to interpret the trends then apply material from the Items and elsewhere to evaluate. This answer requires you to use all skills, so remember to use material from the items provided and other sociological studies or relevant information. Look carefully at all explanations and say what you think and why in order to show good evaluative skills. In terms of attitudes there is now a survey conducted and published as *British Social Attitudes*. Try to look at a copy of this. You might also look at *Typically British?*, a book by E. Jacobs and R. Worcester which is in fact the results of a survey conducted by MORI in April 1991. It is important to note that there is useful material in the other items in the question. Make sure you use this.

e The authors of Item E argue that 'More and more households do not conform to conventional norms. . . . However, these *de facto* relationships are of a form which mirrors the conventional nuclear family' (lines 11–22). Using material from the Items above and elsewhere, assess the extent to which this view is supported by sociological evidence.

(10 marks)

This question again requires demonstration of all skills and here you need to consider the validity of the feminist position outlined in Item E. This topic is dealt with in S. Garrett's book *Gender*. Also see the article by Chandler in *Sociology Review*, April 1993.

2.4 Is the family in decline?

ITEM A

Make sure you refer to the pie chart for persons and not for households in relation to part (a). The data here is also useful in relation to part (e)

Households and people by type of household.* 1990

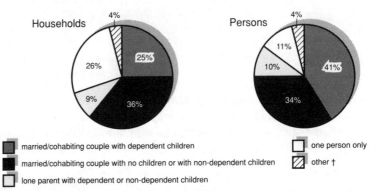

■ married/cohabiting couple with dependent children

■ married/cohabiting couple with no children or with non-dependent children

□ lone parent with dependent or non-dependent children

□ one person only

▨ other †

* Households categorised by the type of family they contain. In the lone parent and married couple households, other individuals who were not family members may also have been present.

† 'Other' includes households containing two or more unrelated adults and those containing two or more families.

Source: General Household Survey 1990, London: HMSO, 1992

ITEM B

This material could be useful for part (c).

Most adults still marry and have children. Most children are reared by their natural parents. Most people live in a household headed by a married couple. Most marriages continue until parted by death. No great change currently seems in prospect.

As headlines, such facts are the equivalent of an earthquake in Chile with nobody killed. They seem a far cry from current pre-occupations about the family. Attention has focused on the rise in divorce, cohabitation, and one-parent families, and the fall in marriage and birth rates. 5

Of course some changes have occurred in marriage and family patterns. Their importance cannot be ignored. But they must be seen in the context of major continuities in family life. 10

The point is that snapshots of household types are misleading about families and they ignore the life-cycle. Even with universal marriage and parenthood, and no divorce or early death, there would always be many non-nuclear family households, because the parents-plus-children unit is a developmental phase. But it is one that is normal and is still experienced by the great majority of people. 15

Source: adapted from R.Chester, 'The rise of the neo-conventional family', *New Society*, 9 May 1985

ITEM C

The material here shows there are clear links between arguments

The possibility that the single-parent family is a distinct and viable family type requires discussion if for no other reason than that in 1990, one in six families in Britain was headed by a single parent, over ninety per cent of whom were women. Any ade-

about the decline of the family and about the development of diverse family structures.

quate sociological discussion of this issue should not be influ- 5
enced by the social stigma which still attach to single parenthood. What it is intended to do is explore whether the
single-parent family, and the Afro-Caribbean single-parent family in particular, can be regarded as an alternative to the nuclear
family and as an exception to its universality. The answer seems 10
to be a qualified 'yes' to both these questions. In no modern society has the single-parent family replaced the nuclear family as
the dominant family form but it is becoming increasingly common.

The number of lesbian and homosexual couples who bring up 15
children is small but increasing. Such cases are unlikely ever to
be more than a small minority of those concerning 'the family'
but they are common enough to require placing within 'the sociology of the family'.

Indeed are such social units 'families'? They do not fulfil 20
Murdoch's definition because they do not include 'adults of both
sexes' and it is debatable whether the sexual relationships within
them are 'socially approved'. As with the case of single-parent
families, a more limited definition of the family is required if lesbian and homosexual families can, in fact, be defined as families. 25

It is historic fact that in almost every society the nuclear family
has been the basic social unit. However, it is not quite true that
the nuclear family is universal to all societies. The main exception
is the single-parent family.

This does not mean that the nuclear family is breaking up, or, 30
to use David Cooper's more dramatic word, 'dying'. Although
the nuclear family survives and often flourishes still as the dominant family form, it is within the context of an increasingly plu-
ralistic or varied pattern of family life.

The above changes can give little comfort to those who favour 35
the extended family type structure. The modern family is typically small and second families especially so. No satisfactory
general alternative to the nuclear family seems to exist.

Source: adapted from M. O'Donnell, *A New Introduction to Sociology*, 3rd Ed., Walton-on-Thames: Nelson, 1992

ITEM D

The material here provides the basis for your answer to part (d).

Most societies have a prevailing image of what desirable family
life would be like; modern Britain is no exception. In our everyday lives we are constantly subjected to such images. The process
of socialization involves forming ideas of family life in children
by a variety of devices including the stories that children read. In 5
the old card game 'Happy Families', every family is made up of a
father, mother and two children. In adult life similar images are
formed.

What does the image of the typical, normal or conventional
family consist of? There are two parents aged between twenty 10
and forty-five, legally married to each other, and not having been
married to anyone else previously. Two children, born of these
parents (and not others), live with them. The husband is in full-
time employment while the wife is not. The wife takes on the
bulk of the household tasks while the husband may help occa- 15
sionally. The family is a self-contained, almost private, institution – a world to itself. Lastly, its members are happy.

Source: adapted from N. Abercrombie and A. Warde *et al.*, *Contemporary British Society,* Cambridge: Polity, 1988

It is doubtful if the image of the conventional family ever accurately described the majority of families in Britain.

ITEM E

There is a clear example here of a difference between behaviour and attitudes, something which psychologists refer to as 'cognitive dissonance'. For sociologists it illustrates the problem that you cannot always assume you are finding something out about the way people live by asking them about their attitudes. This material is useful in answering parts (c) and (e). A similar example is included in the question on Domestic Divisions of Labour, page 80.

It is now a commonplace that the family is changing. There's more cohabitation, and more divorce. There are more single-parent families. More women work and more men stay at home. The family – the conventional couple with two kids idealized by advertisers and moral conservatives – is on its last legs.   5

But if this is the way things are moving why does everyone still bang on about the family?

This year's *British Social Attitudes* survey provides the crucial clue to the answer. For, this year, the survey asked a set of detailed questions on public attitudes to the family. The clear   10 conclusion according to Sheena Ashford of Leicester University, author of this chapter in the survey's report, is that 'in their attitudes towards marriage and other family matters, the British emerge as highly and consistently conventional. The family may be dead but the idea of the family survives unchallenged'.   15

Views on women and work are not very radical either. The survey asked people what working arrangements they thought parents should have. For parents of under fives 76 per cent wanted father to be in full-time work with mother at home.

For parents with children in their early teens, only 19 per cent   20 still insisted that mother should be at home. But still fewer – 17 per cent – favour equality (where both parents work either full or part time) between the parents. A full 60 per cent opt for the father to work full time and the wife part time.

Source: adapted from 'What the British are really thinking' in *New Society,* 30 October, 1987

QUESTIONS

a   According to Item A, what percentage of people lived as part of a married or cohabiting couple in 1990?

(1 mark)

b   Explain in your own words the meaning of the term 'life-cycle' used in Item B, line 14.

(2 marks)

c   The author of Item C argues that 'no satisfactory general alternative to the nuclear family seems to exist' (lines 37–38). Assess the extent to which this view is supported by sociological evidence.

(8 marks)

The key word here is 'general'. You need to interpret the material in Item C and then apply this and other relevant material to an overall evaluation of this issue. The material in the question on Diverse Family Structures (p. 67) might be helpful and relevant here. You could also try Giddens (1989), pp. 410–13 or Bilton *et al.* (1987), pp.253–9.

d Explain what is meant by the 'image of the conventional family' (Item D, line 9).

(3 marks)

e Using material from the Items above and elsewhere, assess the argument put forward in Item E that 'The family – the conventional couple with two kids idealized by advertisers and moral conservatives – is on its last legs' (Item E, lines 4–5).

(11 marks)   Notice that all three skills are required here. The clues are in the wording of the question. See if you can identify them? There is a good discussion of this issue in Wilson (1985) and also Abercrombie and Warde *et al.*, pp. 271–4 or Giddens (1989) pp. 413–16. Also see material emerging from the 1991 Census.

2.5 Domestic divisions of labour

ITEM A

Make sure you are clear what Young and Wilmott mean by 'symmetrical family'. Their work is discussed in Haralambos and Holborn (1991), pp. 500–1, Abercrombie and Warde et al., pp. 284–7 and Wilson (1985), pp. 63–4. The concept of the symmetrical family is also relevant to the question on Power in the Family, p. 87

Source: adapted from: N. Abercrombie and A. Warde *et al.*, *Contemporary British Society*, Cambridge: Polity, 1988

Young and Willmott (1973) argue that, in modern Britain, a new family form – the symmetrical family – which does not require a domestic division of labour is slowly emerging. A whole series of factors have combined to produce the change from families with a high division of labour to those in which domestic tasks are more equally shared. These include the rise in the proportion of married women who work, the trend towards smaller families, the 'privatization' of the family and changing social attitudes about the proper role of men and women.

5

ITEM B

The *British Social Attitudes* survey covers various topics and is a systematic attempt to gather quantitative data on attitudes as opposed to behaviour since as the Item shows these do not always go together. The survey covers various topics and is a useful source for any sociology course. Information on the *British Social Attitudes* survey, is contained in Slattery (1986) pp. 30–2.

Who does the chores? *(percentages)*

	Done mainly by man	done mainly by woman	shared equally
Shopping	8	45	47
Evening meal	9	70	20
Evening dishes	28	33	37
Cleaning	4	68	27
Washing and ironing	3	84	12
Repairing equipment	82	6	10
Money & bills	31	40	28

The contrast between doctrine and practice:
% of respondents in couple households saying

	should share equally	do share equally
Shopping	74	47
Evening meal	54	20
Evening dishes	75	37
Cleaning	60	27
Washing and ironing	36	12
Repairing equipment	29	10
Money and bills	64	28

Since the late 1980s there has been a flattening of the trend towards sex equality. Men professing egalitarian attitudes do appear to take more responsibility for household duties such as making meals, shopping and cleaning than non-egalitarians. But partners of egalitarian women are no more likely than the rest of their breed to take their share of the chores.

There is also a big discrepancy between what respondents say ought to be done and what they do themselves. Since the propor-

5

Source: *British Social Attitudes Survey 1991*, adapted from a report in the *Guardian*, 18 November, 1992

tion saying tasks should be shared has risen, but the proportion actually sharing has remained about the same, the gap between attitudes and practice has widened over the years. 10

ITEM C

The evidence contained here suggests that domestic duties are still not equally shared. This has implications for other aspects of life, for example the amount of time available for leisure activities. In relation to this see Item E on the question on Patterns of Leisure, p. 170.

Source: adapted from A. Warde 'Domestic divisions of labour', *Social Studies Review*, September 1990

Existing evidence suggests that in recent decades the domestic division of labour has become less rigid – the distinction between men's and women's tasks is less exclusive than before. Moreover, where wives are involved in paid employment they spend fewer hours, and their husbands more, doing housework. 5 Nevertheless, women still do a much greater share of domestic work, besides retaining responsibility for its organization. Young and Willmott's image of a 'symmetrical family' is far from reality.There is a strongly gendered division of tasks, with women doing routine household and child care jobs far more often than 10 their male partners.

ITEM D

Source: adapted from Research Roundup, *Social Studies Review*, March 1988

In search of the new man

The 'new man' is reputed to be liberated, caring and determined to share domestic responsibilities – traditionally the preserve of women. But what is the evidence for his widespread existence and influence?

The Family Policy Studies Centre in London recently pub- 5 lished a critical review of the changing roles of men and women, *Inside The Family* (1987). The Centre's conclusions are that stories of widespread 'new manism' are much exaggerated. They question too the notion that increasing work opportunities for women outside the home has led to a massive shift in the balance of 10 domestic responsibilities. Information from the *British Social Attitudes* survey (1985) suggests that the nature of female employment does, indeed, affect domestic responsibilities, but it also shows that women in full-time paid work, as well as those in part-time jobs, perform disproportionate amounts of domestic 15 tasks (see the figures overleaf). Evidence also suggests that while attitudes to domestic roles may have changed somewhat, the sharing of domestic tasks remains markedly inegalitarian and has probably changed little over the past 30 years.

Domestic tasks and women's employment

		Full-time working women %	Part-time working women %
Household shopping	Mainly man	4	4
	Mainly woman	52	64
	Shared equally	43	32
Preparation of evening meal	Mainly man	11	4
	Mainly woman	61	79
	Shared equally	26	15
Household cleaning	Mainly man	6	1
	Mainly woman	61	83
	Shared equally	33	15
Washing and ironing	Mainly man	4	–
	Mainly woman	81	95
	Shared equally	14	5
Repairs of household equipment	Mainly man	83	74
	Mainly woman	5	13
	Shared equally	12	11

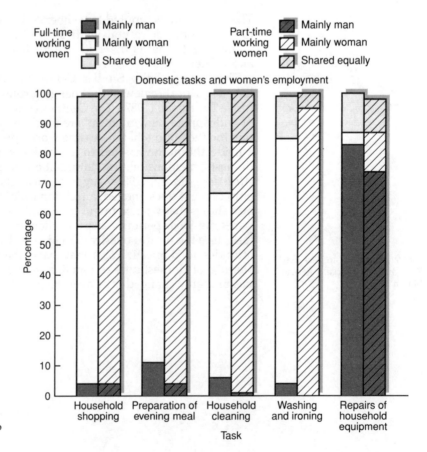

Full-time working women
■ Mainly man
□ Mainly woman
▨ Shared equally

Part-time working women
▨ Mainly man
▨ Mainly woman
▨ Shared equally

Domestic tasks and women's employment

Source: adapted from Research to Roundup, *Social Studies Review*, March 1988

ITEM E

This table is actually compiled from **two** *British Social Attitudes* surveys, thus enabling you to consider trends in the 1980s. If you look at the figures for shopping and doing the evening dishes the percentage reporting the tasks shared equally has actually gone down. This is because the percentage where the task is mainly done by the man is rising. As a result, there is evidence in the table to support both the argument that there is greater involvement by both parties and evidence against this. You need to consider the relative importance of these factors in evaluating the position overall. Notice also that figures are given for attitudes in 1987 so the statement in Item B regarding the growing gap between attitude and practice can be tested.

Household division of labour of married couples[1]: by sex and task, 1983 and 1987

Great Britain							*Percentages and numbers*		
	Actual allocation of tasks						*How tasks should be allocated*		
	1983			*1987*			*1987*		
	Mainly man	*Mainly woman*	*Shared equally*	*Mainly man*	*Mainly woman*	*Shared equally*	*Mainly man*	*Mainly woman*	*Shared equally*
Household tasks (*percentages*)									
Household shopping	5	51	44	7	50	43	1	0	68
Makes evening meal	5	77	17	6	77	17	–	2	45
Does evening dishes	17	40	40	22	39	36	11	17	70
Does household cleaning	3	72	24	4	72	23	1	44	54
Does washing and ironing	1	89	10	2	88	9	–	69	30
Repairs household equipment	82	6	10	82	6	8	73	1	24
Organizes household and bills	29	39	32	32	38	30	22	15	61
Child rearing (percentages)									
Looks after sick children	1[2]	63[2]	35[2]	2	67	30	–	47	51
Teaches children discipline	10[2]	12[2]	77[2]	13	19	67	12	5	82
Household task base (= 100%) (numbers)	1,209[2]			983			1,391		
Child rearing base (= 100%) (numbers)	485[2]			422			1,391		

1 Married or living as married
2 1984

Source: Social Trends 1990,
London: HMSO, 1990

QUESTIONS

a Explain in your own words what is meant by the term 'symmetrical family' (Item A, line 2).

(1 mark)

b Identify the two tasks which are most likely to be shared equally according to the findings of the 1991 *British Social Attitudes* survey (Item B).

(2 marks)

c Using material from the Items above and elsewhere, assess the argument put forward in Item C that the domestic division of labour is affected by the paid employment status of wives.

(8 marks)   Here you need to interpret Item C to see what is actually being said and then apply relevant knowledge to produce an overall evaluation of this issue. Item E from Patterns of Leisure (p. 170) will be helpful here as will Garrett (1987,) pp. 38–59 and Abbott and Wallace (1990), pp. 85–93. See also the article by Leighton in *Sociology Review*, February 1992.

d With reference to Item E, identify four changes in the actual allocation of tasks between 1983/4 and 1987.

(4 marks)

e Item D states that 'while attitudes to domestic roles may have changed somewhat, the sharing of domestic tasks remains markedly inegalitarian and has probably changed little over the past 30 years' (lines 16–19). Using material from the Items above and elsewhere, assess how far this view is supported by sociological evidence.

(10 marks)   This is a question requiring all three skills. 'Using material from the Items above' (*application*), 'Item D states' (*interpretation*), 'and elsewhere' (*knowledge, application and understanding*) 'assess' (*evaluation*). The material relating to the *British Social Attitudes* survey contained in Slattery (1986) will help here as will Haralambos and Holborn (1991), pp. 505–9, Giddens, pp. 176–81, Bilton *et al.*, (1987) pp. 275–80, O'Donnell (1992), pp. 59–60 and Abercrombie and Warde *et al.* (1988) pp. 284–90.

ITEM A

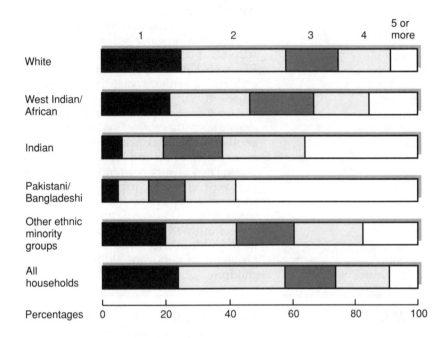

Household size: by ethnic group of head of household, 1985–1987

Number of people in household (*Great Britain*):

Source: Social Trends 1990,
London: HMSO, 1990

ITEM B

The term Afro-Caribbean is itself problematic. It suggests birth in, and direct experience of, the Caribbean. Yet increasingly strict immigration controls have led to a decrease in the proportion of people of Afro-Caribbean descent who were actually born in the Caribbean. Over half of all Afro-Caribbean people are now not only British citizens but born in Britain. 5

The Afro-Caribbean family is discussed within British society as if it is uniformly working class. Yet despite their invisibility in popular and academic discourse, there are middle-class Afro-Caribbean families in Britain. 10

Black families of Afro-Caribbean origin live in various forms of household structure. By comparison with what is known about white households, little is known about black households. In 1982 the Policy Studies Institute surveyed a large representative sample of black people in Britain. Their report provides the best 15 available picture of Afro-Caribbean families in Britain.

Two of the most widely believed characteristics of the Afro-Caribbean family for which there is some evidence are that first, it tends to be 'single parent'. Second that Afro-Caribbean mothers tend to be employed outside the home while their children are young. In many discussions of Afro-Caribbeans these features are reported to produce many of the ills of the black community.

It is however inaccurate to suggest that most Afro-Caribbean households are single parent ones, although the proportion of single Afro-Caribbean parents is high in comparison with white and Asian single parents. In the 1982 PSI survey, only 10 per cent of white households with children under 16 and 5 per cent of Asian households were headed by a lone parent, compared with 31 per cent of Afro-Caribbean households.

But does single parenthood have undesirable consequences for Afro-Caribbean children? Research by the Thomas Coram Research Unit showed no differences in achievement between children of similar social class whose parents were married and those with single parents.

Afro-Caribbean families violate dominant ideological assumptions about the correct situation in which to have children in another way. Black women of Afro-Caribbean origin are much more likely to be employed than their Asian or white counterparts. The PSI survey found that twice as many black women (41 per cent) of Afro-Caribbean origin were employed in 1982 as were white or Asian women. The majority of Afro-Caribbean women of child-bearing years were actually employed. If they were simply to leave the labour market and stay at home with their children they would substitute problems of poverty for problems of childcare. Both sets of problems are damaging to children.

Source: adapted from A. Phoenix, 'The Afro-Caribbean myth', *New Society*, 4 March 1988

ITEM C

Popular images of the Asian family are often selective, prejudiced and riddled with contradictions. Even the term 'Asian' is misleading. It was a colonial invention. Few 'Asians' in Britain identify with the term. They prefer to see themselves as people of Indian, Pakistani or Bangladeshi origin or identify themselves as black people.

For anyone who cares to look, popular images do not match the reality. It is clear that Asian families show similarities and differences across as wide a range as others and that racism, class relations and the importance of gender and generation all have a bearing upon how families are formed.

The Asian population in Britain is over a million, with approximately 40 per cent born here.

There is great ethnic diversity among Asian people in Britain, including Punjabis and Tamils, Gujaratis, Goans and Bengalis.

Generally Asian households are larger with 4.6 members than white or West Indian households with 2.3 and 3.4 members respectively. Seventy-three per cent of Asian households include children (the figures are 31 per cent for whites and 57 per cent for West Indians). Overall the proportion of extended families is 21 per cent – higher than among other groups but not the norm. The trend is in fact towards nuclear families but this does not mean the importance of extended family ties has diminished.

Source: adapted from S. Westwood and P. Bhachu, 'Images and Realities', *New Society*, 6 May, 1988

ITEM D

The term 'matrifocal family' will be used here to refer to female-headed families. In the USA in 1971, 29 per cent of all black families were headed by women. The high level of matrifocal families has been seen as the result of one or more factors. One argument accepts that poverty is the basic cause of matrifocal families but states also that matrifocality has become a part of the subculture of the poor. This view is contained in Oscar Lewis's concept of the culture of poverty. Ulf Hannerz argues that female-headed families are so common that to some degree they have become an expected and accepted alternative to the standard nuclear family. However, many sociologists view the female-headed family as a product of social disorganization and not, therefore, a viable alternative to the nuclear family. It has been accused of producing maladjusted children, juvenile delinquents and high school dropouts.

5

10

15

Source: adapted from M. Haralambos, *Sociology: Themes and Perspectives*, 2nd Ed., London: Unwin Hyman, 1985

QUESTIONS

a   Identify which ethnic groups had the highest and lowest number of households with 5 or more people in the period 1985–87 (Item A).

(2 marks)

b   Illustrating your answer with material from the Items above, explain why the authors of Items B and C consider the terms 'Afro-Caribbean' and 'Asian' inaccurate and problematic.

(5 marks)

c   Using material from the above Items and elsewhere, evaluate the extent to which popular images of ethnic minority households are 'selective, prejudiced and riddled with contradictions' (Item C, lines 1–2).

(8 marks)

d   Briefly explain the meaning of the term 'matrifocal family' (Item D, line 1).

(1 mark)

e   The author of Item D argues that 'many sociologists view the female-headed family as a product of social disorganization and not therefore a viable alternative to the nuclear family' (lines 10–12). To what extent is this view supported by sociological evidence?

(9 marks)

2.7 Childhood and old age

ITEM

Changes in the dependency population

An ageing population

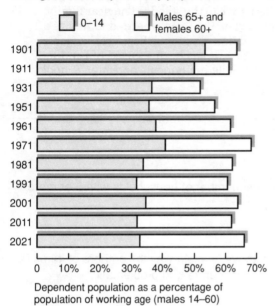

Dependent population as a percentage of
population of working age (males 14–60)

Population projections

Source: M. O'Donnell, *A New
Introduction to Sociology*, 3rd Ed.,
Walton-on-Thames, Nelson, 1992

ITEM B

Source: adapted from an article in
the *Guardian*, 27 March, 1990

Questions of growing old in prosperity

Here are some truly crunchy figures, far beyond the budget, and,
with them, a truly teasing question. Will the Third World War be
a war between generations rather than states? It is not a fanciful
query. Serious academic studies, full of serious statistics, have
recently suggested that the whole notion of the welfare state in   5
the developed world is heading, like a chain letter bowed by too
many promises, towards acrimonious breakdown and collapse.

The populations of all industrialized states are growing old.
The people who, according to the academics' forecast, will lead
the revolt are young adult workers, who are going to have to pay   10
for the health and pension costs of the rising number of elderly
people. That resentment has been fuelled, according to the studies, by the cutbacks which the workers have suffered in child
support, housing and education – while the standard of living of
pensioners, despite their rising numbers, has continued to   15
improve.

ITEM C

Source: P. Aries, *Centuries of Childhood*, Harmondsworth: Penguin, 1973

Our world is obsessed by the physical, moral and sexual problems of childhood. This preoccupation was unknown in the medieval civilization, because there was no problem for the Middle Ages: as soon as he had been weaned, or soon after, the child became the natural companion of the adult.   5

ITEM D

Something of a romantic traditionalist, Aries extols what he sees as the community-based sociability of medieval society into which the young were expected to fit and deplores the obsession of the modern family with its younger members. Not surprisingly, de Mause and others have criticized him for minimizing   5
the evidence of neglect and brutality towards children in the medieval period as well as a general indifference to children's welfare. Nevertheless, Aries does introduce what has become a central feature of much contemporary social scientific analysis of age – that it is substantially a socially-constructed phenomenon   10
rather than simply a biological given.

Ronald Fletcher's insightful comment that both parents and the state have come to take an increasing interest in children suggests the framework within which modern childhood has been moulded.   15

Throughout the nineteenth century a steady flow of legislation first restricted and then prohibited child labour. In parallel, the state increasingly encouraged and financed the education of children until finally compulsory education was enacted.

Modern families are often said to be 'child-centred'. Two   20
trends – both well established at the start of this century – have contributed to this: first, parents have generally had fewer children and, second, the increase in leisure has given them more time to spend with those they do have.

Whatever the outcome, the needs and protection of children   25
rather than the right of parents over children emerge as the dominant theme of post-war legislation in relation to children. The Child Care Act of 1989 re-emphasized the fundamental principle that the prime concern of the state should be the welfare of the child.   30

The matter of child abuse raises profound issues of social policy and sociology. Sociologically, what causes child abuse? From a macro perspective, it is probable that certain widespread cultural attitudes, particularly related to childrearing, may produce a climate more conducive to child abuse. Another large-scale   35
issue for consideration is the relationship between child abuse (and general child welfare) and poverty.

A. H. Halsey is highly critical of the view that the twentieth century has been the century of the child. On the contrary, he considers that a greatly strengthened network of support for chil-   40
dren and parents needs to be put in place to prevent a substantial minority getting into serious difficulties.

Source: adapted from M. O'Donnell, *A New Introduction to Sociology*, 3rd Ed., Walton-on-Thames: Nelson, 1992

QUESTIONS

a   Describe the changes in the age distribution of the British population as shown in Item A.

(2 marks)

b   Evaluate the view that the main consequence of an ageing population will be conflict between young and old as suggested in Item B.

(8 marks)

c   Evaluate the view that there has been a major change in attitudes towards children since the Middle Ages as suggested in Item C.

(5 marks)

d   Identify the two agencies most responsible for the construction of modern childhood (Item D).

(2 marks)

e   To what extent does sociological evidence support the view outlined in Item D that modern families are 'child-centred' (line 20).

(8 marks)

2.8 Power in the family

ITEM A

The nuclear family was a nest. Warm and sheltering, it kept the children secure from the pressure of the outside adult world, and gave the men an evening refuge from the icy blast of competition. And as the nuclear family rose in the nineteenth century, the women liked it too, because it let them pull back from the grinding exactions of farm work, or the place at the mill, and devote themselves to child care. So everyone huddled happily within those secure walls, serene about the dinner table, united in the Sunday outing.

5

Source: E. Shorter, *The Making of the Modern Family*, London: Fontana, 1977

ITEM B

The husband, by virtue of his greater participation in the external economic division of labour compared to his wife, was able legitimately to avoid many household tasks and legitimately to dominate family life. To paraphrase Engels, the fact that not all husbands used their power does not in the least change the position of wives. The wife, by virtue of her relative exclusion from paid work and her major responsibility for the home and the children, was consigned to economic and social dependence upon her husband.

5

In contrast to certain optimistic theorists who claim that the nineteenth-century patriarchal family has been superseded by a more democratic type ... the present study provides abundant evidence of the survival of patriarchalism.

10

Source: adapted from S. Edgell, *Middle-Class Couples*, London: George Allen & Unwin, 1980

ITEM C

As nuclear families become more isolated, the network of kinsfolk becomes dispersed. The young mother can still talk to her mum on the telephone, but she can't ask her to drop in for a few minutes to mind the baby. Ideas about the status of women have been changing; wives are now thought of as companions rather than servants to their husbands, but perhaps they are even more thoroughly enslaved to their children than before.

5

Source: E. Leach, 'The family as an instrument of women's enslavement', the *Sunday Times Magazine*, 10 November, 1986

ITEM D

The family-household system of contemporary capitalism constitutes not only the central site of the oppression of women but an important organizing principle of the relations of production and the social formation as a whole. This is not necessarily inevitable, since the argument that it would not be possible for capitalism's relations of production to be organized in other ways has yet to be proven. Furthermore, it is evident that the contemporary family-household system has incorporated a substantial element from struggles between the interests of men and those of women, by and large in favour of the former. However, it still remains the case that the specific combination of gender and class relations that characterizes this system has entrenched gender division in the fabric of capitalist social relations in a particularly effective way.

5

10

Source: adapted from M. Barrett, *Women's Oppression Today: Problems in Marxist Feminist Analysis*, London: Verso, 1980

ITEM E

Originally, feminist research began with a commitment to exposing the oppression of women and uncovering and claiming women's experiences as valid. More recently it has concentrated on how women resist oppression. Implicit in all this is a critique of male power.   5

Feminists are concerned to improve the situation of women. So they conduct research which provides evidence for the need to instigate change. They disrupt prevailing notions of what is inevitable and ask what is the damage of not changing social conditions. Research on child sexual abuse, domestic violence and   10 marital rape suggests that the longer the ideological myth of the family as a safe haven from the outside world is perpetuated, the greater will be the damage that is done to women and children.

Source: adapted from B. Skeggs, 'Confessions of a feminist researcher', *Sociology Review,* September 1992

QUESTIONS

a According to Item A, how is power distributed within the nuclear family?

(2 marks)

b Explain in your own words the meaning of the term 'patriarchalism' (Item B, line 13).

(2 marks)

c Using material from Items above and elsewhere, assess the view that 'ideas about the status of women have been changing' (Item C, line 4).

(7 marks)

d The author of Item A argues that the family keeps 'children secure from the pressure of the outside adult world' (line 2). Illustrating your answer with material from the Items above, assess the extent to which this view is supported by sociological evidence.

(5 marks)

e Using material from Items D, E and elsewhere, assess the view that the family in contemporary capitalism does not serve the needs of its members.

(9 marks)

2.9 The family and social policy

ITEM A

Population: by selected age bands

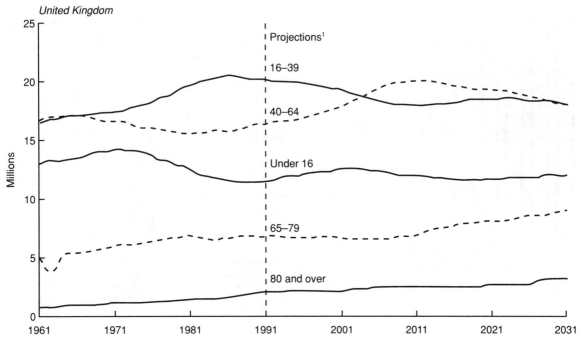

United Kingdom

Projections[1]

16–39

40–64

Under 16

65–79

80 and over

1 1989-based projections.

Source: Social Trends 1992,
London, HMSO, 1992

ITEM B

Source: G.Dalley, 'Women's
Welfare' in *New Society*, 28
August, 1987

Examples from other countries demonstrate that there are
alternative ways of tackling the issues of caring and dependency. The family model of care with the high demands made
on women and lack of choice and frequent loneliness for the
dependents is not the only solution. Policy makers and profes-   5
sionals may support current policies for the 'right' reasons –
the welfare of the dependent – but those policies are associated too strongly with a government-espoused ideology
which often works against the interests of the parties most
centrally involved. There is general agreement that commu-   10
nity care policies need to be reviewed – Sir Roy Griffiths is
doing just that now – but feminists would argue that the fundamental assumptions upon which they are constructed need
to be examined critically. Tinkering with the practical details
is not enough.   15

ITEM C

The disappearing daughters

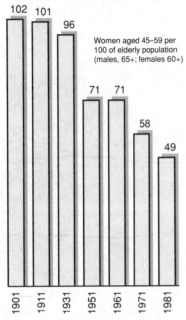

Women aged 45–59 per 100 of elderly population (males, 65+; females 60+)

Source: Annual Abstract of Statistics

How the potential pool of carers has shrunk.

Source: 'The crisis in community care', *New Society*, 18 September, 1987

The rise of the second earner

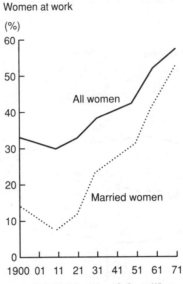

Women at work

(%)

All women

Married women

Source: H. Joshi, R. Layard and S. Owen; *Why are more women working in Britain?* Centre for Labour Economics: LSE. June 1983

The increasing number of women at work gives the lie to the assumption that women are at home and therefore available to provide care.

The low cost* of community care

Care setting: £ per week at 1986 prices

* For a frail elderly single person on a state pension, without substantial savings. The client qualifies for attendance allowance at the lower rate, for a disability incurred after retirement age.

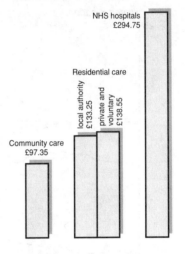

NHS hospitals £294.75

Residential care

local authority £133.25

private and voluntary £138.55

Community care £97.35

Residential care may be unnecessarily expensive as well as inappropriate for many people now forced to make use of it by the absence of alternatives.

ITEM D

The impact of AIDS on family relationships is a reminder that the apparent privacy of the domestic world is no more than a fantasy and that the private realm of domestic relationships carries a public script.

Towards the end of 1986, the government brought the subject 5
of AIDS into the homes of millions.

Ministers adopted more temperate tones and spoke of the need for public education: AIDS was preventable if people knew how it was contracted.

A massive debate was sparked off on the role of AIDS education 10
in schools and in due course the Department of Education and Science itself produced a video on AIDS for use in classrooms.

The responsibilities of state and family sat in uneasy juxtaposition. Ironically, many parents were themselves to become reluctant health educators, unwillingly caught up in the effects 15 of the government's campaign. In January 1987, 'AIDS week' bought mass coverage of HIV and AIDS on television, radio and in the newspapers. Information on AIDS proliferated and in its wake came the questions and the need for clarification, particularly among young people. Some of this was met in the public arena, through helplines and AIDS education agencies of various sorts. But much of it fell at least in the first instance to parents. 20

The cultural anthropology of family life in Britain at that time must have taken some fascinating twists and turns. Conventional codes were turned upside down and the rules of permissible debate were temporarily suspended. Rock singers were seen on TV demonstrating how a condom should be used. Safe sex became a fashionable commodity. 25

Unintentionally sponsored by the DHSS's own campaign, sexuality took a central place on the family agenda. 30

Source: adapted from D. Clark, 'AIDS and the family, *New Society*, 27 May, 1988

ITEM E

Free babysitting, gifts large and small, the loan of the deposit on a first home, caring in times of illness – this kind of help and support appears to be the essence of family life to many people. The expectation that such help will be reliably provided marks the distinguishing line between kinship and other kinds of social relations, including friendship. But does the reality match this image of the family as a reliable source of support? Are people now less willing to deliver this kind of assistance in practice? Do people still feel a special sense 'of obligation' to assist their kin which puts these relationships in a class of their own? 10

Source: J. Finch, 'Family Ties', *New Society*, 20 March 1987

QUESTIONS

a What implications do the trends shown in Items A and C have for the future of the Welfare State?

(5 marks)

b To what extent does the material in Item D challenge traditional functionalist views of the changing relationship between the family and the state?

(4 marks)

c What does Item E suggest is the main distinction between kinship and other social relations and in what way is it changing?

(2 marks)

d   Illustrating your answer with material from Item B and elsewhere, explain what is meant by the 'family model of care' (line 3).

(4 marks)

e   The author of Item B argues that the family model of care leads to high demands being made on women and 'frequent loneliness for the dependents' (lines 4–5). How far is this view supported by sociological evidence?

(10 marks)

2.10 The dark side of the family

ITEM A

The sexual abuse of children is a widespread phenomenon and much of it happens in the context of the family. Sexual abuse can most easily be defined as the carrying out of sexual acts by adults with children below the age of consent (sixteen years old in Britain). Incest refers to sexual relations between close kin. Not all incest is sexual abuse. For example, sexual intercourse between brother and sister is incestual, but does not fit the definition of abuse. In sexual abuse, an adult is essentially exploiting an infant or child for sexual purposes. The most common form of incest is one that is also sexual abuse – incestuous relations between fathers and young daughters.

Incest, and child sexual abuse more generally, are phenomena which have been 'discovered' only over the past ten to twenty years. Of course it has long been known that such sexual acts occasionally occur, but it was assumed by most social observers that the strong taboos which exist against this behaviour meant that it was not widespread. Such is not the case. Child sexual abuse is proving to be disturbingly widespread.

Source: A. Giddens, *Sociology*, Cambridge: Polity, 1989

5

10

15

ITEM B

Child abuse – reported cases

In England and Wales the most systematic studies of this type have come from the research unit of the National Society for the Prevention of Cruelty to Children (NSPCC). Since 1974, cases of child abuse and suspected child abuse have been recorded on child protection registers. In a number of areas, covering almost 10.5 per cent of the population of England and Wales, these are controlled by the NSPCC. By careful examination of cases on their registers each year, the NSPCC is able to provide estimates of the levels of different types of abuse for England and Wales as a whole.

The NSPCC data suggest that in 1989 (the most recent year for which data are available) over 36,000 children in England and Wales were recorded as either having been abused or giving rise to 'grave concern' over their safety. This is an incidence rate of 3.35 per 1000 children. NSPCC records show a dramatic increase of around 30 per cent per year in recorded cases in the early and mid 1980s, levelling out in 1987–88, and increasing again in 1989. The most commonly recorded forms of abuse are physical injury and sexual abuse, but the largest proportionate increases between 1988 and 1989 were in neglect, emotional harm and grave concern cases. Most people feel that while the overall increase in registered cases in the 1980s may be because of an increase in child abuse, it is more likely to reflect increased reporting as a result of greater public and professional awareness of the problem.

5

10

15

20

25

Reported cases provide a readily available source of data on child abuse which has been professionally identified. However critics claim that reported cases understate the true incidence of the problem, as many cases of abuse may not be reported or recorded.

There is some evidence to suggest that reported cases may provide samples which are systematically biased and therefore of little value for projecting guidelines about child abuse in general.

30

Source: adapted from S. Taylor, 'Measuring Child Abuse' in *Sociology Review*, Febuary 1992

ITEM C

Rape profile

Definition: Rape is penetration of the penis into the vagina of a woman against her will. Penetration of the anus or mouth of a woman or a man against their will is termed 'indecent assault', as are most other sex crimes.
The main statistics below are from a sample of 1,236 London women. They were 62% of a random sample of 2,000 approached by the researchers.

1 in 6 women have been raped
This does not include attempted rape or assault or attacks ion children under 16. It does include married women raped by their husbands. Figures extrapolated from police reports give a figure of 1 in 4 for US women.

1 in 12 rapes are reported to the police.
This compares with 1 in 4 of women who seek counselling from UK Rape Crisis Centres. In the US as a whole 51% of reported rapists are caught. 76% of those are prosecuted and 47% of that 76% are acquitted.

3 in 4 attackers are known to the victim
For rapes reported to the police the figure is much lower at around 1 in 2. Women are more likely to report a stranger to the police.

1 in 20 rapes are gang rapes.
For rapes reported to the police the figure is much higher. 30% in Washington, 40% in the UK generally, 43% in Philadelphia, 47% in Malaysia and 50% in Toronto. Women are more likely to report gang rapes to the police.

1 in 2 rapes involve violence in addition to the rape.
For rapes reported to the police the figure is nearer 4 in 5, since women are more likely to report violent rapes.

1 in 2 occur in the home of the rapist or the victim.
This proportion is similar for rapes reported to the police in Memphis and Philadelphia in the US. The figure is likely to reflect women's tendency to avoid dangerous situations *outside* the home.

The rapist who pays the rent

- Over 1 million children in the UK will be sexually assaulted or raped by age 15, many by members of their own family.
- 1 in 3 families in Cairo is incestuous.

- 1 in 4 US children will be raped or sexually assaulted by a trusted adult by age 15.
- 1 in 10 married women in the UK has been forced, with violence, to have sex with her husband.

Source: New Internationalist, April 1986

ITEM D

Jane is defined as schizophrenic. She is in perpetual reverie, her own little dream world, which consists of a game of tennis. It is a mixed doubles; she is the ball. Jane sits motionless and silent and eats only when fed. The adults in her family are in a state of conflict, her father and his mother ranged against her mother and her mother's father. The two halves of the family communicate only through Jane; she is the go-between. The strain eventually becomes too much for her and she escapes into her dream world. However, as her 'dream' shows, even in this world she cannot escape from the clutches of the family. The game of tennis symbolizes the interaction pattern in the family. With examples such as this, Laing shows how the family can be a destructive and exploitative institution.

5

10

Source: adapted from R. D. Laing, 'The politics of the family', in M. Haralambos and M. Holborn, *Sociology: Themes and Perspectives*, 3rd Ed., London: Colins Educational, 1991

QUESTIONS

a   Suggest two reasons for the increase in the number of children registered as at risk by the NSPCC as shown in Item B.

(2 marks)

b   The data in Item C suggest that rape and sexual abuse are more widespread than crime statistics indicate. What explanations have sociologists offered for the extent of rape and sexual abuse in modern Britain?

(5 marks)

c   Using material from the Items above and elsewhere, evaluate the relative importance of the various factors which led to child abuse being 'discovered only over the past ten to twenty years' (Item A, lines 13–14).

(7 marks)

d   Identify the two most commonly recorded forms of child abuse (Item B).

(2 marks)

e   Item D suggests that the family is a 'destructive and exploitative institution' (line 12). To what extent is this argument supported by sociological evidence?

(9 marks)

3

Education

3.1 The role of education

ITEM A

The authors summarize a number of ideas about the role of education. They particularly contrast the difference between those who see education as a socializing force and those who believe that education is about training pupils for their future work roles. This is also covered in Haralambos and Holborn (1991), pp. 229–53.

Durkheim observed that education could play a central role in fostering social integration in societies with a complex division of labour. Following him, sociologists throughout the twentieth century have identified two basic functions of educational systems. Education is on the one hand, an agency of socialization, transmitting social rules and values; on the other hand it is a channel for selecting and training people to fill the many occupations of industrial economies. [5]

However educational systems are only partially successful. This is partly because social classes, political parties, teachers and parents have different views of what elements of culture should be stressed, and what skills are useful. Such disagreement has a fundamental basis in the social structure of modern Britain, there often being a contradiction between the two functions of socialization and training. This is because the two functions are not easily separated in practice. The norms and values transmitted to any group of children have to somehow be related to the kinds of skills they are being taught. To take an extreme example, social problems would be likely to occur if schools taught the kinds of social behaviour appropriate to the aristocracy to children destined to become unskilled manual labourers. Similarly, training for different sorts of work needs to be different: to be proficient in Latin is not useful to the shop assistant, just as expertise in woodwork is irrelevant to a university teacher. [10] [15] [20]

One response to this inevitable contradiction in a class society with a highly specialized division of labour is for policy makers to educate different groups of children in different ways. An example is the tripartite education system which explicitly set about providing a different kind of education for children with 'different abilities and capacities'. Such an arrangement, however, caused a further set of problems. The different cultures being imposed in the different schools tended to perpetuate class hostility rather than integrate children into a common national culture. [25] [30]

So, the intention that schooling should socialize children and foster social integration was undermined; different kinds of preparation for future working lives generated social conflict. It is in this sense then that we talk of contradictions between the functions of socialization and training. It is a far from simple task simultaneously to integrate children into society and to prepare them for their future work roles. [35] [40]

Source: adapted from N. Abercrombie and A. Warde *et al.*, *Contemporary British Society*, Cambridge: Polity, 1988

ITEM B

This is a neat summary of a number of different views about education, you will need to look at them in more depth. The particular publication from which this extract is taken is packed full of extracts from original sociological studies.

Source: R. Gomm, *A Level Sociology*, Cambridge: National Extension College 1990

The national debate on education twists and turns, and changes its shape from year to year. However, we can distinguish two basic positions taken by politicians, educationalists, journalists and so on, according to their ideas about what education is for.

Education should:	
● mould children to serve society **Socialisation** **(Vocationalism)**	● develop each individual's unique personality **Individuation** **(Humanism)**
● prepare children to take their place in an unequal society **Elitism**	● promote equality **Egalitarianism**
● propagate a common national culture **National unity**	● allow for the development of a wide range of different cultures **Cultural pluralism**

ITEM C

Bowles and Gintis' analysis of the correspondence between education and work is a classic of mid-seventies Marxist analysis. Although it has been widely criticized it deserves deeper study and is explained in more detail in any recent text book, for example Bilton *et al.* (1987), pp. 310–12.

Source: S. Bowles and H. Gintis, *Schooling in Capitalist America*, London, Routledge and Kegan Paul, 1976.

The educational system helps integrate youth into the economic system, we believe, through a structural correspondence between its social relations and those of production. The structure of social relations in education not only inures the student to the discipline of the workplace, but develops the types of personal demeanour, modes of self-presentation, self-image, and social-class identifications which are the crucial ingredients of job adequacy. Specifically, the social relationships of education – the relationships between administrators and teachers, teachers and students, students and students, and students and their work – replicate the hierarchical division of labour. 5

  10

ITEM D

The arguments for selection and education for future roles are well expressed in this DES circular. Do you agree with it? The best recent summary of New Right thinking is contained in Mike O'Donnell (1992). Look here and at the other items for a consideration of this view.

Source: G. Walford, *Privatization and Privilege in Education*, London: HMSO, 1990

There has to be selection because we are beginning to create aspirations which society cannot match. In some ways this points to the success of education in contrast to the public mythology which has been created. When young people drop off the education production line and cannot find work at all or work which meets their abilities and expectations, then we are creating frustration with perhaps disturbing consequences. We have to select: to ration the educational opportunities so that society can cope with the output of education . . . 5

We are in a period of considerable social change. There may be social unrest, but we can cope with the Toxteths. But if we have a highly educated and idle population we may possibly anticipate more serious social conflict. People must be educated once more to know their place. 10

ITEM E

A useful summary of two different views on the nature and role of education. Think about which view best describes your own educational experiences. To try to locate these approaches in their broader theoretical context look at the questions on Consensus Theory and Conflict Theory in this book p. 24 and p. 27. Also see Giddens (1989), pp. 705–7.

The table below gives two sociological views on the role of education :

CONSENSUS VIEW	CONFLICT VIEW
Education has:	Education:
1 A selection function	**1 Reproduces inequality**
It selects people and helps to place them in the most appropriate positions in adult life according to their abilities.	It helps to perpetuate existing inequalities.
2 An economic function	**2 Reproduces labour**
It produces people with the general skills and attitudes and (to some extent) the specific skills required by the economy of the society.	It produces a majority of people with the general skills and attitudes and (to some extent) the specific skills required to allow them to be exploited by those who benefit from their labour.
3 A socialization function	**3 Justifies inequality**
It promotes the attitudes and values which people must share if there is to be social stability.	It promotes ideas and values which help those who are powerful to stay powerful, particularly the idea that inequality is the result of differences in individual ability.

Source: R. Gomm, *A Level Sociology,* Cambridge: National Extension College, 1990

QUESTIONS

a   Illustrating your answer with reference to Item A, explain why there may often be 'a contradiction between the two functions of socialization and training' (lines 14–15).

(2 marks)   Two marks for *interpretation* requiring you to identify two differences between these functions. The material is in the passage, but put it in your own words to show you understand it.

b   Identify the similarities and differences between the two sociological views of the role of education shown in Item E.

(4 marks)   A question again asking only for you to use the material provided, but to get all four *interpretation* marks you need to identify at least two similarities and two differences. Reading up on these theories will make that task easier. As a hint, the similarities are to do with the actual effects of the education system. The differences are to do with the desirability of such effects.

c   Item B contains 'two basic positions . . . about what education is for' (lines 2–4). Discuss these positions and assess the relative extent to which they are each reflected in the structure and content of the contemporary British educational system.

(8 marks)   This is quite a complicated question which requires you to use all the skills. You need to demonstrate some knowledge about the current education system and

interpret what each view is saying before you can evaluate how much they have influenced British education. Take your time on this question and structure it carefully.

d Explain the meaning of the term 'structural correspondence' (Item C, line 2).

(2 marks)

Two *interpretation* marks can be gleaned from the passage, but fuller knowledge of the study will make it much easier. An example usually makes any definition clearer.

e Item D quotes a DES circular as arguing that 'People must be educated . . . to know their place' (line 13). Using material from the Items above and elsewhere, assess the extent to which this is the prime role of the education system in contemporary Britain.

(9 marks)

This question requires you to use all skills because you are asked to interpret material in the Items, bring in *knowledge* from elsewhere and in both these cases there will be *application* marks for doing so in a relevant way and you then need to assess the arguments in relation to the question. A well-structured answer covering a number of different studies about the role of education (particularly relating to the views identified in question **a)** is required to get full marks for this question. In particular you need to have information relating to recent changes in the education structure such as are given in the questions in this book on The National Curriculum (p. 116) and New Vocationalism (p. 130). For a comprehensive summary of current trends and issues in education, see the article by Chitty in *Sociology Review*, February 1993.

ITEM A

The *General Household Survey* is a useful source of statistical data, although you need to remember the problems related to official statistics, which are covered in detail in Slattery (1986). This table shows a clear relationship between social class and educational achievement and you need to make sure you understand it before you attempt any questions.

Highest qualification level attained by age, sex and father's socio-economic group

Persons aged 25–49 not in full-time education   *Great Britain: 1989 and 1990 combined*

Age and highest qualification level attained*	Father's socio-economic group							
	Professional	Employers and managers	Intermediate non-manual	Junior non-manual	Skilled manual and own account non-professional	Semi-skilled manual and personal service	Unskilled manual	Total
	%	%	%	%	%	%	%	%
Men								
25–29 Higher education	56	35	48	27	20	14	15	27
Other qualifications	39	55	43	67	59	59	53	56
No qualifications	5	10	9	6	22	27	32	17
30–39 Higher education	63	41	43	36	21	16	10	29
Other qualifications	34	46	48	51	49	43	38	46
No qualifications	4	13	8	13	30	41	52	25
40–49 Higher education	56	38	49	34	22	16	14	27
Other qualifications	37	42	40	46	38	33	34	39
No qualifications	7	20	11	20	39	51	52	34

*'Higher education' = qualifications above GCE A level standard; 'other qualifications' = qualifications at or below GCE A level standard.

Source: adapted from *General Household Survey 1990*, London: HMSO, 1992

ITEM B

Read through this carefully, as the authors summarize most of the key explanations for educational inequality, looking at selection, labelling and upbringing. There are a number of studies in any sociology textbook to support each of these theories, for

In the 1950s and 60s, sociologists advanced several theories of causes of educational inequality.

1   One explanation was that the organization of the schooling system was at fault. The system of competitive selection for secondary schools (the 11-plus examination), the continued existence of elite private schools, and the streaming of school classes, were identified for special criticism. It was hoped that the introduction of comprehensive secondary schools, to which entry was non-competitive, and which had more flexible internal

5

example Haralambos and Holborn (1991), pp. 253–82, and they are worth investigating in more depth. Also look at criticisms of each.

arrangements for teaching, might solve the problem. 10

2 Another explanation was in terms of the teachers' differential expectations of the capacities of children from different social classes. Teachers were said to be inclined to reward and encourage middle-class children, with whom they had affinities in values and styles. This explanation concentrated on the 15 value-system of the school, the role of the teacher and the mechanism of the self-fulfilling prophecy, whereby educational outcomes were produced in accordance with the expectations of educationalists about class differences.

3 A further series of explanations emphasized the role of the 20 family and home environment in determining educational success. Some such explanations emphasized the different extent to which parents of different classes encouraged their children to succeed; others stressed the particular attitudes of working-class communities and peer groups towards school; and the now- 25 famous work of Bernstein identified variable linguistic capabilities among children from different class backgrounds.

Source: N. Abercrombie and A. Warde *et al., Contemporary British Society,* Cambridge: Polity, 1988

ITEM C

This article looks in greater depth at the relationship between social class and educational achievement which seems to have been reinforced by every form of selection. You need to keep up to date with current debates about the need for selection (it allows for the most able to develop their abilities) and the criticisms of it (that it disadvantages lower-class and lower-ability children) which are central to current debates about education. A useful source of material on changes in education, and in particular the 1988 Education Reform Act, sometimes known as the 'Baker Bill', is contained in 'What's Baking in the schools' in *Social Studies Review*, Vol. 3, No. 1.

The Conservatives' election victory and their proposals for educational reform have raised fears of a return to selection and a widening of social class inequalities in education. The arguments for and against the Conservative proposals obscure, however, what research has shown: that class inequalities in British educa- 5 tion have been remarkably stable throughout the century.

There has been constantly rising educational attainment (at least as measured by the acquisition of examination statistics – the only measure available to us) during the course of the twentieth century, a silent revolution that has continued throughout 10 both selective and comprehensive eras. But class inequalities first in access to selective schools, then at GCSE and next perhaps at A level have shown no overall tendency to decline. Chameleon-like they seem to reappear in a new guise but fundamentally unchanged as the educational environment changes around 15 them.

In the face of this remarkable resilience of class inequalities, educational reforms seem powerless whether for good or ill. There are two major reasons for this.

First, the rhetoric of reforms has often been much bolder than 20 the reforms themselves. Thus the 1944 Act provided free secondary education for all, but many local authorities had already provided the bulk of their places free before the war. The act merely reinforced a long-standing trend. Similarly, some protagonists (and some opponents) of comprehensives talk about a 25 common education (or levelling) but there is substantial differentiation both within and between comprehensives. Class differences between comprehensives may often be as great as the class differences between grammar and secondary modern schools.

Second, and relatedly, in a free society educationally ambitious 30 families can adjust their plans so as to maximize their children's chances under any new rules of the game.

Source: adapted from A. F. Heath, 'Class in the classroom', *New Society,* 17 July, 1987

ITEM D

This article expands on the arguments, focusing on the problems of parental choice, one key aspect of the 1988 Education Reform Act. You need to know about this and the other main points of this legislation, which include opting out, National Curriculum and national testing. Try to look at specialist educational publications to explore these changes and debates in more detail. Alternatively you could try looking at Chapman (1986), or Burgess (1985).

Promoting parental choice of schools is a retrograde step that does little to improve the quality of a child's education, according to a five-year study carried out in Scotland.

The Canadian Center for Educational Sociology's findings show that the principle effect of parent's right to choose, intro-   5
duced in Scotland in 1980, has been to increase segregation between working-class and middle-class pupils. The impact on children's academic results was minimal.

It is the first authoritative research to study the effects of the Government's open enrolment policies on schools' intake. The   10
Government claims the reforms will lead to higher standards by forcing schools to compete with each other.

But parental choice was probably having a detrimental effect on the school system. Good schools in poor areas may find themselves losing pupils, while less effective schools in better areas   15
become more popular. Comprehensive reorganization had narrowed the attainment gap between middle-class and working-class pupils. By increasing class segregation schools could lose their more able pupils, who might help to create a strong disciplinary climate as well as high academic standards.   20

Professor Willms, who fears the same effect will lead to a shift into private schools for middle-class pupils, said : 'The losers are the lower social class children and also the teachers in those schools.'

'The really sad result is that pupils in predominantly working-   25
class areas don't have any clout and could be marginalized into ghetto schools which have lost their most talented pupils and their resources,' said Professor Willms.

Source: adapted from a report in the *Times Educational Supplement*, 2 October, 1992.

QUESTIONS

a With reference to Item A, identify differences in the pattern of educational attainment by social class for the three age groups shown.

(3 marks)

b Using material from Item B and from elsewhere, assess the importance of 'the role of the family and home environment in determining educational success' (lines 20–21).

(9 marks)   A question expecting all skills, as the wording tells you. 'Using information from Item B (*interpretation* and *application*) and elsewhere (*knowledge* and *application*) assess' (*evaluation*). Always support concepts and criticisms with sociological studies.

c Explain in your own words two of the aims of the comprehensive reorganization of schooling referred to in Item B.

(2 marks)

d Identify the two social groups who will lose out as a result of the introduction of parental choice according to Item D.

(2 marks)

e   Using material from the Items above and elsewhere explain and evaluate the claim that 'educational reforms seem powerless whether for good or ill' (Item C, line 18).

(9 marks)

You can see that all skills are needed here, so do use material from the Items, do support both sides of the argument with sociological studies and do say whether you agree with the statement expressed or not, and why. In relation to this you could look up the entry for meritocracy in Slattery (1985) or use the table from Gordon Marshall's article quoted in Item A in the question on Education and Social Mobility (p. 112). The book by Chapman (1986) covers this topic on pp. 22–57 and in particular the section referring to the study '15,000 Hours' contained on pp. 55–7.

3.3 Education and gender

ITEM A

A simple but useful chart from *Social Studies Review*, which clearly shows that boys and girls tend to achieve different results at O-level or CSE. You might try to obtain some more up-to-date information on this issue.

School leavers in Great Britain with higher grade results at O-level or CSE in selected subjects: by sex 1980/81 and 1986/87.

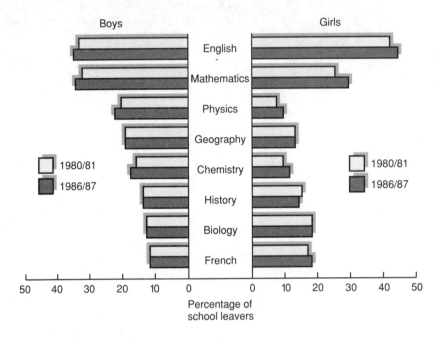

Source: Carol Buswell, 'Gender and sociology', *Social Studies Review*, May 1989

ITEM B

Reynolds provides a lot of recent material to show that girls at school now actually do better than boys at least up to GCSE level, even though it may not benefit them later on. This material is particularly relevant to parts (c), (d) and (e) of this question.

Source: K. Reynolds, 'Feminist thinking on education', *Social Studies Review*, March 1991

Women students are frequently referred to as 'underachieving', that their educational qualifications do not match up to those of men. However this is not the case. In terms of the educational qualifications which girls obtain by school leaving age, girls do marginally better than boys. Girls are more successful in achieving Grade 1 GCSE passes than their male counterparts; according to Department of Education and Science figures, in 1987–1988 42 per cent of girls left school with one or more Grade 1 GCSE passes as compared with 34 per cent of boys. Moreover, 55 per cent of boys left school with lower grade passes or no qualifications compared to 37 per cent of girls.

Yet despite this disparity in educational qualifications at school leaving age, women do not make up the larger proportion of students at further and higher education levels.

ITEM C

Michelle Stanworth was one of the first feminist writers to show how the organization of schools

The most crucial area of comparison for the sexual distribution of attainment is the content of education received by girls and boys – the forms of knowledge, expertise and skill with which women and men were equipped. Whatever the academic or practical merits of particular school subjects, it would be a mistake to

disadvantages girls. There are many studies which support her views, but look through your textbook for criticisms. See for example Bilton *et al.* (1987) pp. 188 (one of the *et al.*'s being Michelle Stanworth), or Giddens (1989), pp. 434–7. Have things changed?

Source: adapted from M. Stanworth, *Gender and Schooling*, London: Hutchinson, 1983

assume that all GCSE or GCE qualifications are interchangeable; on the contrary, in terms of both career opportunities and further training, some subjects carry greater weight than others. Woodwork, metalwork and technical drawing, for example give access to a wider range of careers, and to a greater number of technologically-based courses, than do domestic subjects. Physics and chemistry, too, have a wider currency than the biological sciences into which most girls tend to be channelled. Mathematics at GCSE is a necessary prerequisite for careers in computer programming, textile technology, dentistry, architecture, horticulture, engineering, the police force, market research, printing, radiography, chemistry, economics, surveying, town planning, advertising, banking and astronomy – to name but a few. It is therefore of vital importance that girls as well as boys be fully represented in these subject areas. 20

The differences in school attainments clearly underlie many of the stable patterns of gender differentiation in higher education. 10 ... 15

ITEM D

A useful table from Abercrombie and Warde *et al.* (1988) showing the proportion of women as undergraduates in each subject area. Use a recent edition of *Social Trends* to see how (or whether) things have changed.

Women as a percentage of full-time undergraduates in universities by selected subjects, 1975–83

	Women as a percentage of all students								
	1975	1976	1977	1978	1979	1980	1981	1982	1983
Education	67.1	69.3	65.4	64.6	67.2	65.7	65.4	65.3	65.8
Medicine, dentistry and health	36.3	36.7	37.5	38.6	40.2	41.7	43.2	44.9	44.5
Engineering and technology	4.0	4.4	4.9	5.5	6.1	6.9	7.6	8.6	9.1
Agriculture, forestry and veterinary science	29.1	29.5	32.1	32.9	35.0	36.3	37.3	38.6	38.5
Science	29.6	29.9	30.1	30.5	31.4	32.2	32.7	33.3	33.2
Social, administrative and business studies	37.0	37.3	37.9	39.0	40.0	41.3	42.4	43.8	44.8
Architecture and other professional and vocational subjects	24.0	25.9	26.0	27.9	30.6	32.6	34.4	35.9	36.5
Language, literature and studies	62.4	62.8	63.9	65.0	66.7	67.8	68.5	69.2	69.0
Arts, other than languages	51.9	–	52.2	52.6	53.2	54.3	54.5	54.4	53.8

Source: N. Abercrombie and A. Warde *et al.*, *Contemporary British Society*, Cambridge: Polity, 1988

ITEM E

Chapman outlines the various ways that reading schemes and curricula define certain behaviours as gender-appropriate. Was this true when you were in primary school? Is it only applicable to primary schools? You could try some

Gender stereotyping can be found in all aspects of the primary school curriculum. The basic skills of literacy and numeracy are taught using materials which reflect the reality of the outside world. Reading schemes often show the most extreme examples of bias, the best known being the Ladybird Key Words series. 5 The series has been updated over the years, most obviously in the clothes worn. These books follow the daily lives of Peter and Jane, who appear to have a housewife mother, frequently depicted in a kitchen, and a breadwinning father, rarely shown,

content analysis of the material produced for the introduction of the National Curriculum. The book from which this extract is taken is highly recommended for all aspects of the sociology of education, along with R. Burgess's book, *Education, Schools and Schooling* (1985).

Source: K. Chapman, *The Sociology of Schools*, London, Tavistock, 1986

depicted with a car or mending something. The updating has not acknowledged any changes in the traditional roles of men and women. In book 3a, Peter speaks 30 times, Jane only 15. In the illustrations, Peter is clearly shown as the more active of the two; Jane is generally on the sidelines of any action. The cumulative effect is of a girl who is passive and satisfied by domestic activities, while the boy is shown as physically active and dominant. 10 15

Bias is less obvious in mathematics, yet females are notably absent in junior mathematics textbooks, and mathematical problems are geared to boys' interests, with the result that quite young children regard it as a male subject. 20

QUESTIONS

a Describe the trends in examination results shown by Item A.

(4 marks)

b What percentage of girls left school with one or more Grade 1 GCSE passes in 1987-88 according to Item B?

(1 mark)

c Assess the argument put forward by the author of Item B that women do not underachieve until past the minimum school leaving age.

(5 marks)   Use other studies which both support and challenge this argument to get marks for *knowledge, application* and *evaluation*. Try for example, Garrett, *Gender* (1987), pp. 60–95 or Abbott and Wallace (1990), pp. 49–65. You could also look in Buswell (1989). You can get *application* marks by using material from all the Items as well as other studies even though you are not specifically directed to do so.

d To what extent does the material in Item D support the contention of the author of Item C that there are 'stable patterns of gender differentiation in higher education' (line 22)?

(6 marks)   This question requires careful structuring. Interpret the material in both Items to get *interpretation* marks, and apply it relevantly to get *application* marks. *Evaluation* marks can be gained by showing how these studies support and challenge the view expressed. Give your own views (and the evidence on which they are based) at the end of your answer. Try consulting O'Donnell (1992), pp. 96–101.

e Using material from the Items above and elsewhere, assess how far gender differences in educational achievement can be explained by the content of the school curriculum as outlined in Item E.

(9 marks)   For a discussion of sex roles in children's books, see Research Roundup, *Sociology Review*, February 1993.

3.4 Education and ethnicity

ITEM A

These figures refer to the period before the university/polytechnic division was abolished.

Universities reject half of all their black applicants according to unpublished figures revealing that black students make up just 1 per cent of the university population.

The first ethnic monitoring of university applicants compares unfavourably with polytechnic figures released recently. Black students make up more than 4 per cent of polytechnic numbers, and proportions of black students outweigh applications suggesting positive discrimination in favour of ethnic minorities.

The report from the University Central Council on Admissions claims any 'apparent racial bias' disappears if applicants of similar examination performance are compared. 'It will be seen that applicants from all minority ethnic groups have lower average scores than white applicants' the report says. 'This is particularly marked in the case of black applicants and to a lesser extent Pakistani applicants'.

When the figures are broken down, universities are shown to admit lower proportions of all ethnic minorities when compared to proportions of applicants. But at 92 per cent, they admit almost 3 per cent more white students than applications received.

Almost the exactly opposite picture is revealed in the polytechnics which admit fewer white students compared to applicants and greater proportions of almost all the ethnic minorities.

Source: adapted from a report in the *Times Higher Education Supplement*, 21 June, 1991

ITEM B

This table from *Social Studies Review* shows clearly the relationship between ethnic origin and level of qualification. It also shows a surprising difference between gender patterns for whites and Asians compared to that for West Indians. This shows that it is important to be aware that different sources of inequality can combine together in actual life, though they are often treated separately in sociology books.

		Ethnic origin				
	White	West Indian/ Guyanese	Indian	Pakistani/ Bangladeshi	Other[2]	All[3]
Highest qualification held (percentages)						
Males						
Higher	16	–	20	9	31	17
Other	49	41	39	25	41	48
None[4]	35	53	41	66	28	35
Females						
Higher	14	19	13	–	23	14
Other	40	33	32	14	40	39
None[4]	46	48	54	81	37	46
All persons						
Higher	15	13	17	8	27	15
Other	45	37	36	20	40	44
None[4]	40	50	47	72	32	40

Source: K. Reynolds, 'Feminist thinking on education', *Social Studies Review*, March 1991

Notes (1) Aged 25 to retirement age (64 for males and 59 for females). (2) Includes African, Arab, Chinese, other stated and Mixed. (3) Includes those who did not state their ethnic origin. (4) Includes those who did not know or did not state their qualifications.

ITEM C

Maureen Stone, a black educational researcher, has been one of the severest critics of multi-racial education (MRE) in her book *The Education of the Black Child in Britain*. Although she is committed to improving education for black children, she does not see multi-racial education as fulfilling this aim. She argues that the way multi-racial education is defined by current liberal educationalists is wrong. She feels it is premised on the notion that the under-achievement of black children is the result of their own low self-esteem or negative self-concepts. According to this theory, low self-esteem means low motivation, lack of confidence and therefore low educational achievement. She looks at the research on black self-images and conducts her own survey of 264 children of West Indian origin and their self-concepts. She finds little evidence of low self-esteem. She argues that the main reason for the low attainment of West Indian children is their class position, since many live in inner city areas.

5

10

15

Source: Miriam David 'Education' in M. Haralambos (ed.), *Developments in Sociology*, Vol. 1, Ormskirk: Causeway, 1985

ITEM D

In 1981/2, of school-leavers from the ethnic majority 13 per cent attained one or more pass at A Level, and 9 per cent entered a degree course at university or college. For West Indian school-leavers the comparable figures were 5 per cent and 2 per cent. Although black people are disproportionately concentrated in working-class occupations, these inequalities of educational outcome are not 'simply' the product of social class disadvantage; for a recent study carried out by Craft and Craft (1985) in an outer London borough shows that, even with social class controlled, West Indian children fare less well in school than their white counterparts. Among middle-class pupils, for example, only 14 per cent of the white, but 31 per cent of the West Indian pupils, had a low performance in fifth-form examinations.

5

10

Source: adapted from T. Bilton *et al. Introductory Sociology*, 2nd Ed., London: Macmillan, 1987

QUESTIONS

a Explain in your own words the meaning of the term 'positive discrimination' (line 8) used in Item A.

(1 mark)

b Assess sociological explanations for the patterns of educational performance of pupils from ethnic minorities as shown in Item B.

(8 marks)   This is quite a detailed question which you need all skills to answer fully. Identify two or three patterns in Item B (*interpretation and application*) and suggest at least two sociological explanations of each (*knowledge* and *application*). To evaluate, criticize each view by looking at studies which suggest other explanations. Say which you think is the best explanation, and why, in terms of the data you have examined. This topic is covered in The Swann Report, an extract of which is included in Trowler (1987), pp. 7–10, Abercrombie and Warde *et al.* (1988), pp. 257–68 and Haralambos and Holborn (1991), pp. 290–5.

c   Explain in your own words the criticisms of multi-racial education contained in Item C.

(2 marks)

d   Using material from the Items above and elsewhere, assess the extent to which there are major gender differences in educational achievement between different ethnic minority groups.

(5 marks)   Look at three differences at most, and then bring in arguments and criticisms which attempt to explain them. You can gain *interpretation* marks by using material in the items but you also need to look at other studies such as Fuller. You will gain *application* marks for using them relevantly to explain why West Indian patterns of gender achievement are different to other groups. You need to demonstrate all skills, so be careful to control your time on this one.

e   Using material from the Items above and elsewhere, assess the view expressed in Item D that educational disadvantages experienced by ethnic minorities are **not** mainly due to differences in social class.

(9 marks)   This is the focus of much of the debate about the causes of ethnic differences in educational achievement. The debates are discussed in all recent textbooks, for example Haralambos and Holborn (1991), pp. 290–5 and you need to explore all the different arguments before reaching your own conclusion. All skills. The issues of ethnicity in general are explored in this book in the questions on Ethnicity and Inequality p. 197, Work and Ethnicity p. 161 and The Family and Ethnicity p. 81 and the material included there may be useful. The most detailed summary of the sociology of race is a book of that title written by J. Richardson and J. Lambert, which also forms a part of Haralambos (1985).

3.5 Education and social mobility

ITEM A

This table is taken from a piece of work undertaken using the material gathered by the large scale survey into class by Marshall *et al.* and published as *Social Class in Modern Britain*. An extract from this book is included in the section on Stratification in the question entitled 'Is Social Class Still Central?' (p. 177). This does seem to present evidence that the meritocracy thesis is wide of the mark in relation to contemporary Britain. This relates to the issue of social justice in Britain which was covered in *Sociology Review*, Vol. 2, No. 2, November 1992 in an article by A. Swift, G. Marshall and C. Burgoyne. Notice that the class schema used in this extract is the neo-Weberian model developed by John Goldthorpe.

Mobility trajectories (%)

Educational Attainment		Male destinations			Female destinations			All destinations		
		S	I	W	S	I	W	S	I	W
HIGH	origins S	92	3	5	78	22	0	86	11	3
	I	90	5	5	63	35	2	75	21	3
	W	91	9	0	57	39	4	76	22	2
		S	I	W	S	I	W	S	I	W
MEDIUM	origins S	43	32	25	30	61	9	39	41	20
	I	31	41	29	22	63	16	27	49	24
	W	15	37	43	21	60	19	17	47	36
		S	I	W	S	I	W	S	I	W
LOW	origins S	33	27	40	0	57	43	23	36	41
	I	13	33	54	13	37	50	13	34	53
	W	11	25	64	2	43	56	7	33	60

Goldthorpe class categories

Class		
Service	I	Higher-grade professionals, administrators, and officials; managers in large establishments, large proprietors
	II	Lower-grade professionals, administrators and officials; higher-grade technicians, managers in small business and industrial establishments, supervisors of nonmanual employees
Intermediate	IIIa	Routine nonmanual employees in administration and commerce
	IIIb	Personal service workers
	IVa	Small proprietors, artisans, etc., with employees
	IVb	Small proprietors, artisans, etc., without employees
	IVC	Farmers and smallholders; self-employed fisherman
	V	Lower-grade technicians, supervisors of manual workers
Working	VI	Skilled manual workers
	VIIa	Semi-skilled and unskilled manual workers (not in agriculture)
	VIIb	Agricultural workers

Source: adapted from: G. Marshall and A. Swift, 'Social class and social justice' in *The British Journal of Sociology*, June 1993

ITEM B

One impetus for the development of the sociology of education in Britain came from a number of scholars in the 1950s who were concerned about class inequalities in education. Sympathetic to the Labour Party's professed aim to establish a system of equal educational opportunity, these writers – Halsey, Floud, Banks, among others – sought to document inequalities of achievement, explain their origins, and suggest remedial solutions. They recognized that there were inequalities in both access to education

5

and educational outcomes. The desire for equal access to education was the primary concern of a Labour Party seeking to make entry to selective secondary schools and universities as easy for children of the working class as for those of the middle class. This was the aspiration towards meritocracy, where success, particularly in gaining entry to superior educational institutions, was to be made dependent on ability rather than social status or wealth. Equality of educational outcome remains a more radical aim, implying that schools themselves, and not just their selection procedures, need to be altered to prevent working-class children both leaving education at an earlier age and acquiring disproportionately fewer educational certificates.

10

15

20

Source: N. Abercrombie and A. Warde *et al., Contemporary British Society,* Cambridge: Polity, 1988.

ITEM C

This item suggests that although educational attainment is increasingly linked to occupational success, father's occupation (or class) is still the main determinant of how well children do at school. Although the system seems more open, children of wealthy parents get the best education and, therefore, the best jobs. Compare this to the material presented in Item A

The functionalist view of the relationship between education and occupation argues that educational attainment in advanced industrial societies is increasingly linked to occupational status. There is a steady move from ascribed to achieved status and education plays an important part in this process. Educational qualifications increasingly form the basis for the allocation of individuals to occupational statuses. Thus there is a 'tightening bond' between education and occupation.

5

Using data from the Oxford Mobility Study, A. H. Halsey finds some support for this view. He divided the sample into two age groups: those aged from 40 to 59 and those aged from 25 to 39 in 1972. Comparing the two groups, he found that the direct effect of education on an individual's first job is high and rising (the coefficient of correlation for the first group is 0.468, for the second 0.522), and the direct effect of education on the individual's present job is also rising (from 0.325 to 0.345). Halsey concludes that occupational status is increasingly dependent on educational attainment but he also found that the effect of the father's occupational status upon the son's educational attainment is also rising. He writes 'The direct effect of the class hierarchy of families on educational opportunity and certification has risen since the war'. Thus social background has a greater effect on educational attainment at the very time when the bonds between education and occupation are tightening.

10

15

20

This leads Halsey to conclude that 'education is increasingly the mediator of the transmission of status between generations'. Privilege is passed on more and more from father to son via the educational system. From this viewpoint education can be seen as a mechanism for the maintenance of privilege rather than a means for role allocation based on meritocratic principles.

25

30

Source: M. Haralambos and M. Holborn, *Sociology, Themes and Perspectives,* 3rd Ed. London: Collins Educational, 1991.

ITEM D

The main continuing significance of the public schools lies in the role played by their 'old boy networks' in class reproduction. The importance of such networks of connections is that as society becomes more complex and the circles pull apart, so the people who can make the connections between them become more useful as the fixers, the lubricants and the brokers between one sphere and another.

5

There has been a partial separation of the mechanisms of class reproduction from those of capital reproduction. The capitalist class no longer owes its privileges and advantages exclusively to inherited access to entrepreneurial locations. In the system of impersonal capital the recruitment of executive and finance capitalists depends upon the possession of educational credentials and other attributes deemed relevant to the performance of these tasks. The public schools play an important part in the acquisition of educational credentials. Members of the capitalist class can use their wealth to purchase a privileged education for their children, so ensuring that they are well placed in the educational race and stand a much enhanced chance of attending the universities of Oxford and Cambridge. It is the degrees of these universities which are still regarded by those who recruit executives and directors as being most appropriate for a career in business. Wealthy families are able to convert their wealth into the 'cultural assets' of the educational system, which can then be reconverted into enhanced economic opportunities and prospects for wealth accumulation.

10

15

20

25

Source: J. Scott, *Who Rules Britain?* Cambridge: Polity, 1991

QUESTIONS

a   What differences are there in the social mobility achieved by men and women with high educational attainment according to Item A?

(2 marks)

b   Using information from the Items and from elsewhere, evaluate the argument put forward in Item C that 'occupational status is increasingly dependent on educational attainment' (lines 17–18).

(9 marks)

This question requires a detailed answer. For *interpretation and application* look at Items A, C and D to support the view expressed. *Knowledge* and *application* marks can be gained by looking at these writers in more detail or writers such as Halsey. You need to refer to studies of social mobility – possibly Parkin – and functionalist writers such as Davis and Moore to challenge the view expressed and gain marks for *evaluation* and *application*.

c   Using material from Item B, explain what you understand by the concept of 'equal educational opportunity' and identify two ways in which inequality of opportunity can be measured.

(3 marks)

d   Illustrating your answer with material from Item D, suggest what effect the continuing existence of the public schools is likely to have on the degree of openness in the stratification system.

(2 marks)

e How far does sociological evidence support the view expressed in Item C that 'education can be seen as a mechanism for the maintenance of privilege rather than a means for role allocation based on meritocratic principles' (lines 28–30)?

(9 marks)

Any question asking 'how far . . . ' is expecting you to demonstrate the skill of *evaluation*. You also need to explain the argument presented in Item C to get marks for *interpretation* and *application*. Relating material to the question earns marks for *application*. The *evaluation* marks require your own conclusion, based on the arguments you have examined in relation to this issue see O'Donnel! (1992), pp. 75–109, and Burgess (1985). Bring in evidence from outside for *knowledge* and *application* marks. A large proportion of the marks here are for *evaluation*, so make sure that you detail points for and against and come to an explicit conclusion.

3.6 The National Curriculum

ITEM A

In July 1987 Kenneth Baker, the Secretary of State for Education, published proposals to introduce a core curriculum in schools. He wants pupils between 11 and 16 to be taught three core subjects: maths, English and science.

Sociologists' interest in the school curriculum dates mainly from the publication in 1971 of Michael Young's book *Knowledge and Control*. Drawing on the sociology of knowledge, this book argued that the school curriculum should be treated as problematic. Since it is not self-evident what should be included in it, it is necessary to explain just what is, and why.

The school curriculum is the result of a process involving the production, selection and ranking of knowledge. When this knowledge has been transmitted, pupils are assessed on their ability to demonstrate what they have learned.

How does this insight apply to Baker's core curriculum? It stresses that how knowledge is organized and classified into subjects is a social process. The subject matter of chemistry physics and biology does not exist separately in the natural world, and there is nothing to determine that science has to be taught under these specialist headings. Then there is the question of selection. Obviously, only part of all knowledge can be included in the curriculum.

The point to stress is that curriculum choices are made by those with power, who decide what is appropriate knowledge for school pupils of various ages and abilities. When this selection has been made, and the curriculum fixed, different subjects have different status. In Baker's scheme, maths, English and science are the core.

Basil Bernstein sums up the argument: 'How a society selects, classifies, distributes, transmits and evaluates the educational knowledge it considers to be public, reflects both the distribution of power and the principles of social control'.

Source: adapted from P. McNeill, *Society Today 2*, London: Macmillan, 1991.

ITEM B

What is knowledge is what is defined as knowledge by powerful people or institutions – headteachers, universities and professional organizations for example. One could contrast the elitist and the pool of talent viewpoints. The elitist viewpoint would stress the need to preserve excellence. It accepts the hierarchy of subjects and stresses that access to the highest status subjects, for example the classics, should be limited to the 'excellent'. There is thus an emphasis on exclusion. The pool of talent or equality viewpoint would show that we tend to mystify students with this hierarchical fragmentation of knowledge and thereby exclude able students of lower status. Supporters of this view would emphasise the inclusion of students.

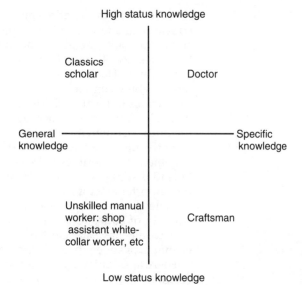

High status knowledge

Classics scholar

Doctor

General knowledge — Specific knowledge

Unskilled manual worker: shop assistant white-collar worker, etc

Craftsman

Low status knowledge

Source: from M. Joseph, *Sociology for Everyone*, Cambridge: Polity, 1986

ITEM C

In terms of gender, the definition and construction of knowledge are very important. Feminists have argued that educational knowledge is defined from a white 'male' perspective whereby the achievements, struggles and even existence of women are omitted from the picture. Radical feminists such as Dale Spender   5 argue that even the language used by schools and wider society reflects and reinforces this marginalization of women.

The option choices which are so much a part of gender differences in schools, have given rise to the idea that all students should study the same subjects throughout their educational   10 career. The National Curriculum with its 'core' and 'foundation' subjects ensures that all students have 'equal access' to the main areas of the curriculum.

The inclusion of maths and sciences in the core curriculum has been welcomed by many people. Maths and science are two of   15 the main areas where women students are under-represented. Yet it is unlikely that merely having 'access' to the same subjects will lead to similar educational 'outcomes' for women and men students.

The National Curriculum further reinforces the hierarchy of   20 educational knowledge whereby maths, English and sciences are seen as important since they are the core subjects, whereas subjects in which women do well are seen as unimportant. Moreover, the areas covered by each subject have been laid down by the DES and this approach has been heavily criticized by   25 teachers and educationalists. In particular the omission of 'community languages' (such as Urdu and Bengali), in preference to 'modern foreign languages' (such as French and German) and the definition of history from a white Eurocentric perspective, have been seen by some as openly racist.   30

Source: adapted from K. Reynolds, 'Feminist thinking on education', *Social Studies Review*, March 1991

ITEM D

Research into the relationship between knowledge, power and educational attainment has suggested that changes in the school curriculum are essential if the ideal of equality of opportunity is to be realized. Dennis Lawton has proposed a 'common culture curriculum'. He accepts that there are important subcultural dif- 5
ferences between social classes, but maintains there are sufficient similarities to form a school curriculum based on a common culture. He claims that 'a heritage of knowledge and belief which includes mathematics, science, history, literature and, more recently, film and television is shared by all classes'. 10

Even if such heritage were shared, which is debatable, Lawton fails to distinguish content from form. As Bourdieu has argued, the important factor is not so much what is known (the content of knowledge) but the manner in which it is presented. To provide equality of educational opportunity, a common culture curricu- 15
lum would have to select from both aspects of knowledge and elements of style which were common to all social classes.

There are similar problems with the decision of the British government in 1988 to introduce a National Curriculum with an emphasis on mathematics, English and science. 20

Source: M. Haralambos and M. Holborn, *Sociology: Themes and Perspectives*, 3rd Ed., London: Collins Educational, 1991

This policy was more concerned with raising standards than promoting equality of opportunity, and no attempt was made to make allowance for competing definitions of knowledge.

QUESTIONS

a Explain in your own words why Michael Young feels that 'the school curriculum should be treated as problematic' (Item A, line 8).

(2 marks)

b To what extent does sociological evidence suggest that the introduction of the National Curriculum has changed the hierarchy of knowledge as outlined in Item B?

(6 marks)

c With reference to the Items above, explain the argument contained in Item C that 'educational knowledge is defined from a 'white "male" perspective' (lines 2–3).

(3 marks)

d Using material from the Items above and elsewhere, evaluate the view that the National Curriculum 'was more concerned with raising standards than promoting equality of opportunity' (Item D, lines 21–2).

(5 marks)

e Using material from the Items above and elsewhere, assess how far sociological evidence supports the view that the content of the National Curriculum 'reflects both the distribution of power and the principles of social control' (Item A, lines 31–2).

(9 marks)

3.7 The hidden curriculum

ITEM A

Source: from M. David, 'Education' in M. Haralambos (Ed.), *Developments in Sociology*, Vol. 1, Ormskirk: Causeway, 1985

ITEM A

Denscombe investigates pupil strategies in 'open classrooms'. He argues that 'Pupils, ever adept at recognising and coping with the hidden curriculum of the classroom can exploit teacher strategies and use them to their own ends – the aim of gaining some influence over the conduct and progress of classroom events. This is a point well illustrated by the case of a teacher strategy of 'flirting . . . [it] is a widely used technique, especially by male teachers with female pupils. Since sex is one of the most prominent interests of the more rebellious girl pupils, it can be a great aid in securing their goodwill and cooperation' (Woods, 1977, p. 283).

Those teachers who use flirting as a strategy however would presumably not be immune to its effects and might be the prime targets of flirting when used as a counter-strategy by pupils. Denscombe goes on to argue that pupil strategies are usually a form of reaction to situations that pupils have not created and where they lack basic rights.

ITEM B

The more complex a society and the more varied the skills possessed by its members, the greater the need for institutions deliberately designed to effect the formal dissemination of specialised skills and knowledge – educational establishments like schools, colleges and universities.

From a sociological point of view however such places are 'learning establishments in a much broader sense than most people would ordinarily recognise and, as such, have to be seen as major agencies of socialisation.'

When a child goes to school he or she is not only confronted with the traditional school subjects, but also with codes of practice governing behaviour. The pupil has to learn not only history and geography, but also how to relate to teachers and fellow students: for example, when it is acceptable to claim the attention of the teacher and to ask questions, or when conversation with friends is allowed. He or she also has to learn which strategies are acceptable in which classroom, since teachers' demands will vary.

Research seems to indicate that pupils are evaluated on their mastery of this 'hidden curriculum' just as they are evaluated on their mastery of the formal syllabus. In some cases mastery of the 'hidden curriculum' can almost compensate for lack of intellectual ability.

Source: adapted from T. Bilton *et al.*, *Introductory Sociology*, 2nd Ed., London: Macmillan, 1987

ITEM C

The hidden curriculum

The phrase was first used by Jackson in *Life in Classrooms* (1964) and refers to all those things pupils learn in schools that are nor overtly taught. These are mainly attitudes, values and principles of behaviour which, though not explicitly spelled out by teachers, are rewarded when pupils display them through their actions. 5

The hidden curriculum can be found in the way that a school is organized, in the way that teachers and pupils interact, and in the content of the subjects taught.

The concept of the hidden curriculum was particularly attractive in the 1970s to those sociologists, often though not always Marxist, who argued that the official rhetoric of schools is often at odds with their real function in a capitalist society. At that time, the dominant view of education stressed that it should be pupil-centred and foster the development of individual potential, with little emphasis on preparation for work. Those who underlined the role of the hidden curriculum were saying that this liberal message was a sham. Mass schooling was in fact in the business of doing what it had always done – reinforcing the values and attitudes which allowed the individual to be easily absorbed into an alienated and unequal society. 10 15 20

Critics have suggested that the hidden curriculum was hidden from academic sociologists more than from its victims, who knew very well what was happening. It is also more useful to think of it as intertwined with rather than concealed behind the mainstream curriculum. But recent and future reforms of how education is organized suggest that some aspects of the hidden curriculum are not so hidden any more. 25

Source: adapted from P. McNeill, 'The hidden curriculum', in *New Society*, 5 January, 1990

ITEM D

R. Sharp and A. Green (*Education and Social Control*) have emphasized the social-control function of education. They attempted to study and demonstrate some of the less subtle ways in which wider social structural forces impinge upon the social processes of the school. Even the child-centred radical teacher with well-intentioned motives may produce effects corresponding to the hierarchical differentiation of pupils as produced by formal methods. 5

Sharp and Green suggest that the radicalism of progressive teachers may be a modern form of conservatism and therefore an effective form of social control. The hidden curriculum is successfully hidden even from the teacher himself; but nevertheless there is no doubt that it effectively inculcates the values, beliefs and attitudes which society wishes to be maintained. 10

Pierre Bordieu argues that the culture that comes from schooling provides individuals with a common body of thought. As the school is the principal transmitter of culture, it is the fundamental factor in the cultural consensus. 15

Source: adapted from J. Nobbs, *Sociology in Context*, London: Macmillan, 1983

ITEM E

The National Council for Vocational Qualifications (NCVQ) detail the aim of vocational education as 'the means of developing people with the skills and quality that industry needs'. (NCVQ, 1990). Much work has been carried out to analyse this process and to explain it, arguing that our education system services the needs of the ruling-class, not always successfully, by perpetuating the family and workplace structures and ideologies. I am particularly concerned with how the teaching of behaviour and attitudes in vocational education contributes to this process.

My research first looked at the methods used by the institution to train students to become productive workers. Integral to this is a corresponding work ethos. This relates to the student's/workers' responsibility to authority. This kind of authority relation between females has the authority figure acting in a supporting but demanding role and allows for socializing.

But this respect for authority, sometimes, has a tone of unquestioning acceptance: 'there's some repetitive work, they have to deal with business documents, they may be doing filing, well most people have to do filing of course' (Secretarial Studies Programme Staff). In fact, it is because managers don't file their business documents when they have finished with them that the secretary has to.

So 'authority relations' are taught as something to expect and accept. For female students this is sweetened with authority based upon friendship, for male students this is shown as unpleasant and 'survival tactics' are offered.

The sexual division of labour is reflected by the 100 per cent female participation of both staff and students in Secretarial Studies Programmes and 100 per cent male in Motor Mechanics courses. This obviously reinforces the sexist preconceptions some students have on entering the college.

For both these sets of working-class students there is a concentration on behaviour and attitudes. Whilst the form of the teaching follows a similar path the content is strongly gendered for the secretaries but only covertly so for the mechanics.

Source: adapted from H.Tucker, 'The not-so-hidden curriculum' in *General Educator*, January 1992

5

10

15

20

25

30

35

QUESTIONS

a Identify three elements of the 'hidden curriculum' (Item B).

(3 marks)

b Suggest two ways in which pupils might be evaluated on their mastery of the hidden curriculum (Item B).

(2 marks)

c Which social group benefits from the hidden curriculum according to the author of Item E?

(1 mark)

d   Using material from Items A and D and elsewhere, assess the validity of the statement made in Item C that 'the hidden curriculum was hidden from academic sociologists more than from its victims' (line 22).

(9 marks)

e   Using material from the Items above and elsewhere, assess the relative importance of the hidden and the official curriculum in explaining differential educational achievement.

(10 marks)

3.8 Pupil–teacher interaction

The framework of identities which derive from the band-labels can be seen in the following composite band-profiles, constructed from teachers' descriptions. These are the stereotypical notions that the teachers hold about the bands. As such they are also situational-expectations, that is, expectations about 'what this form is going to be like'. These stereotypes are constraints which the teacher brings into the classroom and with which the pupil has to deal.

The band 1 child

'Has academic potential . . . will do O levels . . . will probably stay on into the sixth form . . . likes doing projects . . . knows what the teacher wants . . . is bright, alert and enthusiastic . . . can concentrate . . . produces neat work . . . is interested . . . wants to get on . . . is grammar school material . . . you can have discussions with . . . friendly . . . rewarding . . . has common sense.'

The band 2 child

'Is not interested in school work . . . difficult to control . . . rowdy and lazy . . . has little self control . . . is immature . . . loses and forgets books with monotonous regularity . . . cannot take part in discussions . . . is moody . . . of low standard . . . technical ability . . . lacks concentration . . . is poorly behaved . . . not up to much academically.'

The band 3 child

'Is unfortunate . . . is low ability . . . maladjusted . . . anti-school . . . lacks a mature view of education . . . mentally retarded . . . emotionally unstable and . . . a waste of time.'

Source: S. Ball, *Beachside Comprehensive*, Cambridge: Cambridge University Press, 1981

ITEM B

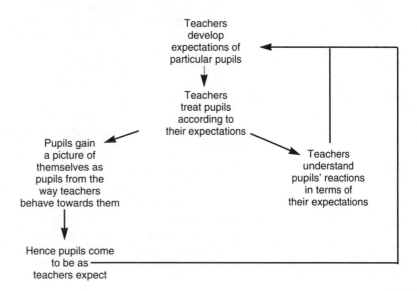

Source: R. Gomm, *A Level Sociology*, Cambridge: National Extension College, 1990

ITEM C

Last year, the American Association of University Women (AAUW) produced a report – 'Shortchanging girls: Shortchanging America' – showing there are still many hurdles to overcome before girls enjoy the same classroom opportunities as boys.　5

The AAUW study centred on the critical loss of self-esteem that occurs in adolescence when boys and girls undergo biological and psychological changes. For girls, loss of self-esteem can be more dramatic and longer lasting. As they grow up declining self-esteem inhibits girls' ambitions. Not only do they have relatively lower career ambitions, but lack of confidence in their abilities makes them more likely to be self-critical, pronouncing themselves 'not good enough' for their dream careers.　10

The American Study also reinforces British observations on the importance of the pupil-teacher interaction. In co-ed classes, boys receive, on average four times more attention than girls. Teachers engage boys in more dialogue and expect boys to grasp, argue and defend more complex ideas. By the time pupils leave school for higher education, the pattern for many girls is set.　15

The AAUW study highlighted the fact that even the brightest girls remained silent in a co-ed class. Such girls tended to submit excellent written work but generally approached the teacher with follow-up questions only after a lesson.　20

Other observations that seem equally valid on both sides of the Atlantic reveal more subtle forms of discrimination. These include teachers addressing boys by name more often than the girls, addressing the class as if no females were present, questioning boys more, dealing with boys' questions at greater length and giving boys more credit and praise.　25

Source: adapted from a report in the *Daily Telegraph*, 13 February, 1992

ITEM D

'Look at him!' mutters Mavis flicking her head in the direction of Brian who is attempting to mould marzipan to the sides of his circular cake. 'Pound to a penny he's a poof!' giggles Mavis. 'He's a right winkle dick, I bet!' she insists. 'Look', she indicates with her hand a small marzipan sculpture of a penis.　5

'You're bloody disgusting you are', scolds Jill. 'Get rid of it! She's [teacher] coming!' With a theatrical raising of the arm Mavis cruelly squashes the sculpture thumping the work top as Mrs Baker [teacher] arrives to police the incident.

The extract presented above forms part of field notes derived from a period of participant observation in an adult evening class. Contrary to researcher expectations, observations in the kitchen classroom revealed that fee-paying adult students needed to be controlled, and that such teaching has problems and tensions of its own.　10　15

Observational data suggested that playing pupil roles was very much tied up with ' 'aving a laugh' and it was clear that Mrs Baker knew this; her mock strict manner contained, but possibly generated, further student 'deviance'. Both teacher and students, it seemed, willingly colluded in taking up stereotyped roles – the students particularly delighting in the classroom game. Perhaps　20 it is possible to see some of the student antics and mucking about as products of the 'teacher expectation' effect. The way teachers perceive pupils has been addressed by several authors. It is argued that typification is inseparable from teaching, assessment, learning and control and that teacher typifications are the means by which teachers achieve the goal of coping in the classroom.

Source: adapted from J. Salisbury, 'Mucking and mixing in a cookery class', *Sociology Review*, September 1991.

25

ITEM E

Some interactionists have come to realize that not all pupils will live up to their labels. In a study of a group of black girls in a London comprehensive school, Margaret Fuller found that the girls resented the negative stereotypes associated with being female and black. They felt that many people expected them to fail, but far from living up to their expectations they tried to prove them wrong. They devoted themselves to school work in order to try to ensure their success. This interactionist then, recognizes that negative labels can have a variety of effects. However, this observation weakens the forcefulness of the labelling theory. It seems that labels will usually have an effect, but the type of effect they have is not predictable. Fuller's work avoids some of the pitfalls of the cruder versions of labelling theory which are rather deterministic in suggesting the inevitability of failure for those with negative labels attached to them. Her views are more in keeping with the non-deterministic interpretations of behaviour which are for the most part typical of interactionist research.

5

10

15

Source: M. Haralambos and M. Holborn, *Sociology: Themes and Perspectives*, 3rd Ed., London: Collins Educational, 1991

QUESTIONS

a With reference to Item A, suggest what effect the teachers' 'composite-band profiles' (line 2) might have on the educational progress of the children in each of the three bands.

(3 marks)

b Item B indicates a process in which 'Teachers develop expectations of particular pupils'. According to sociological research, which types of pupil are particularly susceptible to this process?

(3 marks)

c Using information from the Items above and elsewhere, assess the importance of 'pupil–teacher interaction' (Item C, line 15) in explaining gender differences in education.

(9 marks)

d In what way does the age of the pupils affect their interaction with teachers according to the author of Item D?

(1 mark)

e Using information from the Items and from elsewhere, evaluate the statement made in Item E that 'the cruder versions of labelling theory . . . are rather deterministic in suggesting the inevitability of failure for those with negative labels attached to them' (lines 13–15).

(9 marks)

3.9 Pupil subcultures

ITEM A

Source: adapted from N. Abercrombie and A. Warde *et al.*, *Contemporary British Society*, Cambridge: Polity, 1988.

The culture of 'the lads' expressed their entrenched hostility to authority, though they avoided open confrontations. Their behaviour in school paralleled that outside. Masculinity was a particularly central value, and sexism was prevalent. Racism was also prominent. In an important way, the three characteristics Bowles and Gintis said were penalized in schools – independence, creativity and aggressiveness – find a strong presence in this anti-school sub-culture. 5

The lads' resistance to authority and rejection of some dominant values is typical of elements of working-class culture. Especially of the factory shop floor. Willis suggests that the messing about in school and the resisting of the teachers' authority actually prepared 'the lads', culturally for life on the shop floor. 10

Willis's findings are paradoxical. Some pupils reject the discipline of the school, seeking gratification through informal groups. An independent, oppositional culture is actively created. Such behaviour leads to failure in academic terms but, in the end, it turns out to be 'vocationally relevant', even 'realistic' and it goes some way to explaining the problem with which Willis began: 'The difficult thing to explain about how middle-class kids get middle-class jobs is why others let them. The difficult thing to explain about how working-class kids get working-class jobs is why they let themselves.' 15 20

ITEM B

Source: adapted from C. Buswell, 'Gender and sociology', *Social Studies Review*, May 1989

Sociologists have studied adolescent people with a view to understanding their subcultures, but most of the groups studied have been boys' groups where girls have been either excluded or tolerated on the margins (e.g. Willis, 1977). The boys' subcultures have been shown to be a means of exploring and practising forms of masculinity for those involved – we know far less about adolescent girls. This is not only because of the masculine bias in sociology, but also because adolescent girls are often less publicly visible – which raises sociological questions both about the ways in which the 'masculine' behaviour of males constrains the activities of girls and women and about the methods sociologists expect to use when studying subcultures. 5 10

How do girls learn 'femininity'? Romanticism is an interest that is publicly encouraged as a central interest for girls. The emphasis on romance, however, hides the problem of sexuality. Lees (1986), in her study of adolescent girls, describes the contradictions embodied in the 'slag/drag' dichotomy. Avoiding either of these labels, bestowed by boys (and sometimes teachers), involves girls in walking a tightrope where even their own behaviour and appearance may not be the cause of the labelling but rather based on boys' own reasons for awarding these labels. Girls in fact develop an array of coping strategies. 15 20

ITEM C

I now suggest a model which describes the passage of pupils through the grammar school. Two terms should first be explained: differentiation and polarization. By differentiation I mean the separation and ranking of students according to a multiple set of criteria which makes up the normative, academically orientated value system of the grammar school. Polarization on the other hand takes place within the student body, partly as a result of differentiation but influenced by external factors and with an autonomy of its own. It is a process of subculture formation in which the school-dominated normative culture is opposed by an alternative culture which I refer to as the 'anti-group' culture.

If streaming takes place between the first and second years, it helps speed the process and a new crop of cases of emotional disturbance occurs. Early on, the symptoms are mainly individual; later, after a prolonged period of interaction and the impact of streaming, they are expressed in group attitudes. After six months in the second year this bottom stream was already recognized as a difficult form to teach.

The true anti-group starts to emerge in the second year, and it develops markedly in the third and fourth years. It is then that strenuous efforts are made to get rid of anti-group pupils. Considerable pressure is put on the headmaster by the teachers who take the boys.

5

10

15

20

Source: adapted from C. Lacey, *Hightown Grammar*, Manchester: Manchester University Press, 1970

ITEM D

Ethnographic studies involve gaining an intimate understanding of the people being studied. An important feature of ethnography is that the researcher must be a 'participant observer'. In an educational setting this means either joining the staff of the school as Hargreaves (1967) did, or finding a way of spending as much time as possible with the teachers and/or pupils being studied. The ethnographic approach rejects the traditional procedures of empirical research such as questionnaires and statistical analysis. The aim is for the researcher to observe with an open mind, and with preconceptions suspended, recording the actual language spoken by the subjects under study.

The ethnographic approach is useful for studying pupil cultures, and gives educational insights into the educational experiences of particular groups, such as girls or black pupils. An important feature of this method is that no aspect of human behaviour is considered too insignificant to study.

5

10

15

Source: K. Chapman, *The Sociology of Schools*, London: Tavistock, 1986

ITEM E

I will take issue here with the current focus on sex-role socialization as 'successful'. While it is true that most women learn what is socially approved, and often behave in ways that are expected, I will argue that complete acceptance (as well as complete rejection) of sex-role appropriate attitudes and behaviour is actually rather rare. A more accurate description is what Eugene Genovese has called, a simultaneous process of accommodation and resistance.

5

The process of accommodation and resistance can be observed in   10
schoolgirls. I observed six types of such behaviour:

1   Intellectual achievement. This may not be accommodation on
the girls' part to what is understood or felt to be how girls act.
However, for those girls it was behaviour that resisted passiv-   15
ity and submissiveness.
2   The appropriation of femininity. I observed exaggerated feminine behaviour that was used to resist the flow of work
assignments, and to resist the teacher in other ways.
3   Tomboyishness is another way that some of the girls resisted   20
the feminine stereotype.
4   Appropriation of sexuality is the next type of behaviour that
manifested both accommodation and resistance. I observed
two girls in the working-class school who were using their
nascent sexuality to get attention, to disrupt the class and in   25
one instance, to turn the boys against the teacher.
5   Being a discipline problem is a phenomenon that, for girls
seems to express resistance not only to school, but to what is
expected of them as girls.
6   Distancing and alienation, and staying home from school fre-   30
quently. Girls are more likely to resist the pressures of school
life in ways that are internalized and not so obvious as boys'
resistance.

Source: adapted from J. Anyon,
'Intersections of class and
gender: accommodation and
resistance by working-class and
affluent females to contradictory
sex-role ideologies' in S. Walker
& L. Barton (Eds), *Gender, Class
& Education*, Lewes: The Falmer
Press, 1983

Accommodation and resistance, even when it takes the form of a
turning away or withdrawal, is an active process. The analysis   35
above suggests that most girls are not passive victims of sex-role
stereotypes and expectations but are active participants in their
own development.

QUESTIONS

a   With reference to the Items above and elsewhere, explain how various social groups,
including pupils, might influence 'the process of subculture formation' (Item C, line 9).

(4 marks)

b   Why might ethnographic research be particularly 'useful for studying pupil cultures' (Item
D, line 12)?

(2 marks)

c   To what extent are sociological studies of pupil subcultures invalidated by a 'masculine
bias in sociology' (Item B, line 7)?

(8 marks)

d   Illustrating your answer with reference to the above Items, suggest two possible effects of
subcultural membership on educational performance.

(2 marks)

e   Using material from Item A and elsewhere, evaluate the view that in general members of pupil subcultures 'are not passive victims . . . but are active participants in their own development' (Item E, lines 36–8).

(9 marks)

3.10 New vocationalism

Source: Social Trends 1990,
London: HMSO, 1990

ITEM A

Educational and economic activities of 16 year olds[1]

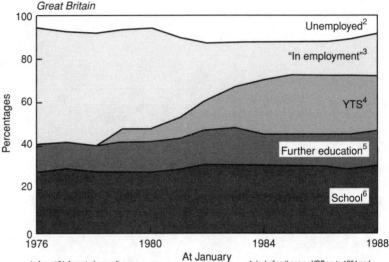

Great Britain

1 Age at 31 August of preceding year.

2 Registered unemployed up to 1982; claimant unemployed in 1983 and thereafter (DES estimates).

3 Mainly those in employment (outside YTS) but including those who were neither employed nor seeking work (e.g. because of domestic responsibilities). Also includes the unregistered unemployed prior to 1983 and from 1983 those seeking work but not claiming benefit.

4 Including those on YOP up to 1984 and those in further education establishments attending YTS/YOP courses.

5 Full-time and sandwich excluding private further education. Excludes those on YTS/YOP within colleges.

6 Pupils attending maintained, independent and special schools.

ITEM B

The changes in the labour market of the 1970s affected young people disproportionately. The collapse in the apprenticeship system, meant that opportunities for such a career route were substantially reduced. For example in the 1960s, 40 per cent of males leaving school at sixteen years or earlier were apprenticed, 5 yet by 1980 this proportion had been halved. The effects of a declining apprenticeship system and economic recession led to large increases in youth unemployment and the emergence of a distinct labour market for young people.

In this changed context, employers refocused their attention on 10 the education system as a whole. Schooling itself came under scrutiny as a major cause of economic decline and the under-employment of youth. The analysis of many industrialists suggested that schools were not equipping students with the knowledge, skills and attitudes which would have enabled them 15 to stimulate economic growth or compete with other groups of workers in the labour market.

Reports showed that for the majority of jobs, the most important qualities for employers were not specific qualifications, but rather such characteristics as punctuality, attendance, timekeep- 20 ing and discipline. That employer demands referred predominantly to characteristics associated with individuals reaching a particular stage of the 'life-cycle', did not prevent them from criticising schools. Industrialists constructed the role of schools to include the inculcation of an appropriate set of attitudes conducive to work in capitalist society. 25

Source: adapted from: C. Shilling, *Schooling for Work in Capitalist Britain*, Lewes: Falmer, 1989

ITEM C

Youth unemployment was treated as an educational problem rather than an employment one for political reasons. The Government could not change the labour process and organization of work to fit existing school leavers but it could try to fit school leavers to the emerging priorities of employers. Thus with 5 school leavers no longer receiving work experience, schools and training programmes had to become the source of the work ethic. In other words in the labour market conditions of the late 1970s and early 1980s the state was to be held responsible for the process of work socialization that had previously been a normal 10 part of leaving school and getting a job.

Since that point and largely organized by the MSC and the Department of Industry, new vocational initiatives and programmes have been introduced across a range of subjects and schools. These innovations and their funding have imposed a 15 new agenda on comprehensive schools. They represent a new ideology of education one which signalled the abandonment of equal opportunity as the central reference point of educational strategy.

In combination with the hidden transformation of education 20 that has been wrought by public expenditure cuts and falling pupil numbers these vocational initiatives have cumulatively undermined some of the achievements of the comprehensive era and are playing a key part in creating a new 'tripartism'. By late 1985 when Lord Young, one of the key architects of the YTS, 25 became the Employment Secretary he was able to outline very clearly this vision of the educational future. He saw a situation: 'at the end of the decade [where] there is a world in which 15 per cent of our younger people go into higher education . . . Another 30 to 35 per cent will stay on doing the TVEI (Technical and 30 Vocational Education Initiative), along with other courses, ending up with a mixture of vocational and academic qualifications and skills. The remainder, about half will go on to two-year YTS.' (*The Times*, 4 September, 1985.)

In complex ways schooling has been (and continues to be) 35 restructured to legitimize traditional social divisions, instil the spirit of enterprise, and resocialize working class youth so that it becomes more acceptable to employers. The primary vehicle for securing this latter objective is the two-year YTS.

Source: D. Finn, 'Education for jobs': the route to YTS, *Social Studies Review*, September 1988.

ITEM D

The imbalance of the sexes (% of males to females, 1985–86)

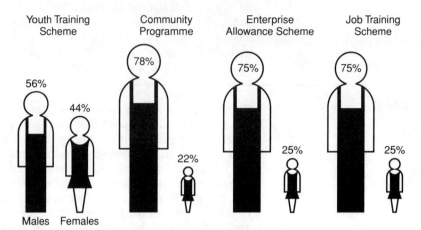

Youth Training Scheme · Community Programme · Enterprise Allowance Scheme · Job Training Scheme

56% 44% 78% 22% 75% 25% 75% 25%

Males   Females

Source: Manpower Services Commission statistics quoted in *New Society*, 27 March, 1987

ITEM E

Over 3 million Youth Training opportunities have been taken up by 16 and 17 year olds. This has added substantially to the amount of high-quality training for young people, while the proportion in apprenticeships has been maintained.

Youth Training offers: 5

- a guarantee of training to all 16 and 17 year olds outside full-time education or employment
- individually planned training
- the first step on a ladder of opportunity within a framework of qualifications: 82 per cent of those who leave training in 10 Great Britain go into jobs or further education
- training for real jobs: an important motivation to continue learning
- an opportunity to reach NVQ Level 2 or higher.

Source: Government White Paper: Education and Training for the 21st Century, London: HMSO, 1991

QUESTIONS

a With reference to Item A, examine the effect of the introduction of YTS on the number of 16 year olds in further education, in employment and unemployed.

(3 marks)

b With reference to Item B, describe how employers view the education system.

(2 marks)

c To what extent does sociological evidence support the view put forward in Item C that vocational initiatives have 'signalled the abandonment of equal opportunity as the central reference point of educational strategy' (lines 17–19)?

(9 marks)

d In which scheme was there the greatest imbalance of the sexes in 1985–86 (Item D)?

(1 mark)

e Item E suggests that Youth Training will provide 'high-quality training for young people' (line 3). Using material from the Items above and elsewhere, consider the arguments for and against this view.

(10 marks)

4

Work and leisure

4.1 Ownership and control of industry

ITEM A

John Scott outlines and then rejects the 'managerial revolution' argument which suggested that companies owned by shareholders would be controlled by managers rather than owners. Try to read more about his ideas in your textbooks, for example, O'Donnell (1992), pp. 135–6. An extract from O'Donnell (1992), pp. 135–6 is included as Item E in the question on The Upper Class (p. 180). Or look at Haralambos and Holborn (1991), pp. 57–62. You could also read John Scotts' articles in *Social Studies Review*, Vol. 1, No. 3; or Vol. 2, No. 1.

Source: adapted from J.Scott, 'The debate on ownership and control', in *Social Studies Review*, January 1986

The modern enterprise is a large and complex social organization formed into a 'corporation' or 'joint stock company'. This form of business enterprise opened up new possibilities of corporate control. The few directors could exercise effective control over the large pool of capital subscribed by the shareholders. It was a recognition of this possibility that led many people to foresee a 'managerial revolution' in which salaried managers could usurp the powers of the capitalists and become the dominant force in society. 5

Berle and Means claimed that the major identifiable trend in the evolution of modern capitalism was a move towards management control in the biggest enterprises in the economy. 10

The central tenets of the managerialist case have come under increased scrutiny in the last decade. The main plank of the attack has been the claim that management control was characteristic of only a very limited stage of capitalist development. Financial intermediaries (banks, insurance companies, pension funds and similar enterprises) have become increasingly important in the ownership of company shares, and it is argued that they are often able to combine their shareholdings to form a large voting block. 15

20

ITEM B

Social Studies Review and *Sociology Review* are invaluable sources for material like this which is easy to understand and relatively up to date. It is easy to see the trends in share ownership.

Source: adapted from J. Scott, 'The debate on ownership and control', in *Social Studies Review*, January 1986

The Stock Exchange survey of share ownership (1983)

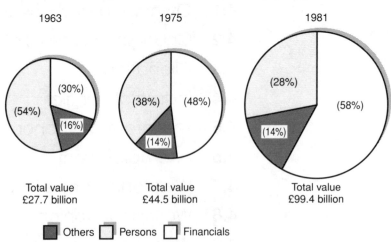

1963	1975	1981
(30%) (54%) (16%)	(38%) (48%) (14%)	(28%) (58%) (14%)
Total value £27.7 billion	Total value £44.5 billion	Total value £99.4 billion

■ Others □ Persons □ Financials

ITEM C

This item from the *Guardian* explains clearly how privatization has increased share ownership, but has not massively broadened the social background of those who own shares. This viewpoint is important in considering whether the government has been successful in creating a share-owning democracy.

Source: adapted from a report in the *Guardian*, 13 December, 1989

Privatization sales only partially extended share ownership to all social groups, suggests the first comprehensive survey of shareholding.

Although the proportion of people owning shares has trebled from 7 per cent to 21 per cent between 1984 and 1987, the typical investor in privatizations is a middle-aged professional man in the South-East.

Share ownership among young people, women, manual workers, people in the North, Wales and Scotland, and non-homeowners remains relatively low . . .

Eight per cent – more than a third of all shareholders – had investments only in privatized companies. A quarter of men owned shares but only 17 per cent of women, 29 per cent of people aged 45–54 and 30 per cent of those aged 55–64 had shares, but only 18 per cent of those aged 25–34.

More than half of all adults earning more than £350 a week were shareowners. The average weekly income of a shareholder was £196 compared to £118 for the survey sample as a whole, although the average of those owning shares in privatized companies only was £168.

5

10

15

20

ITEM D

The *General Household Survey* is a valuable source of statistical data, despite the problems with official statistics. These tables show the social distribution of share ownership in terms of age, sex, class and income. Are they representative of the population as a whole? Does it matter? Think about these issues while you try to understand the tables.

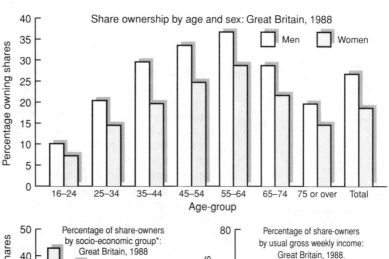

Source: General Household Survey 1988, London: HMSO, 1988

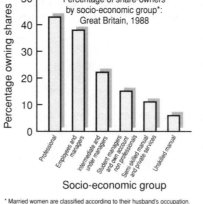

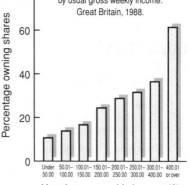

* Married women are classified according to their husband's occupation.

ITEM E

The issue of economic globalization is revolutionizing notions of ownership and control. The idea of the boss as someone aloof may now be geographically correct with the development of transnational corporations. The issue of whether we do live in a global economy and some of the implications of this are covered in J. Fulcher's article in *Sociology Review*, November 1991, an extract of which is included in this book as Item B in the question on Changing Patterns of Work, p. 140. See also Giddens (1989), pp. 519–49.

Economic internationalization means that in certain crucial respects, national economies are increasingly becoming part of a global or world economy. The key feature of economic globalization is that more money is transferred more easily across national boundaries. This process has increased greatly over the past decade. It was made easier by the so-called financial 'big bang' of 1987 which 'deregulated ' or reduced government regulation of the financial functions of the City of London. It is notable that in the period following 'Big Bang' European takeovers in Britain have increased in total value by about twentyfold. According to one estimate, half of the British workforce will be employed by foreign-owned companies by the year 2000.

Britain is a major focal point of global economic change. It is not possible to understand work in contemporary Britain without having at least a basic appreciation of how and why this is so.

London has been and remains a major world financial centre and Britain also remains a major industrial power, although now in relative decline. The role of London as a world financial centre can be readily appreciated by the fact that the annual worth of European, Japanese and United States' financial business done in London dwarfs the value of exclusively British financial business.

The above trend seems set to increase after 1992. What we are witnessing, therefore, is a genuine internationalization of the economy, not simply an increase in 'foreign' investment in British industry.

The internationalization of the British economy has affected different regions differently. London as a world financial centre (and as the seat of central government) has been the main beneficiary from internationalization. The North (and West) have been more peripheral to international wealth and investment. The result of these factors is that the North, by most measures, is at a substantial economic and social disadvantage to the South.

It is possible to exaggerate the differences between South and North. The average differences between the two areas are far less than the extent of the differences that occur within each. There has been Japanese investment in the North East as well as in the South; there is poverty in London as well as in Liverpool and there are millionaires in both cities. Nevertheless, there are substantial and increasing regional differences reflecting the uneven development of the British capitalist economy.

5

10

15

20

25

30

35

40

Source: adapted from M. O'Donnell, *A New Introduction to Sociology*, 3rd Ed., Walton-on-Thames: Nelson, 1992

QUESTIONS

a   Explain what is meant by the term 'managerial revolution' (Item A).

(2 marks)   Two simple *interpretation* marks. Make sure you explain the term clearly and in your own words to get full marks.

b   What trend in personal share ownership is indicated in Item B?

(1 mark)   One sentence will do here.

c Illustrating your answer with material from Items C and D above, discuss the relationship between personal share ownership and five social characteristics.

(5 marks)

This is an *interpretation* question where you have to use the data to identify what type of people own shares. You must indicate five separate social characteristics to get all points. Take your time.

d The author of Item E argues that the process of economic globalization 'has increased greatly over the past decade' (line 5). Assess the sociological explanations of the effect of economic globalization.

(8 marks)

Here you need to interpret firstly what is meant by economic globalization and its rise. You then need to apply material in an *evaluation* of the explanations of the effect of this phenomena. The best outline of this argument Giddens (1989), pp. 517–51. There is also some material in Abercrombie and Warde *et al*, *Contemporary British Society*, pp. 36–43. This whole issue does have links with the notion of post-modernism and post-industrialism. These issues are examined in the question on Modern Social Theory in this book (p. 48).

e Assess the validity of the argument outlined in Item A that management control 'was characteristic of only a very limited stage of capitalist development' (lines 15–16).

(9 marks)

This is a longer question which requires a clearly structured answer. Explain the terms and look at arguments for and against. Include your knowledge of current economic conditions. Say what you think at the end, and why. You do not have to agree with the view expressed in the question. The material in Item E might also be relevant here.

4.2 Changing patterns of work

Weekly hours of work and paid holidays[1]: full-time manual employees (United Kingdom)

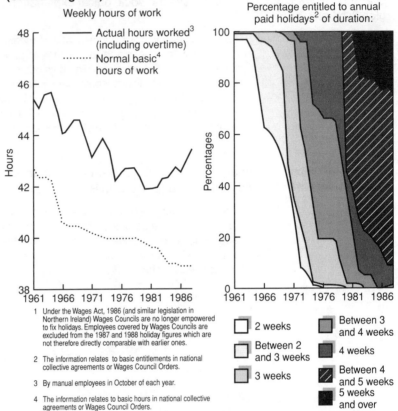

1 Under the Wages Act, 1986 (and similar legislation in Northern Ireland) Wages Councils are no longer empowered to fix holidays. Employees covered by Wages Councils are excluded from the 1987 and 1988 holiday figures which are not therefore directly comparable with earlier ones.

2 The information relates to basic entitlements in national collective agreements or Wages Council Orders.

3 By manual employees in October of each year.

4 The information relates to basic hours in national collective agreements or Wages Council Orders.

Source: Social Trends 1990,
London: HMSO, 1990

ITEM B

Fulcher suggests that production has taken on a global dimension and that capital is now invested where the highest profits can be made. This debate about the possible growth of a 'Global Economy' is central to debates today in both the economics and the sociology of work. Importantly, he also shows the effect it has on the skills required by employers, which also links into the debates around vocational training covered in the question on New Vocationalism (p. 130).

At the heart of the new stage of capitalism is the growing mobility of capital. The rise of the transnational corporation (TNC) has meant that production can be transferred to wherever capital can make the most profit. National economies have become dependent on their capacity to attract and retain this increasingly 5
mobile capital, which prefers countries where wage costs are low, unions are weak, state regulations, whether concerned with health and safety, pollution, or arms control, are minimal, and tax-rates are low. Margaret Thatcher has claimed that one reason for Britain's success in attracting Japanese capital has been the 10
legislation passed in the 1980s to control the activities of the British trade unions.

Increasing international competition and the uncertainties of the global market have led to another kind of deregulation, the introduction of greater flexibility in the employment and man- 15
agement of labour. Specialized craft-workers employed to carry

out specific jobs have been replaced by multi-skilled workers, required to carry out any task and undergo retraining when necessary. Permanent full-time employees are being replaced, where possible, by temporary or part-time workers. Indeed companies increasingly contract out work to smaller firms, to specialized providers of services, using them as they need them and avoiding the costs and regulations involved in employing people directly.

20

Source: adapted from J. Fulcher, 'A new stage in the development of capitalist society?' in *Sociology Review* Vol. 1, No. 2, November 1991

ITEM C

In another *Social Studies Review* article, Warde identifies the difference between the skills needed in an assembly-line as opposed those required in a 'post-Fordist' economy such as that identified in Item A. 'Fordism' is a term used to describe mass production assembly-lines. It originated with the assembly-line manufacturing process first used by Henry Ford to produce the Model T Ford.
The term 'post-Fordist' is linked to the wider concept of postmodernism. On this issue see O'Donnell (1992), pp. 236–41.

Some authors consider the growth of flexible organization and working practices so significant as to constitute the basis for a major new phase in the development of capitalist societies. Various terms are used to describe the new phase – 'flexible accumulation', 'neo-Fordism' and 'post-Fordism' all imply slightly different scenarios – but each identifies a transition away from Fordism to a more flexible system of production, the ideal-type characteristics of which are listed in the table below:

5

		FORDIST	POST-FORDIST
1	Technology	● fixed, dedicated machines	● micro-electronically controlled multi-purpose machines
		● vertically integrated operation	● sub-contracting
		● mass production	● batch production
		● for a mass consumer market	● diverse, specialised products
2	Products	● relatively cheap	● high quality
3	Labour process	● fragmented	
		● few tasks	● many tasks for versatile workers
		● little discretion	● some autonomy
		● hierarchial authority and technical control	● group control
4	Contracts	● collectively negotiated rate for the job	● payment by individual performance
		● relatively secure	● dual market: secure core, highly insecure periphery

Source: A. Warde, 'The future of work', *Social Studies Review*, September 1989

ITEM D

Population of working age: by sex and economic status[1] (United Kingdom)

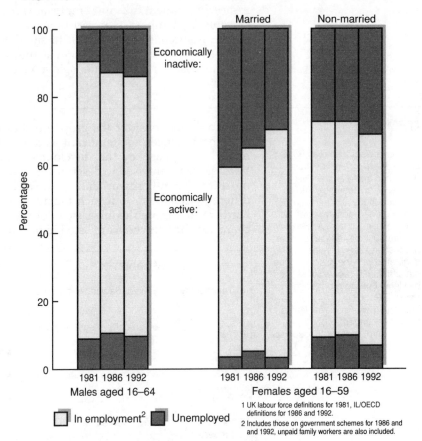

Source: Social Trends 1993,
London: HMSO, 1993

1 UK labour force definitions for 1981, IL/OECD definitions for 1986 and 1992.

2 Includes those on government schemes for 1986 and and 1992, unpaid family workers are also included.

ITEM E

This article highlights the changes in employment and working practices, where staff are seen as more 'flexible'. You need to look in a recent textbook, for example, Haralambos and Holborn (1992), pp. 345–51 to examine in greater detail the concepts of a 'core' workforce with a growing number of 'peripheral' workers. The change is of particular consequence to female employees.

McDonald's secret recipe for success comes not from the Big Mac sauce but from a new production process, using a combination of the Fordist conveyor belt with a Japanese emphasis on flexibility. Each store is a factory where workers' skills have been kept to a bare minimum. No chefs, no apprentices wanted on this burger-line: everyone has been levelled down to the uniform 'crew member' rushing between stations to perform tasks learnt in a day. From Oxford Street to Manila, McDonald's workers follow identical steps to produce identical burgers.

Labour costs should never exceed 15 per cent of an outlet's sales. 'It is very tight,' said one manager. 'If sales are down, labour costs must come down. You have to cut the staff and make those remaining work harder.' Workers hired for busy sessions are later shown the door.

Such 'flexible working practices' are as contagious on the high street as on the industrial estate. By employing part-timers, stores can cover unsocial hours without paying overtime and adjust workers' hours on a weekly, or even daily, basis as sales and staff numbers fluctuate. As one manager put it: 'We don't

5

10

15

Source: adapted from H. Lamb
and S. Percy, 'Big Mac is
watching you', *New Society*, 9
October, 1987

have full and part-timers here. Everyone at McDonald's works   20
flexible hours.'

The new tribe of so-called 'peripheral' workers is becoming
increasingly central to the economy. Today, one in four British
workers are part-time and 90 per cent of them are women.

QUESTIONS

a   Identify three trends shown in Item A.

(3 marks)

b   Using material from the Items and any other material you are familiar with, explain the meaning
of 'flexibility in the employment and management of labour' (Item B, lines 15–16).

(3 marks)   A question where you need to show *knowledge* and *interpretation* skills. Identify
the main argument expressed in Item B and then use data from the Items
(*interpretation and application*) and other sociological studies (*knowledge* and
application) to explain clearly this trend in employment practice.

c   With reference to Item C, suggest one industry characterized by a Fordist environment and one
characterized by a post-Fordist environment.

(2 marks)

d   Assess sociological explanations for the trends shown in Item D.

(8 marks)   An *interpretation* and *evaluation* question. Identify the trends in Item D and look
at a number of reasons why married women are entering the workforce in larger
numbers than hitherto. You can find one explanation in Item E, but there are
others in most textbooks, for example, Abbott and Wallace, pp. 121–51.
Suggest which arguments you find the most convincing, and why.

e   The authors of Item E suggest that 'the new tribe of so-called peripheral workers is becoming
increasingly central to the economy' (lines 22–3). Using information contained in the Items and
elsewhere, assess the extent to which this is now supported by sociological evidence.

(9 marks)   As an extension of this view, there is the idea that the working practices found
in McDonalds are becoming increasingly widespread. The view is not shared
by all sociologists and the situation may be different at times of high
unemployment. A recent textbook such as Abercrombie and Warde *et al*.
(1988), pp. 82–96 will examine the arguments and provide evidence to help you
explain and assess these ideas.

4.3 Alienation

ITEM A

Marx was one of the first writers to grasp that the development of modern industry would reduce many people's work to dull, uninteresting tasks. According to Marx, the division of labour alienates human beings from their work. He describes this phenomenon in graphic terms: 5

> What constitutes the alienation of labour? First that work is external to the worker, that it is not part of his nature; and that consequently he does not fulfil himself in his work but denies himself. The worker therefore feels himself at home only during his leisure time, whereas at work he feels home-   10 less. His work is not voluntary but imposed forced labour. It is not the satisfaction of a need but only a means for satisfying other needs.

For Marx alienation does not refer only to feelings of indifference or hostility to work, but to the overall framework of industrial   15 production within a capitalist setting.

Source: adapted from A. Giddens, *Sociology*, Cambridge: Polity, 1989

ITEM B

This item argues that alienation is a result of the type of technology used, and suggests that a change in technology can increase job satisfaction by giving people more control over their work.

In the early 1960s a succession of books appeared which examined the relationship between technology and job satisfaction. Notable among these are the works of Touraine, Blauner and Woodward. The findings they present are very much in accord.   5

Technology and Alienation

Type of Work →	Craft	Machine Minding	Assembly Line	Process
	↓	↓	↓	↓
Type of Production/ Product →	No standardized product	Mechanization and standardization	Rationalization Standardized product	Rationalization Uniform product
Level of Skill →	High	Low	Low	Responsibility and understanding needed
Level of Alienation →	Low	High	Highest	Low

Blauner's model is virtually self-explanatory. Machine minding is usually required in batch production which is technically less efficient than assembly-line mass production, but usually involves the worker in a slightly more varied way. At the other   10 end of the satisfaction–alienation spectrum is assembly-line work. The phantoms of monotony, repetition and sheer boredom

Source: adapted from M. O'Donnell, *A New Introduction to Sociology*, 3rd Ed., Walton-on-Thames: Nelson, 1992

are never far away. In process work, by contrast, the worker is 'freed' from the machine. S/he oversees much, if not all, of the process of production and therefore has a closer involvement and identity with the whole. The brutal fracturing of the division of labour is partly healed.

15

ITEM C

Taylor believed that the division of labour would benefit everyone involved in the production process and in this extract he shows how it can elevate intelligent workers. Look also at Braverman's criticisms. On both these, see, for example, Giddens (1989), pp. 481–6 or Abercrombie and Warde *et al*, (1988), pp. 44–60.

It is true for instance, that the planning room, and functional foremanship, render it possible for an intelligent labourer or helper in time to do much of the work now done by the machinist? Is this not a good thing for the labourer and helper? He is given a higher class of work, which tends to develop him and gives him better wages. In the sympathy for the machinist the case of the labourer is overlooked. This sympathy for the machinist is, however, wasted, since the machinist, with the aid of the new system, will rise to a higher class of work which he was unable to do in the past, and in addition, divided or functional foremanship will call for a larger number of men in this class, so that men, who must otherwise have remained machinists all their lives, will have the opportunity of rising to foremanship.

5

10

The demand for men of originality and brains was never so great as it is now, and the modern subdivision of labour, instead of dwarfing men, enables them all along the line to rise to a higher plane of efficiency, involving at the same time more brain work and less monotony. The type of man who was formerly a day labourer and digging dirt is now for instance making shoes in a factory.

15

20

Source: F. Taylor, 'Scientific management', 1947, quoted in H. Braverman, *Labour and Monopoly Capital*, New York: *Monthly Review Press*, 1974

ITEM D

Alienation has travelled a course that could be charted on a graph by means of an inverted U-curve.

In the early period, dominated by craft industry, alienation is at its lowest level and the worker's freedom at a maximum. Freedom declines and the curve of alienation (particularly its powerlessness dimension) rises sharply in the period of machine industry. The alienation curve continues upward to its highest point in the assembly-line industries of the twentieth century. In automotive production, the combination of technological, organizational, and economic factors has resulted in the simultaneous intensification of all dimensions of alienation.

5

10

But with automated industry there is a counter-trend, one that we can fortunately expect to become even more important in the future. The case of the continuous-process industries, particularly the chemical industry, shows that automation increases the worker's control over his/her work process and checks the further division of labour. The alienation curve begins to decline from its previous height as employees in automated industries gain a new dignity from responsibility and a sense of individual function – thus the inverted U.

15

20

Source: adapted from R. Blauner, *Alienation and Freedom*, Chicago: Chicago University Press, 1964

ITEM E

The French sociologist Serge Mallet's view of the promise of   5
automation differs radically from Blauner's. Where Blauner sees
automation reducing the possibility of class conflict, Mallet sees
just the opposite. He maintains that automation will highlight the
major contradiction of capitalism: the collective nature of production and the private ownership of the means of production. Since   10
workers in automated industry have greater control over and
responsibility for production, they will tend to see themselves as
the real controllers of industry. Workers will increasingly question the basis of ownership and control and demand worker control of the enterprise.

Source: adapted from M.
Haralambos and M. Holborn,
Sociology: Themes and Perspectives,
3rd Ed., London: Collins
Educational, 1991

QUESTIONS

a Compare and contrast the concepts of alienation used by Marx and Blauner (Items A and B).

(3 marks)   Look at what they have in common and where they differ. Make three clear points to get all
three *interpretation* marks.

b Explain in your own words the advantage of the modern subdivision of labour as seen by
F. Taylor (Item C).

(2 marks)

c Using material from the Items above and elsewhere, assess the statement made by the author
of Item D that alienation 'could be charted on a graph by an inverted U-curve'.

(9 marks)   This is a longer answer that needs to be carefully planned and structured. You know from the
wording that you need to use all skills. Bring in relevant material from the Items (*interpretation
and application*), as well as sociological studies from elsewhere (*knowledge* and *application*),
and assess (*evaluation*) by looking at both sides of the debate. See for example, Slattery (1985)
which includes an entry for Alienation on pp. 2–4, and also O'Donnell (1992), pp. 243–50.

d What sociological perspective is illustrated by Item E?

(1 mark)

e The author of Item A states that 'according to Marx, the division of labour alienates human
beings from their work' (lines 3–4). With reference to the material in the Items and any other
material you are familiar with, examine the arguments for and against Marx's view.

(10 marks)

4.4 Industrial conflict

ITEM A

Stoppages in progress: cause

United Kingdom	12 months to March 1991		
	Stoppages	Workers involved	Working days lost
Pay – wage-rates and earnings levels	150	92,300	322,000
– extra-wage and fringe benefits	20	4,800	12,000
Duration and pattern of hours worked	25	21,200	197,000
Redundancy questions	51	54,300	74,000
Trade union matters	12	2,400	24,000
Working conditions and supervision	65	31,100	58,000
Manning and work allocation	142	34,300	100,000
Dismissal and other disciplinary measures	71	15,400	49,000
All causes	**536**	**256,000**	**836,000**

Source: Employment Gazette, June 1991

ITEM B

Go back to the source to read about this study in more detail. It is interesting because it is one of the few interactionist studies of industrial action. The writers look at the meaning of the act to the actors, rather than any official definition. Why do you think they adopted this method of studying industrial sabotage?

Taylor and Walton classify acts of industrial sabotage in terms of their meanings and motives which direct them. They identify three main sources: 'attempts to reduce tension and frustration'; 'attempts at easing the work process'; and 'attempts to assert control'. They argue that each type of sabotage indicates 'the prevalence of distinctive strains or problems within the workplace'. 5

1 **Attempts to reduce tension and frustration**
   Taylor and Walton argue that such forms of sabotage 'are the signs of a powerless individual or group'. They tend to occur in industries where unions are absent or ineffective, and where there is little or no history of collective industrial action. In this situation there are few opportunities to remove the source of grievances. Sabotage provides a means of temporarily releasing frustration when workers lack the power to remove its source. 10 15

2 **Attempts to ease the work process**
   Taylor and Walton argue that this type of sabotage is typical of industries in which workers have to 'take on the machine', where they work against the clock and wages are dependent on output. By cutting corners, workers can increase output and from their point of view, cut through red tape and get on with the job. 20

3 **Attempts to assert control**
   The third type of sabotage directly challenges authority and is used by workers in an attempt to gain greater control. Usually it is planned and coordinated. Taylor and Walton give the example of car workers in Turin who smashed production lines and intimidated strike breakers. 25

Source: M. Haralambos and M.
Holborn, *Sociology: Themes and
Perspectives*, 3rd Ed., London:
Collins Educational, 1991

Taylor and Walton argue that sabotage directed by a desire to   30
assert control tends to occur in the following situations: where
there is a history of militancy, a general recognition of who's to
blame for grievances and few opportunities for effective protest
through official channels.

ITEM C

This is another way of
summarizing industrial action,
which is very different to the item
above. It shows that the way
something is categorized may
have a considerable effect on our
perception of it.

Until recently, the Department of Employment listed nine
'causes of strikes': claims for wage increases; other wage disputes; hours of labour; demarcation disputes; employment dismissal questions (including redundancy); other personnel
questions; other working arrangements, rules and discipline;   5
trade union status; and sympathetic action. Only four of these
categories of strike issues figured at all prominently: the two
classes of wage disputes, employment and dismissal questions,
and 'other working arrangements'. The remaining five categories
have together accounted for only 10 to 15 per cent of stoppages in   10
recent years, and often less than 10 per cent of striker-days.

Knowles has grouped these categories under three headings:
'basic causes (wages and hours), 'solidarity' (union status and
sympathetic action), and 'frictional' causes (all the other categories).   15

Source: R.Hyman, *Strikes*,
London: Fontana, 1984

ITEM D

Industrial disputes[1]: working days lost and number of stoppages (United Kingdom)

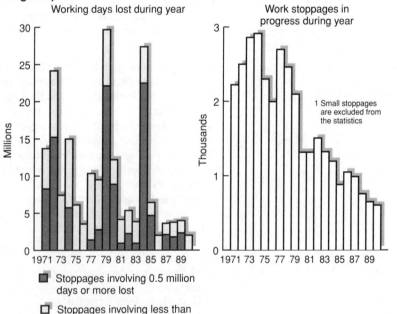

Source: Social Trends 1992,
London: HMSO, 1992

ITEM E

Reasons for striking

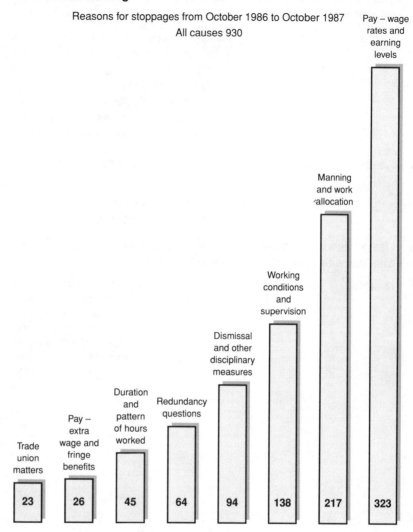

Reasons for stoppages from October 1986 to October 1987
All causes 930

Pay – wage rates and earning levels

Manning and work allocation

Working conditions and supervision

Dismissal and other disciplinary measures

Duration and pattern of hours worked

Redundancy questions

Pay – extra wage and fringe benefits

Trade union matters

Source: Employment Gazette,
January 1988, quoted in *New
Society,* 26 February, 1988

| 23 | 26 | 45 | 64 | 94 | 138 | 217 | 323 |

QUESTIONS

a With reference to Items A and E, identify two changes that have taken place between 1986–7 and 1990–1.

(2 marks) Make sure you identify clearly two trends to get both *interpretation* marks.

b In what way does the level of union organization affect the type of industrial sabotage that occurs in the workplace (Item B)?

(3 marks)

c The author of Item C argues that only four categories of strike issues figured prominently. With reference to Items A and E, assess whether this is still true today.

(4 marks)

This is asking you to extract material from a number of items (*interpretation*) in order to assess a particular statement (*evaluation*). Plan this answer and keep it relevant to gain *application* marks. One problem here relates to the issue of direct comparability of statistics over time. Note this point in your answer. This is an illustration of a potential problem with all statistics. One of the clearest examples of this relates to unemployment statistics, an issue covered in the question on Unemployment in this book (pp. 154–6).

d Assess sociological explanations of the trends shown in Item D.

(8 marks)

Explain the trends in Item D first (*interpretation and application*) and then you can get *knowledge* and *evaluation* marks for suggesting explanations such as changes in legislation or high unemployment.

e Using material from the Items above and elsewhere, evaluate the relative importance of factors that may affect the level of industrial conflict.

(8 marks)

This question requires a longer answer which involves the use of all skills. Identify different factors from the Items (*interpretation*) and elsewhere (*knowledge*). Most of the marks are for *evaluation* and to get these you have to say what you think has the most impact on the level of strikes, based on the information you have available. Don't forget *application* marks are available for using information in a relevant way. Useful material here includes O'Donnell (1992), pp. 255–60 and Abercrombie and Warde *et al.* (1988), pp. 60–75.

4.5 The informal economy

ITEM A

The informal economy consists of undeclared income (known as the black market) and unpaid domestic work. Pahl suggests that rising unemployment has led to the decline of the former at least. This is in contrast to some newspapers who sometimes imply that many of the unemployed are 'on the fiddle'. An example of a 'Moral Panic'.

Source: adapted from R. Deem, *Work, Unemployment and Leisure,* London: Routledge, 1988

Gershuny and Pahl (1985) distinguish between two different aspects of the informal economy, the hidden or underground economy which covers work or production 'wholly or partly for money or barter, which should be declared to some official taxation or regulatory authority, but which is wholly or partly concealed' and the household economy, where goods and services are produced, 'not for money, by members of a household and predominantly for members of that household ... for which approximate substitutes might otherwise be purchased for money'. 5

10

Following his more recent empirical research, Pahl suggested in 1984 that the hidden economy might actually be in decline and gave five reasons for this. First, between 1975 and 1979 self-employment declined. The self-employed are a group with a long tradition of under-reporting of their actual income. Second, 15 unemployment increased – less use of workplace for hidden work. Third, the unemployed are under greater official surveillance. Fourth, more efficient Tax Inspectors. Fifth, the growth of self-provisioning by households where members of the household provide services themselves – DIY. 20

ITEM B

Source: adapted from A. Warde 'Domestic divisions of labour', *Social Studies Review,* September 1990

Ray Pahl and Claire Wallace had interviewed about 750 households, randomly selected, on the Isle of Sheppey about what tasks each household had done and who did the work involved. Pahl's conclusions are now well known. Briefly he discovered:

5

1 Little work is done in the black economy. That which is, is not done by the unemployed.

2 A vast amount of work is undertaken by domestic provisioning. The consequences include domestication and privatization within households which both Gershuny in *After Industrial Society* (1978) and Pahl see as expressions of people's preferences for living home-centred rather than community- or public-centred life-styles. 10

3 Households with two or more earners in them do far more work in the home – more DIY – than those with one or no earner. This leads to sharp differences in life-chances and life-styles as the benefits of income from employment and services provided within the household cumulate to increase inequalities between households. 15

4 Work within the household – the domestic division of labour – is unevenly distributed between men and women, women doing a disproportionate share. Differences in the degree of inequality between couples is explained by the employment status of women and stage of the life-cycle rather than by class or income. 20

ITEM C

This report suggests that the value of the work done by the average (unpaid) housewife in money terms in 1993 was £18,000. This compares with the first survey of this kind, reported in the *Sunday Times* of 29 March, 1987 which showed the value of housework to be £19,253 for a 92-hour week. Look out for the annual updates on this figure.

Should the report make wives feel more secure and valued? In fact, the insurance company was using these figures to try to encourage husbands to increase the value of life-insurance on their wives.

Source: adapted from a report in the *Independent*, 3 February, 1993

The bargain most men take for granted is calculated by Legal and General insurance, which broke down the average housewife's weekly timetable and costed the domestic chores using hourly wage rates from employment agencies. [5]

These are the savings: nanny, 17.9 hours at £5.90 per hour, £105.61; cook, 12.2 at £5.35, £65.27; cleaner, 12.2 at £5.35, £65.27; laundress, 9.3 at £3.80, £35.34; shopper 6.4 at £3.80, £24.32; dishwasher, 5.7 at £3.80, £21.66; driver, 2.6 at £4.50, £11.70; gardener, [10] 1.4 at £5.90, £8.26; seamstress, 1.7 at £3.60, £6.12; other 1.3 at £4.00, £5.20. Total: 70.7 hrs, £348.75.

When comparing the value of a woman's work at home with other jobs, the houswife is worth more than a train driver (£339) and a plumber (£315); while a housewife with one child under [15] one compares favourably with a production manager (£454), or a teacher (£436).

One statistic for men to heed is that women with full-time jobs still work longer hours at home; those with part-time jobs averaged 59 hours at home, while those in full-time work did 48 [20] hours of domestic service, on top of a 40-hour week.

A nationally representative sample of 1,001 married women with dependent children took part in the survey: 47 per cent were not in paid employment, 35 per cent worked part-time and 18 per cent worked full-time. [25]

ITEM D

Read through other feminist writings on this issue to examine a range of different views. Again, the most detailed summary is to be found in Abbott and Wallace (1990)

Source: adapted from H. Wainwright, 'Women and the division of labour' in P. Abrams and R. Brown (eds), *UK Society: Work, Urbanism and Inequality*, London: Weidenfeld and Nicholson, 1984

The absence in sociology of any concerted study of sex and gender reflected the naturalness – until recently – of differences and divisions between men and women in everyday social experience. And this, in turn, is at root a result of the division of labour between men and women; in particular the division between [5] waged labour and domestic labour. In an economy in which a person's capacity to work is bought and sold in exchange for a wage, labour which is performed on the basis of personal and emotional relations rather than on the basis of monetary exchange is not recognized as labour. [10]

What then are the cultural and material relations that underpin the present sex-based organization of domestic labour? An interweaving of economic and emotional dependence is the foundation. The nature of women's unpaid work flows from this. Carried on in isolation, it is in theory a labour of care and devo- [15] tion to particular individuals; in fact it is a major contribution to the economy and to society. But its separation from the economy and its basis in personal relations means that it is not seen as professional, skilled or a source of status. The power relations of sex and gender flow from the same source. It is not that women lack [20] all power, but rather that their direct power and control is limited to the informal sphere of the family.

ITEM E

The view expressed here is that the informal and formal economies are linked and

The informal sector is particularly significant among poorer groups and in areas of high unemployment. Many goods or services that could not otherwise be paid for are provided in this way. Self-provisioning, of course, is not just a matter of economic

decisions are shared between members of the household. Compare the statements in this extract with Item A.

necessity; it may bring satisfactions that cannot be derived from the environment in which paid work is done. 5

The household is usually the main setting in which connections between the formal and the informal economies are handled. Members of households often make collective decisions about what constitutes an overall level of income that will meet their needs, and to some degree – where circumstances allow – distribute paid and unpaid labour tasks accordingly. . . . What counts as work, then, is a complex matter, involving many types of activities in addition to orthodox employment. 10

Source: A. Giddens, *Sociology,* Polity: Cambridge, 1989

QUESTIONS

a   Explain in your own words the changing structure of the informal economy as found by Pahl (Item A).

(3 marks)

b   How does work in the informal economy affect life-chances and life-style according to Pahl and Wallace (Item B)?

(2 marks)

c   What activity do housewives spend most time on according to Item C?

(1 mark)

d   The author of Item D argues that 'labour which is performed on the basis of personal and emotional relations rather than on the basis of monetary exchange is not recognized as labour' (lines 8–10). To what extent is this a valid criticism of the way sociologists have defined labour?

(9 marks)

e   The author of Item E argues that 'the informal economy is particularly significant among poorer people and in areas of high unemployment' (lines 1–2). Using material from the Items and elsewhere, assess the extent to which this is supported by sociological evidence.

(10 marks)
This is a long question which requires quite a long answer using all skills, as you can see from the wording – 'Using material from the Items [*interpretation and application*] and elsewhere [*knowledge* and *application*] assess the extent . . . [*evaluate*]'. To get full marks you need to plan your answer carefully and make sure you understand all the arguments. The material in Items A and E provides a starting point here as does Deem (1988), pp. 41–60. This book is useful for all aspects of the topic of work and leisure.

4.6 Unemployment

ITEM A

Losing your job increases your chances of dying, according to
new evidence. Data from the British Regional Heart Study, which
has spent 10 years studying people from 253 British towns,
shows that unemployment kills.

'We have found that men we were screening who were unem- 5
ployed at any time over a five-year period were more than one-
and-a-half times as likely to die in the next five years as men in
continuous employment,' said Dr Joan Morris, lecturer in med-
ical statistics at St Thomas' Hospital, London.

Last week was one of the worst on record for British industry, 10
with 7000 jobs lost in aerospace, mining, construction and car
making. The losses came as several studies suggested that unemployment poses a threat to life. The Office of Population,
Censuses and Surveys found over a 10-year period that unemployed men were more than one-and-a-third times more likely to 15
die than employed men.

Three weeks ago, the Office of Health Economics published a
compendium of health statistics showing that the number of pre-
scriptions issued in Merseyside (where unemployment stands at
12.5 per cent) was 9.7 per person last year, compared with 6.9 per 20
person per year in South-West Thames (unemployment 4.2 per
cent).

Source: the *Observer*, 27
September 1992

ITEM B

Unemployment by age and duration: Great Britain – January 1991

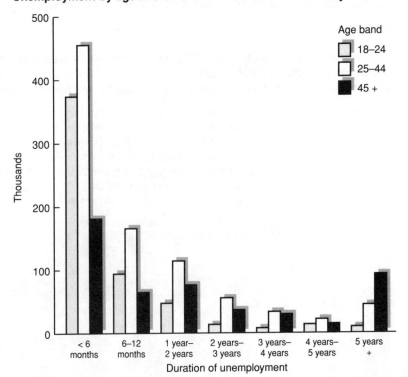

Source: Labour Market Quarterly News, May 1991

ITEM C

Survey of the longer-term unemployed in London: characteristics of the sample

		percent
SEX	male	73
	female	27
AGE	18–24	27
	25–29	20
	30–34	11
	35–39	11
	40–49	19
	50–59	12
ETHNIC ORIGIN		
	white	69
	other	30
MARITAL STATUS		
	married/cohabiting	36
	single	51
	widowed, divorced etc.	13
NUMBER OF DEPENDENT CHILDREN IN HOUSEHOLD		
	none	70
	1	11
	2	10
	3	5
	4 or more	3
HOUSING TENURE		
	owner occupied	21
	council rented	42
	private rented	26
	other	10
AREA OF RESIDENCE		
	Inner London	69
	Outer London	30
STATUS PRIOR TO BECOMING UNEMPLOYED		
	in work	74
	full-time education	9
	Government scheme	6
	looking after family	4
	sick	2
	other	5

Source: Harris survey among the London unemployed in P. Meadows *et al., The London Labour Market*, London: HMSO, 1988

ITEM D

A combination of factors probably explains the sharp increase in unemployment levels in the West in recent years.

An important element is the rise of international competition in industries on which Western prosperity used to be founded. In 1947, 60 per cent of world steel production was carried out in the United States. Today the figure is only about 15 per cent, while steel production has risen by 300 per cent in Japan and the Third World countries (principally Singapore, Taiwan and Hong Kong – which are now undercutting Japanese prices).

There is a worldwide economic recession, which was either

5

10

caused or triggered by the Oil Crisis of 1973 – a recession which is not yet over. The increasing use of micro-electronics in industry has reduced the need for labour-power.

More women than ever before are seeking paid employment, with the result that more people are chasing the limited number of available jobs.   15

Source: A. Giddens, *Sociology,*
Cambridge: Polity, 1989

ITEM E

Jobless – the great divide
Official total:3,094,000

Left-wing critics ADD:		Right-wing critics SUBTRACT:	
Unemployed excluded by statistical changes, October 1982 (net)	189,000	School leavers	168,000
		Claimants who are not really looking for jobs[1]	490,000
Unemployed over-sixties (no longer required to register)[1]	199,000	Severely disabled	23,000
Short-time working	43,000	'Unemployables' – mentally or physically incapable[2]	135,000
Students on vacation	27,000		
Effect of Special Employment Measures	395,000	'Job-changers' – out of work for four weeks or less	360,000
Unregistered unemployed[2]	490,000	'Black economy' workers, illegally claiming benefit[3]	250,000
Total additions	**1,343,000**	**Total subtractions**	**1,426,000**
TOTAL UNEMPLOYED	**4,437,000**	**TOTAL UNEMPLOYED**	**1,668,000**

1. Of whom 37,000 were removed between December 1981 and February 1982 and a further 162,000 as a result of Budget 1983 measures.
2. Estimate based on Dept of Employment survey, 1981.

1. Estimate, based on 1981 Labour Force Survey.
2. Dept of Employment estimate
3. Unknowable estimate based on internal government survey suggesting 8% of claims not justified.

Source: D. Lipsey in the *Sunday Times*, 6 November, 1983

QUESTIONS

a   How does the health of the unemployed compare with the rest of the population according to Item A?

(1 mark)

b   With reference to Item B, examine the relationship between age and duration of unemployment.

(2 marks)

c   Using material from the Items above and elsewhere, assess the relative importance of the various factors given by the author of Item D as explanations for unemployment.

(8 marks)

d   Summarize in your own words the social characteristics that appear to be associated with long-term unemployment in London (Item C).

(4 marks)

e   Item E presents two measures of unemployment. Using any material you are familiar with, examine the arguments for and against each of these measures.

4.7 Work and gender

ITEM A

Many myths about working women's 'improving' circumstances made the rounds in the eighties – while some discouraging and real trends that working women faced didn't get much press.

In Britain, according to figures from the Low Pay Unit, the overall pay gap in 1991 stood at £42.44 billion. A fair distribution of pay between men and women would require the transfer of £21.22 billion in earned income from men to women. Full-time women still earn only around 70 per cent of male earnings. Women's average hourly earnings (excluding overtime) as a percentage of men's actually fell in 1987, and the slow rate of increase since then still leaves them at only 78.3 per cent of men's. Between 1979 and 1991 women's average hourly earnings increased by only 5.3 per cent, compared to a 9.1 per cent increase between 1970 and 1979. And the official New Earnings Survey figures do not even include over 3 million people whose pay is below the PAYE threshold – most of whom are women. The Conservative government undermined women's pay still further by gutting the powers of industry-based wages councils, which had guaranteed a structure of minimum pay rates, as well as overtime and holiday pay, for women in menial occupations from clothing piecework to hairdressing. Three-quarters of the workers under the age of twenty-one who lost the protection of the wages councils were women.

Source: S. Faludi, *Backlash*, London: Chatto & Windus, 1992

ITEM B

The term 'reserve army of labour' refers to a section of the labour force which can be easily and cheaply hired and easily fired and so can be used to facilitate the functioning of capitalism. Black minority workers and female workers are considered to be a disproportionate and, in the latter case, growing proportion of this reserve army. Clearly, if employers can use female labour in this way it would be profitable for them to do so. Further, Veronica Beechey has argued that because females' wages often represent a second source of family income, employers are therefore able to depress male wages.

Irene Breugel's 1982 review of the above thesis in relation to the experience of female labour from 1974–78, provides only mixed support for it. She did find that the rate of unemployment of women rose three times more quickly than that of men and that the decline in female employment in industries experiencing increased unemployment exceeded that of men. Part-time female employees were particularly hard hit. On the other hand, the rapid expansion of the service sector to some extent protected the market position and employment security of women. More recently, Marxist-feminist Juliet Mitchell has speculated that micro-chip technology and the demand for jobs of males displaced from manufacturing industry may weaken the position of women in the service sector. Pessimistically Breugel suggests that women's best protection is the low pay they receive.

Source: M. O'Donnell, *A New Introduction to Sociology*, 3rd Ed, Walton-on-Thames: Nelson, 1992

ITEM C

Total, full-time and part-time female employed workforce participation rates: United Kingdom 1984

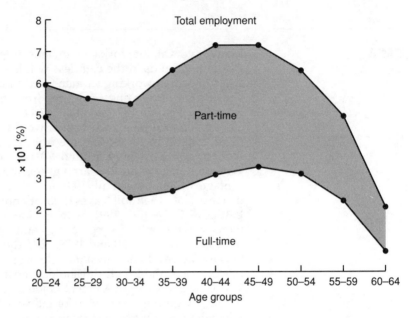

Employment[1]: by sex and hours of work

	Great Britain			Millions
	Males		Females	
	Full-time	Part-time	Full-time	Part-time
1986	12.7	1.1	5.7	4.5
1987	12.7	1.3	5.8	4.7
1988	13.1	1.3	6.1	4.8
1989	13.3	1.4	6.4	5.0
1990	13.3	1.5	6.3	5.2

1. *Includes employees in employment, self-employed, HM Forces (treated as full-time) and work-related government training programmes (treated as part-time)*

Source: Employment Department Statistics and Labour Force Survey 1984 quoted in A. Dale and J. Glover, 'Women's work patterns in the UK, France and the USA', in *Social Studies Review*, September 1987 and *Social Trends 1992*, London: HMSO, 1992

ITEM D

Women's jobs are concentrated in secondary labour markets. The primary labour market consists of work in large corporations, unionized industries or government agencies. In these contexts, workers receive relatively high wages, enjoy good job security and promotion possibilities. Secondary labour markets include forms of employment which are unstable, where job security and wages are low, there are few opportunities for promotion, and working conditions are frequently poor. Waitressing, retail sales work, cleaning, and many other service jobs mostly carried out by women fall into this category.

Women are also much more heavily concentrated than men in part-time paid work. Women make up 90 per cent of part-time workers in the UK; about 40 per cent of all working women are in part-time paid employment. Many women move to part-time work after the birth of a first child, if they do not leave the workforce altogether. Older women who return to paid work once their children are grown up often take part-time jobs – either from choice or because few full-time positions are available to them.

15

Source: A. Giddens, *Sociology,* Cambridge, Polity, 1989

ITEM E

Percentage distribution of persons in employment by occupational grouping and sex (Great Britain, 1987)

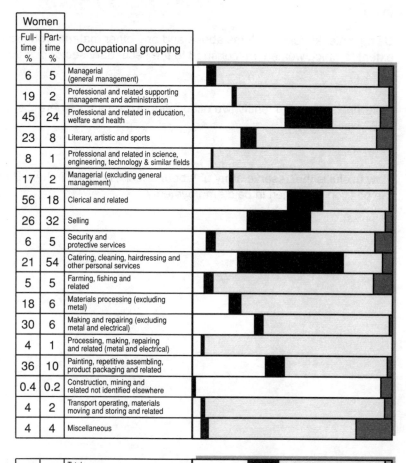

Women		Occupational grouping
Full-time %	Part-time %	
6	5	Managerial (general management)
19	2	Professional and related supporting management and administration
45	24	Professional and related in education, welfare and health
23	8	Literary, artistic and sports
8	1	Professional and related in science, engineering, technology & similar fields
17	2	Managerial (excluding general management)
56	18	Clerical and related
26	32	Selling
6	5	Security and protective services
21	54	Catering, cleaning, hairdressing and other personal services
5	5	Farming, fishing and related
18	6	Materials processing (excluding metal)
30	6	Making and repairing (excluding metal and electrical)
4	1	Processing, making, repairing and related (metal and electrical)
36	10	Painting, repetitive assembling, product packaging and related
0.4	0.2	Construction, mining and related not identified elsewhere
4	2	Transport operating, materials moving and storing and related
4	4	Miscellaneous

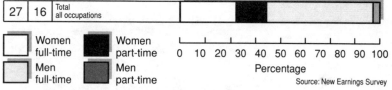

27	16	Total all occupations

Source: New Earnings Survey, quoted in *Social Studies Review,* January 1991.

Women full-time
Men full-time
Women part-time
Men part-time

0 10 20 30 40 50 60 70 80 90 100
Percentage
Source: New Earnings Survey

QUESTIONS

a   How much are women's average hourly earnings as a percentage of men's according to the most recent figures given in Item A?

(1 mark)

b   What explanations have sociologists offered for the patterns of female participation in paid employment as shown in Item C?

(5 marks)

c   Using material from the Items above and any other material you are familiar with, examine the extent to which women are confined to the secondary sector in a dual labour market (Item D).

(8 marks)

d   Referring to Item E, identify two occupational groupings where the majority of the workforce in 1987 was female.

(2 marks)

e   How useful is the 'reserve army of labour' thesis, outlined in Item B (line 1), as an explanation of the position of women in paid employment?

(9 marks)

4.8 Work and ethnicity

ITEM A

The governors of a Leicestershire further education college rejected an Asian candidate for the post of principal even though six of the nine people at the interview thought he was the best man for the job.

An investigation by the Commission for Racial Equality has found that Hinckley College was guilty of direct discrimination in rejecting the candidate who was described by county officials as having given 'by far and away' the best performance.

Leicestershire's director of education warned governors that they would be in breach of the county's equal opportunities policy if they turned the candidate down. But the college still gave the job to the white candidate who had been acting principal at Hinckley.

The investigation found that ethnic minority lecturers are under-represented in FE colleges across the county and in all grades. Only 1.2 per cent of FE lecturers are from minority groups in comparison with an 11 per cent representation in the county population.

The college governors had contended that the new principal needed local knowledge and a local track record. But, according to the commission, this reasoning would in any case have amounted to indirect discrimination.

Source: Times Educational Supplement, 6 September 1991

5

10

15

20

ITEM B

Job levels of men: all employees by ethnic group   *Column percentages*

Job level	White	West Indian	Asian	Indian	Paki- stani	Bangla- deshi	African Asian	Muslim	Hindu	Sikh
Professional, Employer, Management	19	5	13	11	10	10	22	11	20	4
Other non- manual	23	10	13	13	8	7	21	8	26	8
Skilled manual and foreman	42	48	33	34	39	13	31	33	20	48
Semi-skilled Manual	13	26	34	36	35	57	22	39	28	33
Unskilled Manual	3	9	6	5	8	12	3	8	3	6
Base: Male employees (weighted)	1490	972	2167	347	611	177	495	998	571	452
(unweighted)	591	467	1041	401	298	96	227	507	258	213

Source: C. Brown, Black and White Britain: The Third PSI Survey, London: Heinemann, 1984

ITEM C

Stephen Castles and Godula Kosack in a study of immigrant workers in France, Germany, Switzerland and Britain found that immigrants faced similar problems in the labour market to those identified in Handsworth by Rex and Tomlinson. Castles and Kosack claim that in Britain this situation is mainly due to discrimination.   5

Discrimination and restrictive regulations are, however, only the immediate cause of the plight of immigrants. The poor treatment of immigrants ultimately derives from the need in capitalist societies for a 'reserve army of labour'. It is necessary to have a   10 surplus of labour in order to keep wage costs down since the greater the overall supply of labour the weaker the bargaining position of workers. Furthermore, as Marxists, Castles and Kosack believe that capitalist economies are inherently unstable. They go through periods of boom and slump and a reserve army   15 of labour needs to be available to be hired and fired as the fluctuating fortunes of the economy dictate. After the Second World War capitalist societies exhausted their indigenous reserve army of labour; women, for example, were increasingly taking paid employment. Capitalist countries in Europe therefore turned to   20 migrant labour to provide a reserve pool of cheap labour which could be profitably exploited.

Castles and Kosack do not believe that such workers form an underclass outside and below the main class structure. They regard them as being part of the working class. However, they   25 believe that immigrant and migrant workers are the most disadvantaged groups within the working class and as such they form a distinctive strata.

Source: adapted from M. Haralambos and M. Holborn, *Sociology: Themes and Perspectives,* 3rd Ed., London: Collins Educational, 1991

ITEM D

What factors account for the employment distribution of the ethnic minorities? One theory is that the relatively low occupational status of blacks is the result of the fact that they are recent immigrants.

Another explanation of the low occupational status of blacks,   5 not wholly incompatible with the previous one, is that they are discriminated against in the employment market. This is certainly true.

Since 1975, minority unemployment has tended to be proportionately higher than that of the general population. The propor-   10 tion of unemployed blacks has tended to rise in times of economic recession. This gives weight to the theory that, to some extent, minorities serve as a 'reserve pool' or marginal source of cheap labour which, within the limits of the law, can be cut during a slump, and re-employed when expansion occurs.   15

In attempting to put a name to the distinct structural position of blacks, John Rex has suggested the term 'underclass'. We can see arguments for using the term underclass, all of which differentiate blacks from the working class and therefore prevent them from being fully identified with it. Firstly, blacks are subject to   20 racial discrimination and need ways of fighting it. Secondly, blacks as a group tend to be poorer than the working class as a whole and in that sense they are an 'underclass'.

It may, however, still be premature to speak of a black underclass. Matters may not yet be as clear cut as this term suggests.   25

Source: adapted from M. O'Donnell, *A New Introduction to Sociology,* 2nd Ed., Nelson: Walton-on-Thames, 1987

ITEM E

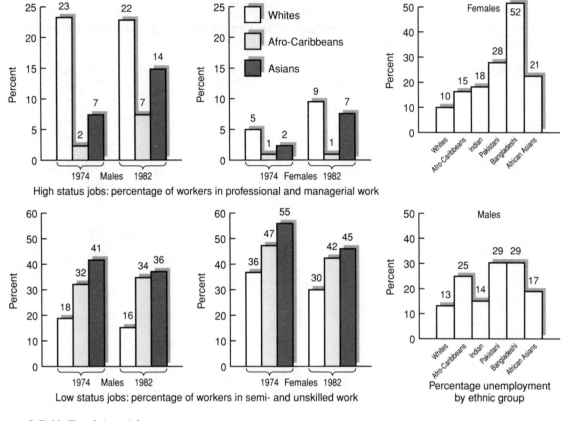

High status jobs: percentage of workers in professional and managerial work

Low status jobs: percentage of workers in semi- and unskilled work

Percentage unemployment by ethnic group

Source: S. Field, 'Trends in racial inequality', *Social Studies Review*, March 1986

QUESTIONS

a   Briefly explain the meaning of the two terms 'direct discrimination' (line 6) and ' indirect discrimination' (line 22) referred to in Item A.

(2 marks)

b   Describe the differences in male job levels for different ethnic groups shown in Item B.

(4 marks)

c   Examine the arguments for and against the view contained in Item C that ethnic minorities form a 'part of the working class' (line 25) in relation to contemporary Britain.

(8 marks)

d Which social group suffered the highest percentage unemployment according to Item E?

(1 mark)

e Using material from Item D and elsewhere, assess sociological explanations for the employment situation of ethnic minorities.

(10 marks)

4.9 Work and non-work

ITEM A

The increasing importance of consumption and of the media in modern societies has given rise to new occupations – or changed the role and character of older ones – associated with the need to encourage people to consume in more frequent, more constant and more varied ways. These occupational groups are involved 5 in both creating and manipulating or 'playing with' cultural symbols and media images so as to get consumers to buy things, even those things which they don't necessarily need but feel they ought to have because this is integral to the consumer ethic.

In view of this argument we cannot only account for the grow- 10 ing occupational importance of advertising, marketing, design, architecture and media professions like journalism and pro- gramme production more generally, but also those occupations like social work, therapists of one kind or another, teachers, lec- turers, and so on, associated with wider definitions of psycholog- 15 ical and personal need and fulfilment.

Source: adapted from D. Strinati, 'Postmodernism and popular culture' in *Sociology Review*, April 1992

ITEM B

The division of existence into work and non-work is very basic. However, there are better categories than work and leisure because much non-work time may be devoted to activities other than leisure. A number of attempts to develop the work/non- work categorization have been made. Stanley Parker makes the 5 following divisions: work; work obligations; existence time; non- work obligations; and leisure.

These types of categorization are useful when considering the lives of males in full-time employment. They give a fair sense of the daily experience of necessity and pleasure. However, they are 10 inadequate for understanding the work/non-work experience of those mainly involved in domestic labour, still overwhelmingly women. Sue McIntosh and her colleagues have criticized Parker sharply on this point.

McIntosh presents a typical work-leisure model of the house- 15 wife. The central feature of it is that domestic activity or concern virtually never ceases: there are few total 'escapes' into leisure, little real 'freetime'.

Source: adapted from M. O'Donnell, *A New Introduction to Sociology*, 3rd Ed., Walton-on-Thames: Nelson, 1992

ITEM C

In much of the literature on the sociology of leisure there is an assumption that leisure and work are inextricably linked. Burns has examined how industrialization bought forward new forms of leisure and consumption. Political struggles by industrial workers not only created a particular form of leisure but also 5 indelibly stamped it with overtones of class and gender divi- sions. The fight for leisure as separate from work was a battle waged largely by the male working class. Women were likely to be heavily engaged in housework and childcare.

Sociologists are similarly divided in their views about leisure– 10
whilst functionalists might stress the complementarity of work
and leisure, and feminists the potentially liberating effects of
leisure and sport, Marxists might point out that leisure is a means
of controlling the population and of ensuring that they consume
vast amounts of capitalist-produced goods and services. 15

Source: adapted from R. Deem,
Work, Unemployment and Leisure,
London: Routledge, 1988

ITEM D

Roberts suggests that leisure needs to be understood
pluralistically. Too many theorists try to explain leisure by
emphasizing one or two variables to the exclusion of others. His
own preference is to acknowledge the great number and range of
factors which influence leisure choice. Gender, age, family and 5
education all have their part to play, but so too do personality
and personal inclination. He admits that totally free choice,
unhindered by social factors, is a sociological impossibility, but it
is in the nature of leisure to be an area of life where we are able to
exercise most choice. 10

A much more radical view is taken by Clarke and Critcher who
argue that leisure was as much an invention of the Industrial
Revolution as the steam engine. In the astonishing restrictiveness
of the licensing laws or the male domination of public leisure, we
find attitudes and practices which have as much to do with the 15
logic of capitalism as with any conception of human freedom. If
people do enjoy themselves, they do so under conditions laid
down by the economic and political structures of capitalist
society.

Source: C. Critcher, 'Leading
lives of leisure' in *Social Studies
Review,* May 1988

QUESTIONS

a   What does Item A suggest are the main effects on occupation of the increasing importance of consumption in modern societies?

(2 marks)

b   Explain the difference between non-work obligations and leisure(Item B), and give an example of each.

(4 marks)

c   The author of Item C argues that 'in much of the literature on the sociology of leisure there is an assumption that work and leisure are inextricably linked' (lines 1–2). How valid is this view?

(5 marks)

d   In Item D, Clarke and Critcher suggest that the structure of modern leisure has little to do with human freedom and choice. Using material from the Items above and elsewhere, assess the extent to which this opinion is supported by sociological evidence.

(6 marks)

e   Item B contains the argument that the concepts of work and leisure are inadequate. Examine the arguments for and against this view.

(9 marks)

ITEM A

Participation[1] in selected social and cultural activities: by socio-economic group[2] and sex, 1986

Great Britain   *Percentages and numbers*

	Profess-ional employers and managers	Inter-mediate and junior non-manual	Skilled manual and own account non-prof-essional	Semi-skilled and unskilled manual	Full-time students	All males[3]	All females[3]	All persons[3]
Percentage in each group engaging in each activity in the 4 weeks before interview								
Open air outings								
Seaside	8	9	6	6	6	6	8	7
Parks	4	5	3	3	3	3	4	4
Country	4	4	2	2	1	3	3	3
Entertainment, social and cultural activities								
Going out for a drink[4]	58	54	61	51	63	65	47	55
Going out for a meal	65	57	39	32	55	47	47	47
Dancing	10	12	9	10	24	9	12	11
Visiting historic buildings/ sites/towns	14	13	7	6	8	9	10	9
Going to the cinema	9	10	6	4	31	8	9	8
Going to the theatre/ opera/ballet	9	8	3	2	8	4	6	5
Going to fairs/amusement arcades	5	5	4	3	6	4	5	4
Going to museums/art galleries	6	5	2	2	7	4	4	4
Amateur music/drama	5	5	2	1	11	4	3	4
Home-based activities								
Listening to records/ tapes[4]	70	73	63	59	96	69	65	67
Reading books[4]	68	71	45	47	81	52	64	59
Gardening[4]	54	44	44	38	17	47	39	43
House repairs/DIY	55	37	50	29	22	54	27	39
Needlework/knitting/dressmaking[4]	16	40	12	31	19	3	49	27
Sample size (= 100%) (numbers)	2,969	5,940	4,048	5,098	603	8,891	10,318	19,209

1 Annual averages of participation of people aged 16 and over
2 Full-time students are covered separately
3 Includes armed forces and persons who have never worked. These are excluded from the analysis by socio-economic group
4 The high participation levels are partly attributable to the fact that these items were prompted.

Source: Social Trends 1990,
London: HMSO, 1990

ITEM B

It's 7.50. Play is about to begin. The caller, known to all as John, takes his place at a glittery green pulpit suspended half-way to the ceiling. The 'Slots of Fun' arcade empties as players scoot to their seats. John, a mixture of master of ceremonies and stand-up comic, is in full evening dress, including bow tie. He quickly dispenses with the preliminaries: 'Good evening ladies and gentleman, and you Elsie.' We sit, pens poised and the real business of the evening begins: The Game. 'Four and eight, forty-eight on its own, number nine.' 5

All heads are bowed during this brisk litany. The only noise is the soft scribble of hundreds of felt-tip pens. 10

Bingo is a game of pure chance. It requires no skill. That's why bingo players are ridiculed as moronic (*The Times* once described bingo as a 'cretinous pastime'). But it's the whole point of the game's appeal. Liz explains: 'There's no skill in it, which means I don't have to work hard'. 15

Frances endorses this: 'I come here for a break, to get out of the house'.

In a supposedly post-class society, bingo remains emphatically, undeniably, exclusively, a working-class pursuit. An analysis done in 1981 found that 85 per cent of players came from social classes C2, D and E. It is also a game predominantly played by women, typically middle-aged or older women. 20

As such, bingo has been the target of much snobbery and sexism. In 1980 the *Glasgow Evening Times* warned that 'bingo palaces' are taking over and 'more and more women are being drawn into the world of gambling'. 25

Among the women I spoke to, there was no evidence of compulsive gambling or family neglect. On the contrary, they are far too shrewd. Playing bingo is their right. Besides, it is the social side that is important. Betty explained that it was the only place where you could go to at night on your own without feeling self-conscious or embarrassed. Nobody bothered you, and there was always someone you knew to talk to if you felt like it. 30

Source: adapted from M. Manning, 'Sweating on numbers', *New Statesman and Society*, 16 March 1990

ITEM C

Gender divisions and gender power relations between men and women do exert a significant influence over the kind of leisure that is possible for women. Leisure is a political as well as a socially constructed phenomenon.

Although I have said that leisure cannot be fully understood as something which occupies a time slot different from that of other activities and experiences, nevertheless, the amount of time that women potentially have available for separate leisure is important. The Henley Centre for Forecasting has estimated that in general men in this country have more leisure time available to them than women, after taking into account time devoted to paid and unpaid work, travel and essential activities like washing and eating. The least leisure time available is found amongst employed women, followed by employed men. 5 10

Many women, especially those with young children, spend a good deal of time in the home. In practice, this may give them less leisure time than men, since the typical female day at home – 15 including work, such as childcare, cooking and cleaning – is unstructured, unpredictable and time-consuming.

Even though women may spend a lot of time at home, they may not always be able to determine the conditions under which they live. For example, when I was doing fieldwork on my leisure research, I was surprised to find that a number of women, both middle and working class, said that their husbands turned off the central heating when they went out to work, leaving them in unheated houses.

Source: adapted from R. Deem, 'Women and leisure – all work and no play?', *Social Studies Review*, March 1990

ITEM D

Question: why are girls twice as likely as boys to be written off by their peers as boring, quiet and posh? Answer: because they are twice as likely as boys to have their noses buried in a book, writes Adrian Caudrey. A survey into how children spend their free time, carried out by the market researchers, Millward Brown, shows that 97 per cent of boys are glued to the television every day, whereas only 57 per cent read a book on an average day.

Both sexes give watching television as their favourite pastime. But while 36 per cent of girls cite reading a book as their second favourite activity, this is true of only 14 per cent of boys. Book reading wanes with age. For while 37 per cent of eight and nine-year-olds read avidly in their spare time only 15 per cent of 14 and 15-year-olds do so. This may be partly because book worms are perceived as dull, introverted and old-fashioned by their peers.

The survey – carried out among 1,000 eight to 15-year-olds shows that middle-class children are only slightly more hooked on books than their working-class peers. For while 64 per cent of those from the top social brackets had read a book the previous day, this was also true of 54 per cent of the working- class young-sters. Middle-class children, however, are twice as likely as working-class children to frequent public libraries. Girls are three times more likely to do so than boys.

While girls are reading, boys are likely to be engaged in sport - 51 per cent do so three times a week compared with only 27 per cent of girls. Boys are also far more likely to relax in front of a home computer because 73 per cent of boy-only households possess one as against 44 per cent of all-girl homes.

Source: New Society, 29 May 1987

ITEM E

Time use in a typical week: by employment status and sex, 1991–1992

Great Britain (hours)

	Full-time employees		Part-time female employees	Housewives	Retired
	Males	*Females*			
Weekly hours spent on					
Employment and travel[1]	48.9	43.7	21.1	0.4	0.2
Essential activities[2]	26.8	42.3	57.0	65.5	36.0
Sleep[3]	49.0	49.0	49.0	49.0	49.0
Free time	46.5	33.0	41.0	53.5	83.0
Free time per weekday	4.8	3.3	4.7	7.0	11.6
Free time per weekend day	11.3	8.3	8.7	9.0	12.6

Source: Social Trends 1993,
London: HMSO, 1993

1 Travel to and from workplace.
2 Essential domestic work and personal care, including essential shopping, child care, cooking, personal hygiene and appearance.
3 An average of 7 hours sleep per night is assumed.

QUESTIONS

a What research method is being employed by the author of Item B?

(1 mark)

b What explanations have sociologists offered for the patterns of participation in leisure activities shown in Item A?

(5 marks)

c Using material from the Items above and elsewhere, assess the arguments put forward by the author of Item C that 'Gender divisions and gender power exert a significant influence over the kind of leisure that is possible for women' (lines 1–3).

(9 marks)

d Which social group had the least free time in a typical week in 1991–2 according to Item E?

(1 mark)

e The author of Item D suggests that a process of labelling is associated with certain leisure activities. Using material from the Items above and elsewhere, assess the validity of this argument.

(9 marks)

5

Stratification

5.1 Distribution of income and wealth

ITEM A

The *New Earnings Survey* provides up-to-date information about income and is very useful because it highlights class, gender and regional differences. Use this information for other pieces of work.

However be aware of the limitations of this survey – see for example the extract from Susan Faludi's book in the question on Work and Gender (p. 157).

Source: adapted from *New Earnings Survey 1990*, London: HMSO, 1990

Average gross weekly pay for full-time workers on adult rates whose pay was not affected by absence

Region	Male Manual	Male Non-manual	Female manual	Female Non-manual
South East	255.30	404.00	164.90	244.60
East Anglia	237.20	333.90	141.90	198.30
South West	227.00	326.60	141.90	199.50
West Midlands	229.40	322.30	143.10	195.00
East Midlands	231.60	322.80	140.10	198.90
Yorks & H'side	230.70	316.80	140.80	193.50
North West	233.10	322.60	143.80	199.80
North	231.60	314.50	141.00	192.50
Wales	224.70	306.20	143.50	193.00
Scotland	231.70	327.40	141.20	200.60

ITEM B

Social Studies Review and *Sociology Review* are invaluable for articles like this one which not only look at current information but also indicate many of the problems and pitfalls connected with it. The writer shows how problematic the concept of an 'average' wage is for understanding anything about the distribution of income. However, it also shows how it is possible to analyse information in much greater detail if all types of average figure are readily available: the problem is that they often aren't. Similar points are made in Giddens (1989) pp. 666–7.

Source: adapted from 'Averaging out inequality', Research Roundup, *Social Studies Review*, May 1989

Social Trends, an annual official publication, presents data on gross weekly earnings of full-time employees. This shows the mean figure for men in 1987 to be £224 (equivalent to £11,648 per annum). This estimate relates to all adult male full-time employees, and it is clear that the inclusion of women or young workers would have pulled the average down considerably. This figure also masks some important class differences: the mean for male manual workers is £185.50 (£9,646 per annum), while that for non-manual workers is £265.90 (£13,826.80 per annum). What this shows is that a mean figure can often obscure as much as it shows. An overall figure for the whole population will give a distorted picture of the real distribution.

In order to overcome these distortions, alternative measures of average are used. The median is the 'middle' value in a distribution and so divides it cleanly in half. In a distribution of income, there would be as many earners above the median as there are below it. In 1987 the median weekly earnings of male workers were £198.40 (£10,316.80 per annum). This means that exactly half of all male earners receive less than £198.40 per week; conversely, exactly half of earners receive more than this figure.

You will see that the calculated median is lower than the calculated mean for the same category: the mean for male earners is £224 and the median is £198.40. In general terms, the discrepancy tells you that income distribution is skewed towards the top of the scale: the mean is higher than the median because the 50 per cent of earners above £198.40 have an aggregate income which is higher than that of the 50 per cent of earners below £198.40. If the mean were lower than the median, this would show that the skew was towards the bottom of the scale.

ITEM C

The CPAG chart shows clearly that someone with an income of £40,000 p.a. receives only £1 less in state benefits than someone with no other income.

For further details on this issue see T. Cole *Whose Welfare*.

Source: the *Observer*, 17 March, 1991

Benefits for wealthy equal handouts for jobless

Married couple with a single earner (aged 44) on £40,000 p/a	£/week	Unemployed married couple with two children aged four and six	£/week
Married couple's and personal allowance at 40%	13.64	Income support	57.60
			12.35
			12.35
			7.35
Mortgage interest tax relief	33.46	Rent rebate	23.43
Personal pension relief	61.54	Community Charge benefit	10.58
Nat. Ins. personal pension subsidy	8.11	Free school meals	2.85
2% personal pension incentive	6.08	Free welfare milk	2.10
Personal equity plan dividend	4.62		
Total	**127.45**	**Total**	**128.61**

ITEM D

This article is packed full of statistics which look at the key issue of how the distribution of income changed during the 1980s under the Conservative Government.

The key issue is not whether people have more money in their pockets now, but whether the difference between the rich and the poor has increased or decreased. Notice the original source of the material quoted in the article.

The truth gap over the poverty gap . . .

One voter who . . . phoned the BBC's *Election Call* put this question to the Chancellor of the Exchequer. After 13 years, he said, more than one fifth of the poorest people in Europe lived in Britain. The gap between the lowest and highest paid was greater than in Victorian times. To which Norman Lamont replied: 'I [5] don't accept your statistics. I don't recognize them and they are not correct.'. . .

'But hadn't the gap between rich and poor increased?', pressed Jonathan Dimbleby. 'I don't believe it has,' said Lamont. This was an astonishing thing for him to say. It is not true. [10] Information produced by his own government has repeatedly demonstrated it is untrue . . .

In 1990, a government survey, *Households Below Average Incomes*, showed that between 1981 and 1987, average income increased ten times as fast as that of the poorest 10 per cent . . . [15]

In January this year, *Economic Trends*, produced by the Government Statistical Service, revealed that in 1979 the poorest fifth of the population had just under 10 per cent of post-tax income and the richest fifth had 37 per cent. By 1989 the poorest fifth had only seven per cent while the richest had 43 per cent . . . [20]

As for his [questioner's] comparison with Victorian times, the Low Pay Unit this week published a table based on the Government's *New Earnings Survey* which showed that the gap between the highest and the lowest full-time male manual earners was wider in 1991 than it was in 1886, a gap which only started to [25] widen appreciably during the 1980s.

So what the Chancellor said on the income gap was utterly untrue. What he and the rest of the government like to stress is that even the poorest people have seen their real incomes grow over these years . . . [30]

Now let's look at what John Major has said on this issue . . . 'At every level people have had more net disposable income'. [He went on to stress that] many people had done well by their own efforts and that people who were relatively poor had their net disposable income increased. He dismissed the 'envy factor'   35 which led people to measure how they were doing against other people . . .

The Prime Minister is said to be a decent man. On the basis of these remarks, however, he is incapable of distinguishing between envy and justice . . . Inequality is unjust. Denying some   40 people an equal share in the country's prosperity is immoral. The Institute for Fiscal Studies showed this week that tax and benefit changes since 1979 have given on average an extra £87 per week to the richest 10 per cent while denuding the poorest tenth of an average £1 per week. To dismiss or even deny the government's   45 record of taking a great deal of money from the poor to give to the rich is to pile cynicism on moral degeneracy.

Source: abridged from a report in the *Guardian*, 3 April, 1992

ITEM E

Social Trends is a valuable source of statistical data, despite the problems with official statistics, covered in detail in Slattery (1986). This table shows that there has been a certain amount of redistribution of wealth, at least from the very rich. The amount of wealth in the economy as a whole as measured by GDP has increased massively. The data also suggests that redistribution is significantly different when we have taken into account private and state pensions. Remember the problems involved in measuring the wealth, particularly of the very rich and notice the original source of the data.

Distribution of wealth[1]

United Kingdom		*percentages and £ billion*		
	1971	1981	1986	1987
Marketable wealth				
Percentage of wealth owned by[2]				
Most wealthy 1%	31	21	18	18
Most wealthy 5%	52	40	36	36
Most wealthy 10%	65	54	50	50
Most wealthy 25%	86	77	75	74
Most wealthy 50%	97	94	92	93
Total marketable wealth (£ billion)	140	546	1,017	1,199
Marketable wealth plus occupational and state pension rights				
Percentage of wealth owned by[2]				
Most wealthy 1%	21	12	11	11
Most wealthy 5%	37	24	24	24
Most wealthy 10%	49	34	35	35
Most wealthy 25%	69-72	55-58	58-61	59-62
Most wealthy 50%	85-89	78-82	82-87	82-87

1. Estimates for 1971 and 1981 are based on the estates of persons dying in those years. Estimates for 1986 and 1987 are based on estates notified for probate in 1986/87 and 1987/88. Estimates are not strictly comparable between years.
2. Percentages are of population aged 18 and over.
3. Estimates vary with assumption.

Source: Inland Revenue statistics in *Social Trends 1990*, London: HMSO, 1990

QUESTIONS

a With reference to Item A, identify the social groups which received the highest and lowest average gross weekly pay.

(2 marks) Two *interpretation* marks: be sure to identify them both in terms of gender, class (manual/non-manual) and region to get full marks.

b Explain why the author of Item B feels that a 'mean figure can often obscure as much as it shows' (line 10).

(3 marks) Explain the term 'mean figure' (remember it is a type of average) and then summarize the views of the author about low paid groups and the distribution of income in your own words.

c Using material from Item D and elsewhere, examine the arguments for and against the view expressed in Item C that the state helps the rich just as much as the poor.

(9 marks) This is a longer question which requires a clearly structured answer. The wording shows that you need to demonstrate all skills: 'Material from Item D' (*interpretation and application*), 'elsewhere' (*knowledge* and *application*), 'arguments for and against' (*evaluation*). Look at the statistical information provided as well as the work of Julian Le Grand and/or Tony Cole. You may wish to bring in the idea that high earners pay higher income taxes, but you will also need to look at the burden of taxation overall. In your evaluation, say what you think at the end, and why.

Useful material here includes: Haralambos and Holborn (1991), pp. 213–16, Bilton *et al.* (1987), pp. 75–7, O'Donnell (1992), pp. 358–62, and the extracts on Social Policy included in Trowler (1987) pp. 126–58. You could also look at Graham (1989).

d What trend in the distribution of wealth is shown in Item E?

(1 mark) One *interpretation* mark for a well-summarized sentence or two. Take your time (you have about two minutes) to get it right.

e Assess sociological explanations for the differences in income shown in Item A.

(10 marks) The key to success here is to identify the trends first and then to concentrate on the ones you mention. As this question requires you to use all skills and specifically mentions 'sociological explanations', you must use your textbooks to look at different explanations of class, gender or regional difference in income. One problem here is selecting out the evidence and you may find that a plan will help. A plan will also ensure material is used in a relevant way, thus gaining *application* marks. The best summary of the material relevant to this issue is contained in Saunders (1990). This book is useful for all aspects of the stratification topic.

5.2 Is social class still central?

See also the material contained in the question on the Working Class p. 187. This is also in some cases related to the ideas of postmodernism, particularly in the case of Lash and Urry, so look at the question on Modern Social Theory pp. 48–51.

ITEM A

Sociology Review offers an up-to-date analysis of the whole question of whether class is still an important concept. Many writers argue that status (gender, ethnicity, age, etc.) is now a more important division between social groups than class. In particular this examination of status is focused on the behaviour of working-class people. See also the material contained in the question on the Working Class p. 187. This is also in some cases related to the ideas of postmodernism, particularly in the case of Lash and Urry, so look at the question on Modern Social Theory pp. 48–51.

The centrality of class as a basis for identity has been challenged by Lash and Urry. They argue that economic and cultural changes have dislodged class as a key identity for the majority of the population. They have termed this process 'decentering'. The economic changes include the emergence of core and peripheral labour markets for all classes. Core workers have full-time secure jobs with a career structure whereas peripheral workers are temporary, often part-time with no job security or chance of promotion. This new structuring of the workforce cuts across class lines. For example, women, ethnic minorities and the young are more likely to be in the peripheral labour market. Additionally, the decline of manufacturing industry and the increasing size of the service class have led to changes on a cultural level. Moreover, within a generation there are more likely to be changes in employment and marital status. So it would seem that, for some groups, class is becoming less significant as a source of identity.

Bryan Turner has also highlighted the importance of status groups rather than classes. He argues that society is becoming structured into 'status blocs' which cut across traditional class divisions. Tables 1 and 2 demonstrate how status blocs such as housing tenure and ethnicity affect voting behaviour.

Table 1: Housing tenure and voting

Conservative lead over Labour by class and housing tenure, 1983

Salariat		Intermediate classes		Working class	
Owner-occupiers	Council tenants	Owner-occupiers	Council tenants	Owner-occupiers	Council tenants
+44	−3	+45	−25	+2	−42

Source: *Heath* et al. *(1985, p. 46).*
Note: *Each figure is % Conservative minus % Labour in the group concerned.*

Table 2: Ethnicity and voting

	Labour support	
White	Afro-Caribbean	Asian
43%	86%	80%

Source: Adapted from the Commission for Racial Equality findings (1983).

Source: adapted from J. Clarke and C. Saunders, 'Who are you and so what?' in *Sociology Review*, September 1991

ITEM B

The emphasis has shifted from groups to individuals, from classes to categories and from producers to consumers. Collectivities in the class war are replaced by individuals in an 'open market'. This shift in social imagery from the military to the market does seem likely to affect the way that sociologists see the world: but it does not follow that the social world has changed as much as the language used to describe it. Lifestyle categories are based upon clusters of common attitudes gathered from regular surveys. They are *ad hoc* and pragmatic and do not derive from any clear theoretical orientation but they seem a better guide to what people will do with their money than categories based on socio-economic groupings. So market researchers have abandoned class for empirical, not theoretical reasons.

In summary then, firstly class as a force for social and political change is problematic. Secondly, as a classificatory device class does little to help us understand the lifestyles of the privileged and adds nothing to the brute facts of poverty when considering the other end of the social spectrum. And thirdly, it is well nigh impossible to operationalize the concept in order to make international comparisons.

I am not of course saying that we should forget about class: I am simply stating that if the concept does not do any useful work for us we should cease behaving as if it does.

Lest I be misunderstood, I must make it absolutely clear that nothing I have written so far should be taken to imply that capitalism does not produce a class society. Modern capitalist society is based upon an inherent conflict of interests between capital and labour and each, in turn, is fractioned within itself. This I take to be axiomatic. My purpose in casting doubt on the practical usefulness of class is not to say that the concept does not have value at a higher level of analysis in comparative and historical sociology. However its frequent incantation is often misplaced and the concept has been debased through inappropriate and uncritical usage.

10

15

20

25

30

35

Source: adapted from R. Pahl, 'Is the emperor naked?', *International Journal of Urban and Regional Research*, Vol. 13, 1989

ITEM C

Marshall *et al.* reject the view that other differences in society are more important in understanding society than are class differences. They find that class is still the main (although not the only) factor influencing the way people see and understand the world. This book was written as part of an international research project on social stratification which will hopefully allow more comparative comments to be available in future. See also O'Donnell (1992), pp. 113–26.

Our analysis suggests, then, that modern Britain is a society shaped predominantly by class rather than other forms of social cleavage, no matter whether the phenomena under scrutiny are structural or cultural in nature. Further evidence to substantiate this claim is readily available from data elsewhere in our survey. These make it clear, for example, that awareness of class is not a function of class location. Among the factors which show no significant variation across classes (by whichever schema these are identified) are the proportions of respondents claiming a class identity; that class is an inevitable feature of modern society; and that there are important issues generating class conflict. Men show no signs of being more class conscious than women; private sector and public sector workers are, in this respect as in others we have examined virtually indistinguishable; and home-ownership is not associated with a heightening or lessening of class awareness.

These points are especially pertinent in the context of sociological discussions about the demise of social class. It has been argued recently that Britain is a society increasingly divided by sectoral and other cleavages which encourage the pursuit of narrow sectional interests in a wholly instrumental fashion. These cleavages cut across social class boundaries and so have under-

5

10

15

20

mined older loyalties to class itself, and to class-related organisa-
tions, such as those of union and party. We would disagree with
this interpretation of consensus and conflict in recessionary   25
Britain on the basis of the twin findings reported in the previous
paragraph. To repeat, our data suggest that, in so far as identities
beliefs and values investigated in this study are socially structured, then the source of this structuring lies in social class differences rather than more fashionable sectoral cleavages.   30

Source: adapted from G. Marshall
*et al., Social Class in Modern
Britain,* London: Unwin Hyman,
1988

ITEM D

Make sure you are clear on
exactly what is meant by the
classless society, since it has
many different meanings. There is
an excellent article on this by
Geoff Payne in *General Studies
Review*, November 1991.

Eight out of 10 people reject the concept of a classless society in
Britain. And just as many Tory Party supporters – 80 per cent –
are convinced there will never be a classless society.

And even the 53 per cent of people who describe themselves as
classless do not believe John Major's dream will ever come true.   5

These are the alarming findings for the Prime Minister in the
Sunday Express/MORI poll.

Twenty-five years after TV's classic *Frost Report* sketch in
which an upper-class John Cleese looked down on a middle-class
Ronnie Barker who in turn looked down on a working-class   10
Ronnie Corbett, Britons are now more aware of class.

The survey found that 34 per cent of people now think of
themselves as belonging to a particular social class. In 1981 the
figure was 29 per cent.

Source: adapted from a report in
the *Sunday Express,* 1 September,
1991

ITEM E

This article highlights the problem
of categorizing identities if, as
postmodernists suggest, there
are no real ways to categorize
people except, perhaps, in terms
of what they consume.

You can link the material here
to the extract on postmodernism
in the question on Modern Social
Theory (p. 48).

But how is it possible to understand modern society if the slip-
pery ground is characterized by the full force of postmodernity?
And how is it possible to begin to consider what a better society
would look like when social and political theory is dominated by
relativism? The answer might lie in simply sustaining debate,   5
analysis and critique . . .

Modern society is relatively unbounded and borderless. A
national economy is nothing more than a site for the flow of capital, an element in the chain of interlocking parts which constitutes the international division of labour.   10

Today, the social relationships and social movements which
breathe life into society cannot be mapped with the predictability
which sociologists used to look for. Such a search is doomed to
fail in a situation where, for example, rapidly changing patterns
of consumption offer a better sense of social identity than the old 15
markers of occupation or class.

Source: adapted from 'How to
cope when class and nation
aren't everything' in the
Guardian, 22 August, 1992

QUESTIONS

a Suggest two identities, other than those mentioned in Item A, which may act as the basis for the 'status blocs' identified by Bryan Turner.

(2 marks)

b What problems have sociologists faced when trying to 'operationalize the concept' of class (Item B, line 20)?

(4 marks)
A *knowledge* and *interpretation* question where you need to identify the main problems involved in categorizing people (perhaps especially women) in terms of class. Make four clear points to get all the marks available. Make them relevant to obtain the *application* marks.

c Using material from the Items and elsewhere, examine the arguments for and against the view that 'it does not follow that the social world has changed as much as the language used to describe it' (Item B, lines 6–7).

(6 marks)
This question requires you to use all skills. Explain what Pahl is saying (i.e. that class remains important but other groupings are easier to identify) and then find material to support and criticize the view. You can get some information from the Items but also look at any textbook to check out the basic Marx–Weber debate. you could try, for example, Giddens(1989), pp. 205–24.

d Explain what the authors of Item C mean when they state that 'awareness of class is not a function of class location' (lines 6–7).

(3 marks)
You need to explain what the writer means (that subjective class awareness does not always match objective class position) and expand on the idea to get all three marks. Use your own words. Are people more likely to behave on the basis of how they categorize themselves or on the basis of how sociologists categorize them? On this issue see O'Donnell (1992), pp. 145–6 or Haralambos and Holborn (1991), pp. 83–100.

e Item A contains the argument put forward by Lash and Urry that 'economic and cultural changes have dislodged class as a key identity for the majority of the population' (lines 2–4). With reference to material in Items D and E, examine to what extent this view is supported by sociological evidence.

(10 marks)
This is the key debate around this issue – do people still identify themselves in terms of class? Use material from the passages and elsewhere and examine arguments for and against to get full marks. Why do you think that, as Item D suggests, people might now be becoming more class conscious? All skills are being tested here.
   A lot of material has been published on this subject and the following extracts from this book provide a good starting point: Conflict Theory, Item C; Modern Social Theory, Items A and B; Bias in Sociology, Item C; Changing Patterns of Work, Items B and C; The Informal Economy, Items C and D; Work and Gender, Item C; Distribution of Income and Wealth, Item A; Gender and Inequality, Items C and D.

ITEM A

Scott's highly readable neo-Marxist analysis of class society is neatly summarized in this extract, where he shows the continuing influence of the major public schools and the 'old boy network' on society. His ideas are also relevant to questions on education and politics.

The public schools collectively take just 5 per cent of the male school population, and a half of these pupils are themselves the sons of former public schoolboys. Over a third of public schoolboys go on to university, overwhelmingly to either Oxford or Cambridge.

Eton was the richest of all the public schools, and its leading figures were, both officially and informally, at the heart of the capitalist class.

In 1983, Old Etonians were to be found as the Governor of the Bank of England, the Chief of the Defence Staff, the editor of *The Times*, the head of the Home Civil Service, and the head of the Foreign Service. The heads of the top 200 wealthiest families of 1990 included 35 Old Etonians, and 25 men who had been officers in the Brigade of Guards were from Eton. Eton remained highly selective in its recruitment from the higher circles, though rather less self-recruiting than before: in 1961, 60 per cent of its pupils were the sons of Old Etonians, but by 1981 this figure had fallen to 43 per cent.

The main continuing significance of the public schools lies in the role played by their 'old boy networks' in class reproduction. This network of connections and contacts, rooted in a similarity of social background and experience, provides the basis for a myriad of other informal contacts and connections.

Source: adapted from J. Scott, *Who Rules Britain?* Cambridge: Polity, 1991

ITEM B

The importance of inheritance, and the barriers to gaining substantial wealth through saving or employment mean that the upper class has maintained a considerable degree of social closure. That style of life and demeanour characteristic of Britain's dominant class are a result of its peculiar history. Unlike many other European countries, the ancient British aristocracy has managed to preserve and transmit its wealth through judicious marriage and inheritance. Far more important however has been the merging of the new bourgeoisie with the traditional aristocracy.

The landed rich became economically active, especially in the eighteenth century, through the rise of commercialized farming, banking and trade with the colonies. When the new class of bourgeois manufacturers and traders arose in the nineteenth century, it was able to merge with the commercialized aristocracy through marriage, and through the newly reformed public schools and universities. Old values and class patterns of behaviour became grafted on to a new economic class. The rise of the Empire and British trading dominance allowed a gentlemanly upper class of senior colonial administrators and City financiers to sustain and nurture distinctly upper-class characteristics. The continued dominance of the City and Civil Service élites has often been seen as a barrier to dynamism in British industry; in

Source: adapted from T. Bilton *et al. Introductory Sociology*, 2nd Ed., London: Macmillan, 1987

fact, it has merely been one aspect of a secure and integrated dominant class, linked by kinship, ownership of wealth and distinctive patterns of education.

ITEM C

This article suggests that the rich have improved their position in relation to the poor over the last decade. This is due mainly to wages rising more rapidly than benefits and a reduction in higher rates of income tax. Not everyone would see this as a bad thing, many people argue that these changes are ultimately good for the economy because wealth and income trickle down from the rich to the poor. To put it simply, the way to make the poor richer is to start by making the rich richer. These ideas were the basis of the policies of Margaret Thatcher, Ronald Reagan and the New Right.

Source: adapted from J. Lawrence 'To those that have' in *New Society*, 15 January, 1988

The top one per cent of earners has seen its income (before tax) rise from £16,000 in 1975–6 to £48,000 in 1984–5. The income of the next 9 per cent has grown from £6,500 to £19,000. The poorest 50 per cent has crawled up from £1,300 to £3,300.

Not everyone has shared equally in the boom. The gap   5
between rich and poor is growing. The distribution of income over the last ten years has become 'steadily more unequal' according to *Social Trends*. After the payment of taxes and the receipt of benefits, the share of disposable income of the bottom 20 per cent of households fell from 7 per cent of the total to 6.5   10
per cent.

The richest have of course been most helped by the tax cuts. The top 1 per cent of tax payers have seen their tax chopped from 46 per cent in 1975–6 to 36 per cent in 1984–5. But the rich have also enjoyed the biggest increase in earnings. The net effect is that   15
the disposable earnings of the top tenth of earners has risen by 18 per cent after inflation since 1980 compared with a 6 per cent rise for the bottom tenth.

ITEM D

These figures come from the *Sunday Times'* annual survey into the rich. Although not produced by sociologists, it is nonetheless a valuable source of material on the upper class in our society. Look out for the latest survey material published in April or May each year.

Source: adapted from a report in the *Sunday Times Magazine*, 10 May, 1992

Britain's Rich – The top 300, the *Sunday Times'* fourth annual survey reveals total wealth of the top 200 equals £47.1 bn, equal to 9.4 per cent of GDP, and of the entire 300, £50.09 bn, equal to 10.03 per cent of GDP. Property is no longer the most common source of wealth. This year it has been superseded by food.   5
Twenty-eight of the people on the list made their money from food and drink. Fifty-nine people on the list went to Eton and 8 to Harrow, 28 to Oxford University and 26 to Cambridge University. Included in the list are 12 Dukes, 7 Marquesses, 7 Viscounts, 17 Earls, 23 Barons and 25 Knights. Of the 300 people,   10
50 were not even worth £1 million before 1979. The top 300 includes 21 women. One hundred and thirty-six of the 300 are from London and the South-East, 26 from Scotland, 25 from Yorkshire, 22 from the North-West, 21 from the South-West, 17 from the East Midlands, 12 from the West Midlands, 6 from East   15
Anglia, 4 from the North-East and 2 from Wales.

ITEM E

This material shows the link between 'the ownership and control of industry' debate and debates on the upper class. You might therefore wish to look up the material on that question in this book (p. 136).

The Weberian, Ralf Dahrendorf, has made a significant contribution to the debate about where power lies in modern societies. He argues that, with the development of large scale joint stock companies which enable the public to buy shares in a company, much control is exercised by top salaried managers and less   5
by capitalist owners. He refers to this process as the decomposition of capital. Dahrendorf therefore sees modern societies as

'managed' societies. He further contends that the rise of managers has produced considerable potential for conflict within the economic élite (that is, between owners and management).   10

Anthony Giddens criticises Dahrendorf sharply on two counts. First he points out that, even though the growth of joint stock companies has broadened the basis of ownership, profit remains the purpose of capitalist enterprise: thus the system is still a capitalist one. In addition, only a minority still gains substantial profit   15
from shareholdings. Giddens' second point is related to his first. He suggest that far from there being a conflict of interest between capitalists and top managers, there is more likely to be a close identity of interest. This is intensified by the fact that many managers are themselves large shareholders in the companies they   20
work in. They are both primarily concerned with the success and profitability of the company.

Source: adapted from M. O'Donnell, *A New Introduction to Sociology*, 3rd Ed., Walton-on-Thames: Nelson, 1992

QUESTIONS

a What does the author of Item A suggest is the main reason for the continuing importance of the public schools?

(2 marks)

b What factors, according to Item C, have contributed to the unequal rise in disposable income for the richest and poorest sectors of the population since 1980?

(2 marks)

c The author of Item B states that 'Old values and class patterns of behaviour became grafted on to a new economic class' (lines 17–18). To what extent does this mean that sociologists cannot define the upper class on solely economic grounds?

(9 marks)   There are marks here are for *evaluation*, *application* and *interpretation* as well as *knowledge*, so focus on the passage. Look at any textbook, such as Haralambos and Holborn (1991), pp. 53–5, to examine the arguments for and against the measurement of class in terms of economic categories. The debate about the continuing importance of the 'old' upper class (i.e. the landed aristocracy in this country), involves issues such as the continuing importance of tradition embodied in feudal hangovers like, for example, the monarchy and the House of Lords.

d According to Item D, what percentage of the top 300 richest people in Britain in 1992 were women? What number went to Eton?

(2 marks)

e The author of Item A refers to the 'capitalist class' (line 7). Using material from Item E and elsewhere, assess the validity of the argument that such a distinct capitalist class exists in the UK today.

(10 marks)

This question clearly requires you to use all skills. Apart from material in the Items (*interpretation and application*), bring in data to support the statement (*knowledge* and *application*) and criticisms such as the constraints on ruling-class power and evidence of social mobility (*evaluation* and *application*). Say what you think and give your reasons to gain full *evaluation* marks. Again material from the question on The Ownership and Control of Industry (p. 136) might be helpful here. You could also try Bilton *et al.* (1987), pp. 90–100 or O'Donnell (1992), pp. 132–6.

5.4 The middle class

ITEM A

Saunders suggests that the middle class is easily identifiable today because it has grown so much this century. He identifies the main groups as professionals, managers and (mainly female) routine non-manual workers. Do you agree with him? Is it middle class or middle *classes*? Does it matter?

Source: adapted from P. Saunders, *Social Class and Stratification*, London: Routledge, 1990

It may be difficult to identify a distinct capitalist class in modern Britain, but there is no such problem in finding the middle class. The middle class (or perhaps more accurately the middle classes) has mushroomed during the twentieth century in all advanced capitalist countries, and Britain is no exception. Figures based on the 1981 Census indicate that 26 per cent of the working population of Great Britain is accounted for by professional and managerial occupations. The growth of the middle class has come about almost entirely as a result of the expansion of professional, managerial and administrative occupations. For many members of this class, the state has become the major source of new employment opportunities as it has expanded its activities to areas like health, education and social welfare. 5 ... 10

The biggest single grouping in the lower middle class is that of routine non-manual employees in clerical, secretarial and similar occupations. By 1981, clerical and related occupations had expanded to account for 16 per cent of the working population. Not only has clerical work expanded enormously during the twentieth century, but it has become overwhelmingly a female occupation. 15 ... 20

ITEM B

This report from the *Sunday Express* suggests that the middle class has continued to grow over the last decade. Can you see any problem with the way class is defined here?

Source: adapted from a report in the *Sunday Express*, 1 September, 1991

'When Mrs Thatcher took office in 1979 one third of the British public – 33 per cent – was objectively classified as middle class' says Professor Robert Worcester, Chairman of MORI. 'A decade later 41 per cent was middle class. That represents the biggest change in society's class structure in over 1,000 years of British history.' And more people would now describe themselves as upper or middle class rather than working class. Ten years ago a similar survey found that 28 per cent opted for upper or middle class and 63 per cent for working class. Today's figures, are respectively, 30 and 61 per cent. 5 ... 10

ITEM C

Westergaard and Resler suggest that the term middle class has become almost meaningless because it covers such a range of workers, including the upper class. Their book is now quite old but it is still a classic example of Marxist analysis.
Source: J. Westergaard and H. Resler, *Class in a Capitalist Society*, Harmondsworth, Penguin, 1975

'Middle class' is often used as an umbrella term of startling elasticity to describe all sections of the population who are not manual workers; from routine-grade office labour, increasingly indistinguishable in market position from manual workers, to the very top. If an upper crust is distinguished, it is as likely to be defined by traditional criteria of social esteem, or by way of indiscriminate occupational bracketing, as by those criteria of economic position and power which are relevant for a diagnosis of class 'in itself'. But in many instances, 'middle class' covers the whole span beyond 'working class' (itself usually conceived as embracing only the mass of manual workers): nonsensically 'middle' between a lower group and a vacuum. 5 ... 10

ITEM D

From a study of images of class, Roberts, Cook, Clark and Semeonoff claim that 'The days when it was realistic to talk about the middle class are gone'. They argue that the middle class is increasingly divided into a number of different strata, each with a distinctive view of its place within the stratification system. They found a number of different images of class. Some 27 per cent of the white-collar sample had a 'middle mass' image of society. They saw themselves as part of a middle class made up of the bulk of the working population. The second image, held by 19 per cent of the sample, was that of a 'compressed middle class'. They saw themselves as members of a narrow stratum which was squeezed between two increasingly powerful classes. A third group saw society in terms of a finely graded ladder containing four or more strata. Although this was assumed to be the typical middle-class image of society, it was subscribed to by only 15 per cent of the sample. Finally, 14 per cent of the sample held a 'proletarian' image of society. They defined themselves as working class and located themselves in what they saw as the largest class as the base of the stratification system.

The diversity of class images, market situations, market strategies and interests within the white-collar group suggests that the middle class is becoming increasingly fragmented.

Source: adapted from M. Haralambos and M. Holborn, *Sociology: Themes and Perspectives,* 3rd Ed., London: Collins Educational, 1991

ITEM E

This article neatly summarizes the argument about the class position of clerical workers. The Marxist view is that due to deskilling they are becoming working class, while non-Marxists point to differences in their position and perception compared to manual workers. Does the fact that most of them are women make a difference? For more information on this debate see the entry for the Middle Class in Slattery's *ABC of Sociology*, pp. 66–8 or O'Donnell (1992), pp. 136–44 or Abercrombie and Warde *et al.* (1988), pp. 169–85. Also look at the material on the question on Work and Gender in this book (p. 157).

Source: R. Pawson, 'Social stratification' in M. Haralambos (Ed), *Developments in Sociology,* Vol. 1, Ormskirk: Causeway, 1985

The thesis that clerical workers are becoming incorporated into the working class represents perhaps the most long-standing debate in the stratification literature. Traditionally the fight has been between, in the red corner, sociologists like Westergaard who have pointed to the progressive loss of advantage of clerical over manual workers in terms of wage levels, routinization of work, fringe benefits and, more recently, even their resistance to unemployment; out of the blue corner, have come the responses, beginning with Lockwood, which point out that though the economic or market situation of clerical workers may be weakened, there are still a range of important work and status differences such as qualification requirements, regular interaction with management, superior work conditions, relative prestige of 'brain work', which act as a spur to their separate class identification.

QUESTIONS

a   What explanations have sociologists given for the expansion of the middle class (Item A)?

(4 marks)

b   With reference to Item B, what was the rise in the percentage of people describing themselves as either upper or middle class between 1981 and 1991?

(1 mark)

c   Item C suggests that white-collar workers are 'increasingly indistinguishable . . . from manual workers' (lines 3–4). Using material from Item E and elsewhere, assess the extent to which this view is supported by sociological evidence.

(9 marks)   This question requires you to use all skills, as it asks you to use 'material in the Items' (*interpretation* and *application*) and 'elsewhere' (*knowledge* and *application*) and to 'assess the extent' (*evaluation*). Use 'sociological evidence' to support both sides of the argument and to draw your own conclusions. Material on the proletarianization debate is included in Haralambos and Holborn (1991), pp. 75–80, Bilton *et al.*, 2nd Ed., pp. 105–7 and the articles by May, Crompton and Jones in Trowler (1987), *Active Sociology*, pp. 49–56.

d   Item B refers to people being 'objectively classified as middle class' (line 2). Suggest two criteria which might be used to make such a classification.

(2 marks)

e   Item D contains the argument that 'the days when it was realistic to talk about the middle class are gone' (lines 2–3). Examine the arguments for and against this view.

(9 marks)   This question requires you to use all skills to analyse the argument about whether there is one middle class or many. Making a plan will help you to produce a clear answer. You can gain *application* marks by demonstrating the relevance to the question of a particular study. Helpful material can be found in Haralambos and Holborn (1991), pp. 63–83, or O'Donnell (1992) pp. 136–44.

ITEM A

Self-rated social class in Britain, 1986

Social class (%)	Self	Parents
Upper middle	1	2
Middle	24	17
Upper working	21	12
Working	48	59
Poor	3	8
Don't know/no response	3	2
Sample size (= 100%) (numbers)	3,066	3,066

Source: A. Giddens, *Sociology*, Cambridge: Polity, 1989

ITEM B

This item suggests that many working-class people now have a more instrumental view of work than in the past. Relate this to the Affluent Worker study conducted by Goldthorpe and Lockwood. You will find information on this in O'Donnell (1992), pp. 141–4 or Haralambos and Holborn (1991), pp. 88–92. There is an extract from their work in Trowler (1987), pp. 56–58.

Source: adapted from A. Giddens, *Sociology* Cambridge: Polity, 1989

A classic discussion of class imagery was developed by David Lockwood in the 1960s. Lockwood's discussion concentrates on the working class, distinguishing three main types of working-class image of society:

1 **Proletarian traditionalism**. Workers holding this type of class imagery see the world in terms of a division between 'us' and 'them'.   5

2 **Deferential traditionalism**. Such workers see the class structure in more co-operative and harmonious terms. These workers are deferential towards their superiors and aware of the class hierarchy, but accept it as legitimate and necessary.   10

3 **Privatized workers**. These workers have broken with both of the other types of outlook. They see work mainly as a way of achieving a satisfactory lifestyle for themselves and their families, and feel few of the old class loyalties.

ITEM C

This extract from Saunders' book suggests that the number of people defined as working class has declined. He also claims that some writers are beginning to revive the issue of embourgeoisement.

Goldthorpe and Lockwood's work on the Affluent Worker sought to test the validity of this thesis when it first emerged. You will need to look at the relevant studies carefully to engage fully in this debate. To be recommended is Marshall *et al.* (1988). If you can't get hold of the actual book there is an extract from it in *The New Modern Sociology Readings*

The OPCS divides the manual working class into three categories – skilled workers such as fitters, bus drivers and trained coalface workers; semi-skilled workers like machinists, bus conductors and storekeepers; and unskilled workers such as labourers, refuse collectors and cleaners. The manual working class as a   5
whole has been shrinking and by the 1981 Census it accounted for just 51 per cent of the employed population. This shrinkage has been particularly marked in the unskilled stratum as technological change has reduced demand for sheer muscle power: unskilled manual workers made up less than 7 per cent of the   10
workforce. This compares with skilled workers who still represent one quarter of all those employed (and 36 per cent of all the men employed) in Britain.

The Affluent Worker study effectively killed off academic concern with the issue of embourgeoisement for nearly twenty   15
years. Recently, however, the thesis has re-emerged, though in a rather different form. As in the 1950s, so too in the 1980s work-

edited by Peter Worsley. Again in Worsley the article by A. H. Halsey is also relevant. There is an entry for Embourgeoisement in Slattery (1985), *ABC of Sociology*, pp. 30–1. Note when this material was first published and think about the relevance of embourgeoisement during an economic recession.

Source: adapted from P. Saunders, *Social Class and Stratification*, London: Routledge, 1990

ing-class living standards have been rising and a sustained consumer boom has meant that many working-class people have bought their houses and made them into the principal focus of their lives. The old staple industries have been run down over the years while new technologies have generated new kinds of working-class employment. On top of all this, the Conservative Party has secured three successive general election victories since 1979 just as it did from the years 1951 to 1959. [20] [25]

All this has led some sociologists to ask whether the embourgeoisement thesis was perhaps developed a quarter of a century in advance of its time. If the workers of the sixties were not shedding their class skin, what of the workers of the eighties and nineties? [30]

ITEM D

Lukes (1984) argues that technological change, the increased participation of women in paid employment, and 'politicization of the market' via state intervention in economic processes, together with the shift from manufacturing to service industries, have made the distinction between manual and non-manual labour largely irrelevant. Indeed, with the rise of mass production and consumption, labour or work itself has become less central to the identity and consciousness of workers. More and more, the working class is concerned with issues of consumption. British workers having come to terms with the acquisitive society, have settled down to seek their private satisfactions at home and in leisure and to pursue conflicting sectional demands in the workplace. [5] [10]

The Marxist historian Eric Hobsbawm, in a controversial and much debated volte-face, has arrived at similar conclusions based on a review of British labour history (Hobsbawm, 1981). According to his account the solidarity of shared lifestyle and common political objectives among the traditional British working class have been undermined since the 1950s by the growth of public-sector employment and of multinational corporations. This, together with the increased but uneven participation of women in paid labour, the expansion of non-manual employment, and postwar immigration from the new Commonwealth, has encouraged 'a growing division of workers into sections and groups, each pursuing its own economic interest irrespective of the rest'. Everywhere, according to Hobsbawm, solidaristic forms of political consciousness have given way to 'the values of consumer-society individualism and the search for private and personal satisfactions above all else'. [15] [20] [25]

Source: adapted from G. Marshall 'What is happening to the working class?' in *Social Studies Review*, January 1987

ITEM E

Little support is provided for the views of Goldthorpe and Lockwood in a more recent study of the British stratification system carried out by Gordon Marshall, Howard Newby, David Rose and Carolyn Vogler. Based on a national sample of 1,770 adults, the study found that 'sectionalism, instrumentalism, and privatism among the British working class are not characteristics somehow peculiar to the recent years of economic recession'. [5]

Source: adapted from M. Haralambos and M. Holborn, *Sociology: Themes and Perspectives*, 3rd Ed., London: Collins Educational, 1991

Marshall *et al.* claim that historical studies demonstrate the existence of artisans who put primary emphasis on their home life, and who had an instrumental attitude to work, well back into the   10
nineteenth century. Furthermore, their data on contemporary workers suggests that they retain some commitment to their work, and do not lead completely privatized lifestyles. Marshall *et al.* claim in relation to instrumentalism and privatism 'There are no grounds to suppose that these phenomena have been   15
increasing or changing in any significant way'.

QUESTIONS

a According to Item A, what percentage of the population described itself as either working or upper working class in 1986?

(1 mark)

b What criticisms have sociologists made of the categories used by Lockwood as outlined in Item B?

(4 marks)

c According to Item C, which section of the working class has seen the greatest decline?

(1 mark)

d Eric Hobsbawm claims that there has been 'a growing division of workers into sections and groups, each pursuing its own economic interest irrespective of the rest' (Item D lines 24–6). Examine the evidence for and against the view that there is no longer a unified working class in Britain.

(9 marks)

A longer answer is required here, using all skills. You need to look at several writers, including those in the Items, to argue for and against the view that the working class is becoming more divided. See for instance Abercrombie and Warde *et al.* (1988), pp. 144–69 or Bilton *et al.* (1987), pp. 108–15. Refer any conclusions to sociological studies as well as current economic conditions and political events to get *application* marks.

e The author of Item C states that the embourgeoisement thesis re-emerged in the 1980s. With reference to material in Item E and elsewhere, examine the extent to which sociological evidence supports the notion of embourgeoisement in contemporary Britain.

(10 marks)

Another long answer requiring planning and research to make it effective. Refer to the sources of the Items to guide your reading. Make sure you define and understand the terms used and the arguments presented before offering your conclusions. Notice that the material in the Items does not give a full explanation of the idea of embourgeoisement so consult other textbooks for guidance, for example Bilton *et al.* (1987), pp. 111–12. Look up Devine (1992) for an update of the Affluent Worker Study. Always examine arguments and evidence critically. You must demonstrate all skills in your answer. Remember to use the material provided here and in other studies to support both sides of the argument and to apply them to the question.

5.6 The underclass

ITEM A

In recent years the idea has developed that some of these people who do not regularly participate in the formal economy might validly be said to represent an 'underclass' in British society.

There are four key features of the underclass: it suffers multiple deprivation, it is socially marginal, it is almost entirely dependent upon state welfare provisions, and its culture is one of resigned fatalism.

Inactivity breeds apathy. Empty hours are filled with sleep, and days go by in a dull haze of television programmes and signing on. Sooner or later, the unemployed become unemployable, and even when jobs are found they are swiftly lost.

Source: adapted from P. Saunders, *Social Class and Stratification*, London: Routledge, 1990

ITEM B

Why people are poor?			%
Why in your opinion are there people who live in need? Here are four opinions – which is closest to yours?	1976 (UK)	1983 (GB)	1990 (GB)
Because they have been unlucky	10	13	10
Because of laziness and lack of willpower	43	22	19
Because there is much injustice in our society	16	32	40
It's an inevitable part of modern progress	17	25	19
None of these	4	5	3
Don't know	10	3	8

Source: H. Frayman, *Breadline Britain 1990s*, London: Domino Films/LWT, 1991

ITEM C

Despite the fact that the notion of an underclass has been propagated by writers who favour a cultural view and question the need for structural changes or, indeed, the value of a welfare state, it should not be assumed that the concept is used only in this way. One American sociologist, for example, has argued that structural changes have created an underclass of poor black families who live in inner city ghettos and are effectively isolated from the rest of society (Wilson, 1989). The 'deplorable behaviour' of such people 'should be analysed not as a cultural aberration but as a symptom of class inequality', for 'if underclass blacks have low aspirations or do not plan for the future, it is not ultimately the result of different cultural norms but the product of restricted opportunities'.

Of the two major approaches which seek to account for the growth of an underclass – the cultural and the structural – it is the latter which has been more prominent in Britain.

Source: adapted from A. Pilkington, 'Is there a British underclass' in *Sociology Review*, February 1992

ITEM D

'Underclass' is an ugly word, with its whiff of Marx and the lumpenproletariat. Perhaps because it is ugly, 'underclass' as used in Britain tends to be sanitized, a sort of synonym for people who are not just poor, but especially poor. So let us get it straight from the outset: the 'underclass' does not refer to degree of poverty, but to a type of poverty. 5

Britain does have an underclass, still largely out of sight and still smaller than the one in the United States. But it is growing rapidly. Within the next decade, it will probably become as large (proportionately) as the United States' underclass. It could easily become larger. 10

I am not talking here about an unemployment problem that can be solved by more jobs, nor about a poverty problem that can be solved by higher benefits. Britain has a growing population of working-aged, healthy people who live in a different world from other Britons, who are raising their children to live in it, and whose values are now contaminating the life of entire neighbourhoods – which is one of the most insidious aspects of the phenomenon, for neighbours who don't share their values cannot isolate themselves. 15

20

There are many ways to identify an underclass. I will concentrate on three phenomena that have turned out to be early-warning signals in the United States: illegitimacy, violent crime, and drop-out from the labour force.

Source: adapted from C. Murray, 'Underclass', in the *Sunday Times Magazine,* 26 November, 1989

ITEM E

The categorization of poor people in statistics is normally according to family and employment status. Traditionally, there has always been a tendency to categorize poor people, albeit not statistically, according to their respectability or 'deservingness', i.e. according to moral rather than economic or demographic characteristics. 5

Recently we have seen a revival of such thinking on the New Right, spearheaded by US writers such as Charles Murray. They are attempting to revive moral distinctions, using the concepts of 'behavioral poverty' and the 'underclass'. In other words, it is argued that their poverty is the product of their own behaviour, such as having illegitimate children or avoiding work. This behaviour is then, the theory goes, reinforced by the social security system itself, which encourages and perpetuates dependency on the State. 10

15

The danger is that the concept of the underclass is so imprecise that it gets stretched to describe the poor generally, and so value-laden and emotive that it stigmatizes them as a group apart.

Source: adapted from R. Lister 'Concepts of poverty', *Social Studies Review,* May 1991

QUESTIONS

a State two of the characteristics of the underclass, according to the author of Item A.

(2 marks)

b According to Item B, what was the reason for people being poor given by the largest number of people in 1976 and in 1990?

(2 marks)

c   The author of Item C argues that there are two versions of the underclass thesis. Using material from the Items above and elsewhere compare and contrast these two approaches.

(7 marks)

d   Using material from the Items above and elsewhere, assess the argument put forward by the author of Item D that 'Britain has a growing population of working-aged healthy people who live in a different world from other Britons' (lines 14–16).

(6 marks)

e   Examine the arguments for and against the view that 'the concept of the underclass is so imprecise that it gets stretched to describe the poor generally, and so value-laden and emotive that it stigmatises them as a group apart' (Item E, lines 16–18)

(8 marks).

5.7 Gender and inequality

How much do they earn?

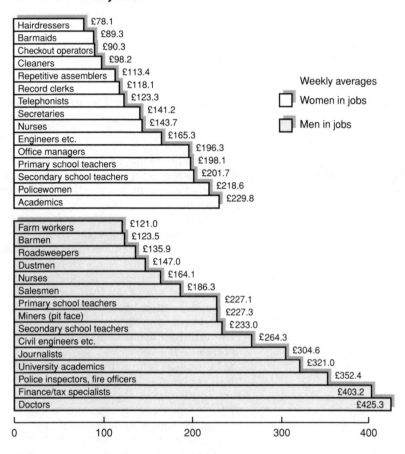

Weekly averages
- Women in jobs
- Men in jobs

Women in jobs:
- Hairdressers £78.1
- Barmaids £89.3
- Checkout operators £90.3
- Cleaners £98.2
- Repetitive assemblers £113.4
- Record clerks £118.1
- Telephonists £123.3
- Secretaries £141.2
- Nurses £143.7
- Engineers etc. £165.3
- Office managers £196.3
- Primary school teachers £198.1
- Secondary school teachers £201.7
- Policewomen £218.6
- Academics £229.8

Men in jobs:
- Farm workers £121.0
- Barmen £123.5
- Roadsweepers £135.9
- Dustmen £147.0
- Nurses £164.1
- Salesmen £186.3
- Primary school teachers £227.1
- Miners (pit face) £227.3
- Secondary school teachers £233.0
- Civil engineers etc. £264.3
- Journalists £304.6
- University academics £321.0
- Police inspectors, fire officers £352.4
- Finance/tax specialists £403.2
- Doctors £425.3

(axis: 0 100 200 300 400)

Source: *New Earnings Surveys,*
1970–9 and 1986 quoted in
'Levels of pay', *New Society
Database,* New Society, 23
January, 1987 and *Social Trends
1992, Employment Gazette,* June
1992 quoted in A. Anderton, *The
Economy in Focus,* 1992/3,
Ormskirk: Causeway, 1992

Wage inequality between males and females (ratio of female to male gross weekly earnings, full-time employees)

	1971	1976	1981	1986	1991
Manual employees	0.53	0.62	0.62	0.62	0.63
Non-manual employees	0.52	0.61	0.61	0.59	0.63
All employees	0.57	0.66	0.67	0.66	0.70

The 1984 amendment to the Equal Pay Act, requiring employers
to pay men and women equally for work of equal value, has had
little impact, according to an Equal Opportunities Commission
study published today.

Men and women are still routinely grouped in different pay
structures which reflect the continuing job segregation in the
labour market.

5

Even women in the same pay structure as men are often marginalized in the lower grades, the report finds . . .

The report, which surveyed public and private sector industries,   10
finds that few employers have assessed their pay practices against
the equal value legislation, and that job evaluation schemes have
brought only marginal improvements in women's pay.

Bonuses and premium payments for overtime and shiftwork
are often out of reach for women because of domestic commit-   15
ments. Part-timers miss out on payments because of their work
patterns, and merit pay schemes are commonly limited to managerial grades, dominated by men.

Source: adapted from a report in
the *Guardian*, 25 March, 1991

ITEM C

Feminists challenge and oppose patriarchal ideologies by
demonstrating their partial and distorted view of the world.
Patriarchal ideologies have the effect of disguising the actuality
of male power. Men defined themselves as powerful because
of their ability to master nature – to be dominant. Women, because   5
of their biological role in reproduction, are defined as being closer
to nature than men, thus justifying their domina-
tion by men. Male ideology confirms and reinforces men's
dominant status by devaluing women's work and reproductive
functions while at the same time presenting male work as of   10
cultural importance and as necessary. Masculinity is equated with
the public sphere; to be a man is to be a person who does important
things outside the domestic sphere – who does man's work.

All feminists agree that women's oppression is primary.
However, radical feminists argue that women have shared   15
interests because they are all exploited and oppressed by men.
Women, then are said to form a class that is in conflict with
another class – men.

The radical feminist position has mainly been developed by
the French feminist Christine Delphy. Delphy argues that while   20
sociologists have regarded occupational class inequalities as
primary, their own research demonstrates that sexual inequality
is primary and more fundamental than occupational inequality.
Thus women's oppression cannot be regarded as secondary to,
and therefore less important than, class oppression.   25

Abbott and Sapsford argue that their analysis of the data on
the female respondents in the Open University 'People in
Society' survey demonstrates that women do have a subjective
class identification and that this is no better predicted from the
husband's or head of household's occupation than from the   30
woman's own occupation and/or personal and 'pre-marital'
attributes such as class of origin (determined by father's
occupation) and educational level. Women's overall social
imagery, whether they saw society as conflictual or harmonious
and divided or homogeneous, was again no better predicted by   35
the head of household's class than by a woman's own attributes.
They conclude that the view that a woman's class sentiments are
solely and necessarily determined by the occupation of the man
with whom she lives is not sustainable.

Source: adapted from P. Abbott
and C. Wallace, *An Introduction
to Sociology: Feminist Perspectives,*
London: Routledge, 1990

ITEM D

The view that class inequalities largely govern gender stratification was often an unstated assumption until recently, but the issue has now become the subject of some debate. John Goldthorpe has defended what he calls the 'conventional position' in class analysis – that the paid work of women is relatively insignificant compared to that of men, and that therefore women can be regarded as being in the same class as their husbands. This is not, Goldthorpe emphasizes, a view based upon an ideology of sexism. On the contrary it recognizes the subordinate position in which most women find themselves in the labour-force. Since the majority of women are in a position of economic dependency on their husbands, it follows that their class position is most often governed by the husbands' class position.

Goldthorpe's argument can be criticized in several ways. First, in a substantial proportion of households the income of women is essential to maintaining the family's economic position. Second, a wife's employment may strongly influence that of her husband, not simply the other way round. Third, many 'cross-class' households exist, in which the work of the husband is in a higher class category than that of the wife, or (less commonly) the other way round. Fourth, the proportion of families in which women are the sole breadwinners is increasing.

Source: adapted from A. Giddens, *Sociology* Cambridge: Polity Press, 1989

5

10

15

20

ITEM E

Married couples with both partners economically active, by social class of husband and wife

Husband's social class	Percentage of wives whose social class is different from husband's
I	93.8
II	66.2
III non-manual	48.7
III manual	87.8
IV	63.5
V	77.6

Source: A. Oakley, *The Sociology of Housework*, Oxford: Martin Robertson, 1974

QUESTIONS

a With reference to Item A, identify two occupations where there was unequal pay for men and women in 1986.

(2 marks)

b Illustrating your answer with material from the Items above and elsewhere, examine the arguments for and against the proposition that the Equal Pay Act has had little impact (Item B).

(5 marks)

c Item C puts forward the view that 'sexual inequality is primary and more fundamental than occupational inequality' (lines 23–24). How far this view is supported by sociological evidence?

(7 marks)

d Briefly explain the meaning of the term 'patriarchal ideologies' (Item C, line 1).

(2 marks)

e Items C and D contain very different views on the social class categorization of women. With reference to material in Item E and elsewhere, discuss these points of view and assess their relative merits.

(9 marks)

5.8 Ethnicity and inequality

ITEM A

Ethnic minority population: by age and whether UK-born or overseas-born, 1985–87 (Great Britain)

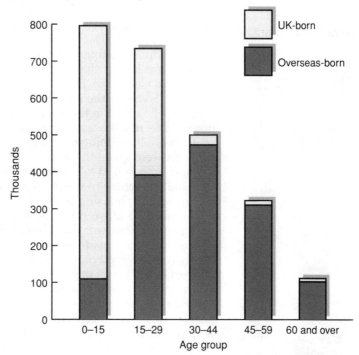

Source: Social Trends 1990,
London: HMSO, 1990

ITEM B

Britain is the only country in the world to refuse entry to its own nationals to the national territory.

The most recent Act, the 1981 British Nationality Act, epitomises the nature of these laws. For example Section 39 of the Act gives several million (almost all white) existing 'partial' government citizens the same right of abode in the UK that British citizens are to have. At the same time, British Dependent Territory Citizens, British Overseas Citizens, British Protected Citizens and British subjects without citizenship of any commonwealth country are to have no right of abode under the Act. The vast majority of people in these categories are of Indian, Chinese, Afro-Caribbean or other non-European descent.

Effective controls on the immigration of people from the commonwealth began in 1962. The policies which were developed at this time were based very much on what has come to be known as the 'numbers game'. Essentially, the 'numbers game' works on the premise that the fewer black people live in Britain, the better race relations will be. Implicit in this theory is the belief that black people, and not the response of white people to black people, are the source of race conflict.

This ethos in British society, however, does not just affect the unfortunate 'illegal' immigrant but all black people.

Source: adapted from 'White attitudes: the rhetoric and the reality' by Pam Nanda in A. Bhat, R. Carr-Hill and S. Ohri (Eds) *Britain's Black Population,* 2nd Ed., Aldershot: Gower, 1988

ITEM C

As we systematically compare the jobs, incomes, unemployment rates, private housing, local authority housing, local environments and other aspects of the lives of people with different ethnic origins, a single argument emerges in respect of the way the circumstances of black people came to be and continue to be   5
worse off than those of white people. In its most general form, the argument runs as follows. Asian and West Indian immigrants came to Britain not as a result of a migratory fever, but as a result of the availability of jobs that offered rates of pay that were higher than those that could be obtained by the migrants in their   10
countries of origin. There were openings for immigrants because the expanding economy of the 1950s and early 1960s created demands for labour that could not be satisfied from within the indigenous workforce. However, these openings were located at the lower levels of the job market, in jobs left behind by white   15
workers who could in this period more easily become upwardly mobile. The result was that even highly qualified immigrants found themselves doing manual work, while those without qualifications were given the very worst jobs. The same mechanism operated with regard to housing and residential area. Asians and   20
West Indians settled in the areas that white people were leaving, and in the poor housing stock no longer wanted by whites who could afford to move on or who were housed by the council. Black people came from the former colonies into this country to a position of ready-made disadvantage; their entry into British   25
society was a replacement for the lost battalions of urban manual workers, not, as it might have been, as a group of newcomers with a varied range of qualifications, skills and abilities who could make contributions at all levels of society. And perhaps the most serious aspect of this movement of immigrant workers into   30
the unwanted jobs and housing at the foot of the social pyramid was that the patterns of disadvantage were bound to reproduce themselves rather than gradually disappear.

Source: C. Brown, *Black and White Britain – The Third PSI Survey*, London: Heinemann, 1984

ITEM D

On the basis of their study of Handsworth in Birmingham, Rex and Tomlinson argued that there were clear differences of life chances between ethnic minorities and the white British, which meant that the former had 'a different kind of position in the labour market, a different housing situation, and a different kind   5
of schooling'. Subject to racism and distinctly disadvantaged in these three sectors, the minorities constituted an underclass in British society, increasingly conscious of their subordinate position and the need to pursue their interests in a distinct and militant fashion. Given the increasing racism among white people,   10
who saw the newcomers as responsible for the deterioration of the inner city, and the absence of any community-wide organizations, the authors pessimistically concluded that 'the greatest likelihood is that conflict in the community will grow'.

Source: adapted from A. Pilkington, 'Is there a British underclass?' in *Sociology Review*, February 1992

ITEM E

Source: adapted from a report in
Labour Research, August 1991

Racial attacks in the London Borough of Greenwich in the first five months of this year increased by 140 per cent compared to the same period in 1990. Earlier this year the borough's Thamesmead area was the focus of anti-racist marches following the murder of two black men, Rolan Adams and Orvil Blair. Figures supplied by Greenwich Council for Racial Equality (GCRE) in its 1990–91 annual report show an increase in attacks from 52 between January and May 1990, to 125 in the same period in 1991. Nine black families have been forced to leave their homes in the face of threats of racial attacks.

5

QUESTIONS

a Suggest one reason for the pattern shown in Item A.

(1 mark)

b Explain in your own words the effect of the 1981 British Nationality Act (Item B).

(3 marks)

c Using material from the Items above and elsewhere, assess the view that ethnic minorities are over-represented in manual jobs largely because they are 'a group of newcomers' (Item C, line 27).

(6 marks)

d The author of Item D argues that racism among white people is increasing. Referring to material in Item E and elsewhere, assess how far this view is supported by sociological evidence.

(7 marks)

e How useful is the concept of the underclass (Item D) in explaining the position of ethnic minorities in contemporary Britain?

(8 marks)

ITEM A

In the last 30 years the greatest single influence on the sociological study of childhood has been the work of the French demographic historian Phillippe Ariès.

The basis of this impact has been the growing acceptance that childhood, like so many other vitally important aspects of social life – gender, health, youth and so on – was socially constructed. Contemporary researchers now see this as the main bulwark of a new paradigm (or conceptual framework) through which to study children and childhood. 5

There are a number of important implications which flow immediately from this new approach. First, as Prout and James point out, a great deal of conventional thinking about childhood, particularly in the fields of medicine and psychology, is called into question. This thinking has in general been biological and evolutionary in its orientation. 10

Secondly, within sociology, similar objections will be made from within the new paradigm to functionalist accounts of childhood. These accounts place heavy emphasis on the importance of a socialization process, through which the child learns its prescribed social role(s). According to the new view, this renders the child merely as a passive recipient. 20

Ariès' basic proposition that childhood is socially constructed has been developed to the realization that it is constructed by adults, with little regard to how it is, or might be, constructed by children themselves. In the new paradigm, notions of fixed roles or biologically based sequences of development are inadmissible. It also means more attention will be paid to the objectification of children: how, in other words, they are framed as passive, both by the adults who wield power directly over them and by theorists who have written about their social world. Children are always having things done to them: being loved, abused, protected, played with or not played with. They are much discussed but never consulted. They are not seen as people, nor as active in their own lives. 25 30

Source: adapted from S. Wagg, 'I blame the parents: childhood and politics in modern Britain' in *Sociology Review*, April 1992

ITEM B

In British society, becoming old is linked to economic and legal definitions associated with pension rights, and especially for men, definitions of economic productivity. Entry to old age is unlike many other important status changes, such as graduating or getting married, in a number of ways. It is not generally a valued status, and there are few 'rites of passage' to signal entry into it, especially for those not previously in full-time paid employment. There is little prior socialization for the role, which is amorphous and unstructured: there are very few social rules for 'being old'. 5 10

Entry to old age is defined primarily by an 'emptying out' of roles and activities which is largely irreversible as a result of such things as job loss, the death of a spouse and reduced income. Whereas other status changes typically involve new roles and responsibilities as well as the relinquishing of previous roles and responsibilities, the entry to old age is characterized primarily by the loss of roles, activities and responsibilities, but without the acquisition of new ones. Over time, the cumulative effect is to generate and encourage the loss of independence, particularly where there are financial and health difficulties. This creates problems for old people who wish to retain their autonomy and control over life. 20

It is also important to be aware of individual and social variations within the broad picture outlined above. In particular there are clear gender and social class differences. 25

Source: adapted from D. Field, 'Elderly people in British society', in *Sociology Review*, April 1992

ITEM C

A stereotype is an oversimplified belief which tends to persist despite contradictory factual evidence. The table below shows a high level of negative stereotypes about old age among the American public.

Differences between personal experiences of Americans aged 65 and over, and expectations held by other adults about those experiences

	Very serious problems experienced by the elderly themselves (percentage)	Very serious problems the public expects the elderly to experience (percentage)	net difference
Fear of crime	23	50	+27
Poor health	21	51	+30
Not having enough money to live on	15	62	+47
Loneliness	12	60	+48
Not having enough medical care	10	44	+34
Not having enough education	8	20	+12
Not feeling needed	7	54	+47
Not having enough to do to keep busy	6	37	+31
Not having enough friends	5	28	+23
Not having enough job opportunities	5	45	+40
Poor housing	4	35	+31
Not having enough clothes	3	16	+13

Clearly many old people find old age less problematic than younger people expect. For every one elderly person who found things worse than expected, three found them better. Hendricks and Hendricks comment that on the whole: 'Income and racial background have been identified as having a greater impact on life satisfaction than does age'. 10

This last point is important. The old are stratified in social-class terms as are other age groups. For a substantial minority of the old in the United States, and perhaps a larger one in Britain, their 'problems' are caused by poverty rather than by age.

Source: adapted from M. O'Donnell, *Age and Generation*, London: Routledge, 1985

ITEM D

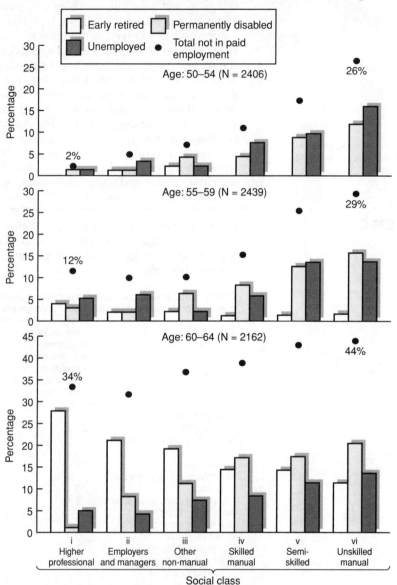

Proportion of men not in paid employment by social class and age

Source: S. Arber, 'Class and the elderly' in *Social Studies Review,* January 1989

ITEM E

The Government is to block new laws to protect child workers across Europe despite evidence of widespread illegal employment of youngsters. But the move has provoked outrage from child welfare experts and charities, who have discovered:

- children as young as 10 leaving school at 3.30 pm for factory shifts
- a 12 year-old boy working for less than £1 an hour in a dangerous lighting factory

5

- schoolchildren absconding to work
- thousands of children working in fields and farm enterprises 10
  – some illegally, others legally but on rock-bottom wages.

The proposed EC directive would increase the minimum working age for children from 13 to 15, with a few exceptions such as paper rounds. And it would revive safeguards on working conditions for 16 to 17-year-olds recently removed in Britain. 15
A spokesman for the Department of Employment refused to reveal Britain's position on the directive – due to be discussed by Employment Ministers early next year.

But the Government's tough stance on teenage labour is confirmed in a letter obtained by the *Observer*. It was written by Eric 20 Forth, then an Employment Minister. 'To legislate in this area would constitute unwarranted interference and put unnecessary burdens on business. It was for precisely these reasons that the Employment Act 1989 removed existing restrictions on young people's terms and conditions of work' he wrote. 25

The Low Pay Unit estimates that about 43 per cent of children aged between 10 and 16 have jobs. Many are employed illegally; about 25 per cent are believed to earn £1 per hour or less.

In Birmingham, Britain's second largest education authority, teachers are reporting a worrying trend of schoolchildren 30 absconding to work.

'There is now a glut in the market for 14 to 16-year-olds, who often work very hard, for a pittance' said Ann Searle, principal child employment officer. 'They think they are getting a foothold in the jobs market. Then they get to 17 and are sacked before their 35 wages go up. Our laws have not changed much since we sent children up chimneys, and we are slipping backwards.'

Source: adapted from a report by S. Lonsdale and P.Ghazi in the *Observer*, 15 November, 1992

QUESTIONS

a Explain in your own words the differences between the new and old paradigms of childhood as outlined in Item A.

(5 marks)

b In relation to which aspect of life were the stereotypical views about old aged people most unrepresentative of the way old people felt (Item C)?

(1 mark)

c According to Item E, what percentage of children aged between 10 and 16 have jobs and what percentage earn below £1 per hour?

(2 marks)

d Illustrating your answer with material from Item E and elsewhere, assess the relative importance of the various agencies involved 'in theobjectification of children' (Item A, lines 27–8).

(7 marks)

e   The author of Item B argues that in relation to old age there are clear 'Gender and social class differences' (line 25). Using material from Item D and elsewhere, consider to what extent this means age itself is unimportant as a basis for inequality in relation to all age groups.

(10 marks)

5.10 Social mobility

ITEM A

Given the very considerable degree of movement between classes, it might be imagined that Britain has become a fairer, more open society, with opportunity becoming less and less dependent on class origins. In an important sense, though, this is a misleading impression. Much of the upward mobility into the service class is merely the consequence of changes in the occupational structure. What Goldthorpe *et al.* point out is that the service class increased in size to such an extent that, even if every son of a service-class father had obtained a service-class job, there would still have been more men with origins in other classes in the service class in 1972.

This fact led Goldthorpe *et al.* to try to separate out absolute mobility, of which we have seen there is a great deal, from relative mobility, which is a measure of whether class differentials have narrowed. In other words, if there had been no change in the occupational structure would there still have been an expansion of opportunities for the lower classes? Goldthorpe *et al.* suggest that, relatively, speaking, the capacity of service-class fathers to transmit privilege did not decline between 1928 and 1972.

The Nuffield study examined only men, as have other studies of mass mobility. It is very doubtful whether the same kind of study could be undertaken if it included women, because women's experience of social mobility is so different from men's. Women's intra-generational experience is likely to be much more varied and hard to capture with orthodox sociological categories. It is equally problematic to analyse women's inter-generational mobility. Should a daughter's occupation be compared with that of her mother, rather than her father, for instance? Our present state of knowledge allows us to say very little about women and mobility. This implies however, that we do not understand a major experience of one half of the British population.

Source: adapted from N. Abercrombie and A. Warde *et al.*, *Contemporary British Society*, Cambridge: Polity, 1988

ITEM B

We have seen that systems of stratification based on social class tend to be more 'open' than those based on status. There is movement between class positions. This movement may occur within one individual's lifetime, in which case sociologists refer to intra-generational mobility. Or movement may occur between generations, in which case we refer to inter-generational mobility

Goldthorpe's study concentrates on inter-generational mobility, although he found that for working-class men, intra-generational was still more common as a route out of the working class. Thus, three-quarters of the sons of working-class males started work in working-class occupations, but one-third of them subsequently rose into higher class positions. Looking at those who made it into the salariat, many more did so by working their way up than by direct entry on the strength of qualifications earned at school or colleges.

Comparing older and younger age cohorts in his sample, he shows that the younger group had enjoyed greater opportunities of upward mobility through education while retaining the same chances of upward mobility within employment. The system has become more open.

The previous section has outlined the evidence on social mobility in Britain. The puzzle is why this evidence has not led to a substantial revision in the image that so many sociologists and political commentators continue to portray of class in modern Britain.

Their commitment to a relativistic perspective sometimes leads these left-wing sociologists to make statements about British capitalism which are patently misleading. The Essex team, for example, conclude their discussion by asserting: 'The post-war project of creating in Britain a more open society . . . has signally failed to secure its objectives' (Marshall *et al.*, 1988). Yet this is untrue.

20

25

30

Source: adapted from P. Saunders, *Social Class and Stratification*, London: Routledge, 1990

ITEM C

Sons' status category in 1949

		1	2	3	4	5	6	7	Total
	1	38.8	14.6	20.2	6.2	14.0	4.7	1.5	100.0
		48.5	11.9	7.9	1.7	1.3	1.0	0.5	129
	2	10.7	26.7	22.7	12.0	20.6	5.3	2.0	100.0
		15.5	25.2	10.3	3.9	2.2	1.4	0.7	(150)
	3	3.5	10.1	18.8	19.1	35.7	6.7	6.1	100.0
		11.7	22.0	19.7	14.4	8.6	3.9	5.0	(345)
Fathers' status category	4	2.1	3.9	11.2	21.2	43.0	12.4	6.2	100.0
		10.7	12.6	17.6	24.0	15.6	10.8	7.5	(518)
	5	0.9	2.4	7.5	12.3	47.3	17.1	12.5	100.0
		13.6	22.6	34.5	40.3	50.0	43.5	44.6	(1510)
	6	0.0	1.3	4.1	8.8	39.1	31.2	15.5	100.0
		0.0	3.8	5.8	8.7	12.5	24.1	16.7	(458)
	7	0.0	0.8	3.6	8.3	36.4	23.5	27.4	100.0
		0.0	1.9	4.2	7.0	9.8	15.3	25.0	(387)
	Total	100.0	100.0	100.0	100.0	100.0	100.0	100.0	
		(103)	(159)	(330)	(459)	(1492)	(593)	(424)	(3497)

Status categories
No Description
1   Professional and high administrative
2   Managerial and executive
3   Inspectional, supervisory and other non-manual (higher grade)
4   Inspectional, supervisory and other non-manual (lower grade)
5   Skilled manual and routine grades of non-manual
6   Semi-skilled manual
7   Unskilled manual

Source: D. Glass and J. Hall, *Social Mobility in Great Britain*, London: Routledge and Kegan Paul, 1954

ITEM D

Sons' class in 1972									
		1	*2*	*3*	*4*	*5*	*6*	*7*	*Total*
	1	45.7 / 25.3	19.1 / 12.4	11.6 / 9.6	6.8 / 6.7	4.9 / 3.2	5.4 / 2.0	6.5 / 2.4	100.0 (680)
	2	29.4 / 13.1	23.3 / 12.2	12.1 / 8.0	6.0 / 4.8	9.7 / 5.2	10.8 / 3.1	8.6 / 2.5	100.0 (547)
	3	18.6 / 10.4	15.9 / 10.4	13.0 / 10.8	7.4 / 7.4	13.0 / 8.7	15.7 / 5.7	16.4 / 6.0	100.0 (687)
Fathers' class	4	14.0 / 10.1	14.4 / 12.2	9.1 / 9.8	21.1 / 27.2	9.9 / 8.6	15.1 / 7.1	16.3 / 7.7	100.0 (886)
	5	14.4 / 12.5	13.7 / 14.0	10.2 / 13.2	7.7 / 12.1	15.9 / 16.6	21.4 / 12.2	16.8 / 9.6	100.0 (1072)
	6	7.8 / 16.4	8.8 / 21.7	8.4 / 26.1	6.4 / 24.0	12.4 / 31.0	30.6 / 41.8	25.6 / 35.2	100.0 (2577)
	7	7.1 / 12.1	8.5 / 17.1	8.8 / 22.6	5.7 / 17.8	12.9 / 26.7	24.8 / 28.0	32.2 / 36.6	100.0 (2126)
	Total	100.0 (1230)	100.0 (1050)	100.0 (827)	100.0 (687)	100.0 (1026)	100.0 (1883)	100.0 (1872)	(8575)

Classes
No Description
1   Higher professionals, higher grade administrators, managers in large industrial
    concerns and large proprietors
2   Lower professionals, higher grade technicians, lower grade administrators, managers
    in small businesses and supervisors of non-manual employees
3   Routine non-manual – mainly clerical and sales personnel
4   Small proprietors and self-employed artisans
5   Lower grade technicians and supervisors of manual workers
6   Skilled manual workers
7   Semi-skilled and unskilled manual workers

Source: adapted from J.
Goldthorpe *et al., Social Mobility
and Class Structure in Modern
Britain,* Oxford: Oxford
University Press, 1980

ITEM E

Despite the general omission of women from mobility surveys, there is fortunately one recent source which we can utilize. This is the General Household Survey conducted for the government by the OPCS.

The occupational distribution for women is very different from that of men, it is a 'bimodal' one with women heavily concentrated in lower white-collar work and semi- or unskilled manual work. There appears to be gross inequality of opportunity between men and women here. Among both there is a surplus of upward over downward mobility, but the surplus is much smaller for the women, 27 as against 32 per cent moving up and 26 as against 19 per cent moving down.

Our first view of the material suggests that women have considerably poorer mobility chances than men.

An alternative view sheds a very different light on the inequalities between men and women. Overall 37 per cent of the single women but only 27 per cent of the single men were upwardly mobile; and 17 per cent of the single women as against 25 per cent of the men were downwardly mobile. The picture we now see is the mirror image of the earlier one.

Source: adapted from A. Heath,
The Social Mobility of Women,
London: Fontana, 1981

QUESTIONS

a Why might women's intra-generational mobility be 'hard to capture with orthodox sociological categories' (Item A, line 25)?

(2 marks)

b Explain the difference between inter-generational mobility and intra-generational mobility (Item B) and suggest an example of each.

(4 marks)

c Referring to Items C and D, compare and contrast the patterns of social mobility discovered by Glass and by Goldthorpe.

(4 marks)

d Using material from the Items above and elsewhere, assess the view that 'women have considerably poorer mobility chances than men' (Item E, lines 13–14).

(6 marks)

e Using material from the Items above and elsewhere, examine the arguments for and against the view that 'the system has become more open' (Item B, line 19).

(9 marks)

Select bibliography

Abbot, P. & Wallace, C. *An Introduction to Sociology: Feminist Perspectives*, London: Routledge, 1990
Abercrombie, N. *et al. Contemporary British Society*, Cambridge: Polity, 1988
Aries, P. *Centuries of Childhood*, Harmondsworth: Penguin, 1973

Ball, S. *Education*, London: Longman, 1986
Bauman, Z. *Thinking Sociologically*, Oxford: Basil Blackwell, 1990
Bilton, T. *et al. Introductory Sociology*, 2nd Ed., London: Macmillan, 1987
Bottomore, T. & Nisbet, R. (eds) *A History of Sociological Analysis*, London: Heinemann, 1979
Brown, C. *Black and White Britain: The Third PSI Survey*, London: Heinemann, 1984
Brown, C. H. *Understanding Society*, London: John Murray, 1981
Bulmer, M. *Sociological Research Methods*, London: Macmillan, 1984
Burgess, R. *Research Methods*, Walton-on-Thames: Nelson, 1993
Burgess, R. *Education, Schools and Schooling*, London: Macmillan, 1985
Buswell, C. *Women in Contemporary Society*, Walton-on-Thames: Nelson, 1989

Chapman, K. *The Sociology of Schools*, London: Tavistock, 1986
Cuff. E. E. & Payne, G. C. F. (eds) *Perspectives in Sociology*, 3rd Ed., London: Routledge, 1992

Deem, R. *Work, Unemployment and Leisure*, London: Routledge, 1988
Devine, F. *Affluent Workers Revisited: Privatism and the Working Class*, Edinburgh: Edinburgh University Press, 1992

Faludi, S. *Backlash*, London: Chatto and Windus, 1992
Fletcher, R. *The Family and Marriage in Britain*, Harmondsworth: Penguin, 1973
Frayman, H. *Breadline Britain 1990s*, London: Domino Films/LWT, 1991

Garrett, S. *Gender*, London: Routledge, 1987
Giddens, A. *Sociology: A Brief but Critical Introduction*, 2nd Ed., London: Macmillan, 1986
Giddens, A. *Sociology*, Cambridge: Polity, 1989
Glass, D. & Hall, J. *Social Mobility in Great Britain*, London: Routledge and Kegan Paul, 1954
Goldthorpe, J. *et al. Social Mobility and Class Structure in Modern Britain*, Oxford: Oxford University Press, 1980
Gomm, R. *A Level Sociology*, Cambridge: National Extension College, 1990
Graham, H. *Health and Welfare*, Walton-on-Thames, 1989

Haralambos, M. (ed.) *Developments in Sociology* Ormskirk: Causeway, 1985
Haralambos, M. *Sociology: A New Approach*, 2nd Ed., Ormskirk: Causeway, 1986
Haralambos, M. *Sociology: New Directions*, Ormskirk: Causeway, 1985
Haralambos, M. and Holborn, M. *Sociology: Themes and Perspectives*, 3rd Ed., London: Collins Educational, 1991
HMSO *British Social Attitudes Survey*, London: HMSO, annually
Employment Gazette
General Household Survey
Labour Market Quarterly News
New Earnings Survey
Social Trends
Horne, J. *Work and Unemployment*, London: Longman, 1987

Hyman, R. *Strikes*, London: Fontana, 1984

Jacobs, E. & Worcester, R. *Typically British?* London: Bloomsbury, 1991
Jones, P. *Studying Society: Sociological Theories and Research Practices*, London: Collins Educational, 1993
Joseph, M. *Sociology for Everyone*, Cambridge: Polity, 1986

Langley, P. (ed.) *Discovering Sociology*, Ormskirk: Causeway, 1988
Lawson, T. *Sociology for A Level: A Skills-Based Approach*, London: Collins Educational, 1993
Lawson, T. *et al.* (eds) *Sociology Reviewed*, London: Collins Educational, 1993
Lee, D. & Newby, H. *The Problem of Sociology*, London: Hutchinson, 1983
Leonard, D. & Hood-Williams, J. *Families*, Walton-on-Thames: Nelson, 1988

Marshall, G. *Social Class in Modern Britain*, London: Unwin Hyman, 1988
Mayes. P. *Gender*, London: Longman, 1986
Maynard, M. *Sociological Theory*, London: Longman, 1989
McNeill, P. *Research Methods*, London: Routledge, 1985
McNeill, P. *Society Today* 2, London: Macmillan, 1991
Morison, M. *Methods in Sociology*, London: Longman 1986

Nobbs, J. *Sociology in Context*, London: Macmillan, 1983

Oakley, A. *The Sociology of Housework*, Oxford: Martin Robertson, 1974
O'Donnell, M. *Age and Generation*, London: Routledge, 1985
O'Donnell, M. *Race and Ethnicity*, London: Longman, 1991
O'Donnell, M. *A New Introduction to Sociology*, 3rd Ed., Walton-on-Thames: Nelson, 1992

Saunders, P. *Social Class and Stratification*, London: Routledge, 1990
Scott, J. *Who Rules Britain?* Cambridge: Polity, 1991
Shorter, E. *The Making of the Modern Family*, London: Fontana, 1977
Slattery, M. *ABC of Sociology*, London: Macmillan, 1985
Slattery, M. *Official Statistics*, London: Routledge, 1986
Stanworth, M. *Gender and Schooling*, London: Hutchinson: 1983

Townley, C. & Middleton, M. 'Sociological perspectives' in P. McNeill & C. Townley (eds), *Fundamentals of Sociology*, London: Macmillan, 1986
Trowler, P. *Active Sociology*, London: Collins Educational, 1987

Walker, S. & Barton, L. *Gender, Class and Education*, Lewes: The Falmer Press, 1983
Westergaard, J. & Rester, H. *Class in Capitalist Society*, Harmondsworth: Penguin, 1975
Williams, M. *Society Today*, London: Macmillan, 1986
Willmott, P. and Young, M. *Family and Kinship in East London*, Harmondsworth: Penguin, 1962
Wilson, A. *Family*, London: Routledge, 1985
Worsley, P. (ed) *The New Modern Sociology Readings*, Harmondsworth: Penguin, 1991

Journals

Sociology Review is published four times a year and is available on subscription from the Subscriptions Department, Philip Allan Publishers, Market Place, Deddington, Oxon, OX15 0SE.

Sociology Update is published annually and is available from Dr Martyn Denscombe, 32 Shirley Road, Stoneygate, Leicester, LE2 3LJ.

Social Science Teacher is the Journal of the Association for the Teaching of the Social Sciences (ATSS). The ATSS is the professional body for teachers of sociology and social science. Further information can be obtained by writing to: ATSS, PO Box 461, Sheffield, S2 2RH.

Author index

Subject index